Working with Parents

Working with Parents

Establishing the Essential Alliance in Child Psychotherapy and Consultation

Diana Siskind

JASON ARONSON INC.
Northvale, New Jersey
London

Production Editor: Judith D. Cohen

This book was set in 11 pt. Fairfield Light by Alpha Graphics of Pittsfield, New Hampshire and printed and bound by Book-mart Press, Inc. of North Bergen, New Jersey.

Library of Congress Cataloging-in-Publication Data

Siskind, Diana.
    Working with parents : establishing the essential alliance in
child psychotherapy and consultation / Diana Siskind.
        p.   cm.
    Includes bibliographical references and index.
    ISBN 0-7657-0060-3 (alk. paper)
    1. Child psychotherapy—Parent participation.   2. Therapeutic
alliance.   I. Title.
RJ505.P38S57   1997
618.92'8914—dc21   96-40017

Printed in the United States of America on acid-free paper. Jason Aronson Inc. offers books and cassettes. For information and catalog write to Jason Aronson Inc., 230 Livingston Street, Northvale, New Jersey 07647-1731. Or visit our website: http://www.aronson.com

For Elliott

Contents

PART III
Ongoing Work with the Parents of Children in Treatment

Acknowledgments

Writing a second book to be published by Jason Aronson is like re-entering the memory of a friendly and welcoming place and discovering that in this instance reality and memory are a perfect match. I thank Jay Aronson for the constancy of his enthusiasm and for the intelligence and wisdom that guide it. I thank his staff for their contribution to the smooth process of getting this book published. I feel lucky to have had once again the pleasure of working with Judith Cohen, a most gifted editor.

Some of my friends have read parts of my book and have made valuable comments. I thank Beatrice Weinstein, Helen Goldstein, Renee Goldman, and Anne Marie Dooley for their involvement and help. I thank my husband Elliott for his support throughout this project and for his outstanding care in reading my manuscript and making excellent comments.

Finally, I would like to thank the parents I have come to know professionally, some directly and some through my work as supervisor. These parents taught me to take nothing for granted, to be ready for the unexpected, and to combine confidence and humility in the proper proportions to fit each situation. After many years spent trying to meet the challenges they presented I decided to explore and conceptualize the complexity of this work. In the pages that follow you will meet some of the parents I helped and failed, while others play a silent role in shaping this book. I thank them all for what they have taught me.

Prologue

In working with parents, experience and wisdom are paramount but sometimes brashness and determination get the edge. I remember an intake I did a long time ago when just starting as a child therapist. At the time I was on the staff of a very fine child guidance clinic. Our work there was based on sound psychoanalytic principles and the evaluation of a child was lengthy, painstakingly thorough, and included a diagnostic assessment of the parents.

During the many months that I met with Mr. and Mrs. Ford and observed their 3-year-old daughter Tina, I struggled to maintain a professional attitude towards Mrs. Ford whose hostility towards me was expressed through sarcasm and a refusal to answer any of my questions directly. Since Mr. Ford was quite willing to cooperate, and Mrs. Ford would supply information he lacked by addressing it to him, I was able to assemble an extensive developmental history of this fascinating and highly atypical little girl.

Finally, reports of a psychiatric interview, psychological tests, and my diagnostic evaluation were all complete and the case was conferenced. It was decided that treatment for the child and weekly individual child guidance sessions for each parent would be the treatment plan, and I would be the therapist for all three family members. My pleasure at this assignment was dampened by the problem I now faced. How was I to get Mrs. Ford to attend individual sessions with me when she would not speak to me and mocked my presence?

It was an absolute rule of this agency that no child could be in treatment without the full participation of both parents. Mr. and Mrs. Ford knew this from the onset. Mrs. Ford accepted the plan that her child be in treatment and it was easy to arrange Tina's twice weekly sessions, but when I called her to set up a regular weekly time for *our* sessions I ran into total unwillingness. I reminded her that we had a rule about parental participation. She whispered that she knew that. "Well then," I asked, "What are we going to do?" She didn't know. She sounded a little sad and a little defeated. Perhaps it was this uncharacteristic genuineness that gave me hope. I had never before seen her unarmed.

"We both want Tina to do well," I said. "We have the same goal, but I have to see you every week and I know that you don't want that. Is there anything I can say or do to change your mind?"

"Yes," she answered softly, sounding very young. "You have to promise that every time I come to see you, you will give me a gem, a gem of wisdom to take home and put to use. If you promise to do that I will come."

"Well," I said, "if that's the only way you'll come then I will have to produce a gem for you every week."

With this vignette I begin my book on work with parents. When I come to the end, both you, the reader, and I will understand a little better what happened during that exchange. But I will tell you now that from that moment on everything and anything I said to this mother was placed by her in the gem category. Much time has passed since that conversation. Tina is married and mother to her own daughter. But the working alliance was so firmly cemented by my rash (novice that I was) promise of "gems," that Mrs. Ford still calls me about once a year under some pretext or other. The last time she asked whether I was still in practice. I think she wants to make sure that I'm still alive and have my wits intact in case she suddenly needs an infusion of "gems." There is something almost uncanny about the timing of her calls. They always come when I am exceptionally busy and haven't a minute to spare, but I don't mind. After all, we have done a lot for each other. I became for her someone she created, a partner she could absolutely count on, a partner in the deepest sense. And I learned to carry the role she gave me. I learned to tolerate her idealization and to leave it undisturbed, one of the hardest tasks of our profession.

The Working Alliance: Obstacles and Objectives

1

⤵

Questions and Dilemmas in Work with Parents[1]

Establishing and maintaining a working alliance with the parents of our child patients is an essential dimension of the work of child therapists and the one that the majority of us find the most difficult to achieve. This difficulty exists for child therapists[2] at all levels of experience, including those who have devoted many years to the study, practice, and teaching of child treatment.

Despite the many pleasures and challenges of treating children and the satisfaction in facilitating their growth and development, many child therapists eventually limit, reduce, and even give up the practice of child psychotherapy. The cumulative frustrations encountered in contacts with the child's parents sometimes grow to be so taxing and impose such stressful con-

---

1. Portions of Chapters 1, 2, and 3 appeared in Edward and Sanville (1996).

2. *Therapist* will be used throughout this book to denote psychotherapist and *analyst* to denote psychoanalyst.

ditions that even the most committed practitioners often feel defeated.

Why do so many professionals have such difficulty in this area? This book will explore this question and analyze the factors that serve as obstacles to establishing a working alliance with the parents of the children we treat. My hope is to achieve a shift of attitude in the way we view parents and a concomitant deepening of awareness of how we respond to them from the first moment of contact.

When we review literature on the therapist's work with the parents of child patients, it quickly becomes apparent that this is a neglected subject. It is surprising that this topic has failed to be represented as a complex and important treatment issue, one requiring a theoretical framework and careful discussion of its clinical application.

Some articles have been written that have work with parents as their primary focus (Bernstein and Glenn 1988, Elkisch 1971, Ferholt and Gurwitt 1982, Fraiberg 1980, Glenn et al. 1992, Sandler et al. 1980) but these are the exceptions. More often one has to look to books and articles on child treatment to find mention of this aspect of our work. And then we typically find these references to the child's parents to be brief, cursory, and confined to what are viewed as practical considerations: how often to see the parents, how much to tell them, how to gain their cooperation. Not infrequently these references carry a cautionary tone: parents can be dangerous if one does not find a way to get along with them, parents can undermine the therapist's work, and in some situations parents can even take their child out of treatment. There is frequently an attitude of resignation, one that suggests that parents are the special burden that the child therapist must bear.

Not only is working with parents often subsumed under the subject of child therapy rather than being considered a category in its own right, it is often relegated to second-class status, a bothersome aspect of our work.

Not surprising, given the professional community's inattention to work with parents, is the dearth of seminars on this subject. While such breach of attention only attests to the fact that the lack of popularity of a topic in no way reflects its clinical importance or degree of complexity, this shrinking away from a difficult area of our work becomes interesting in its own right because it is so unusual in our field.

Our profession has at its center a pull towards the expansion of knowledge. The number of books and periodicals we produce is boundless. We write about everything that crosses the path of our consciousness. Worry about duplication seems relatively absent as attested to by the constant flow of journal issues and books on similar subjects that arrive in our offices. No topic appears too big or too small for serious investigation. So why not this one?

Could it be that the frustrations encountered in working with parents might extend to an avoidance of this topic as a subject for articles and seminars? If so, what is it about these frustrations that is so crippling and silencing? In so many aspects of our work we feel challenged by what we do not know and mobilize ourselves to look deeply and learn. Why not here? What is different about this arena of knowledge? What stops our customary quest for insight and clarity?

In contrast to the reluctance among professionals to write on this subject is the ease with which it takes center stage when child therapists meet for seminars or conferences. It is paradoxical that child therapists are so verbally outspoken about their dilemmas concerning work with parents and so reticent about recording their experience in this area of their work. Is there still the notion that in order to write one must have the answers rather than the wish to explore? Most likely the reason for this omission is deeper and more obscure.

Here are some of the questions and general issues typically raised at seminars on child treatment. I will list some of these to convey the complexity of this therapeutic role and the dilemmas it creates.

1. Should the child's therapist also work with the parents or should the parents be seen by a different therapist? Should the parents be seen as a couple, individually, or should they each be seen in individual treatment by separate therapists? If other therapists are involved in treating the parents, how much communication, if any, should take place among the various therapists?

2. When the parent of a child in treatment is seen by his or her child's therapist, is the parent to be viewed as a patient or as something other than a patient?

3. Should parents be given direct advice regarding their children or would this represent the therapist as an authority figure who might undermine parental prerogative?

4. At what age should we consider the child too old for us to continue to maintain regular contact with his parents?

5. What is the child's right to confidentiality and what is the parents' right to know what is going on in their child's treatment?

6. Should the parents' participation in their child's treatment be mandatory or voluntary?

7. What happens with divorced parents in regard to confidentiality, contact with both parents or with stepparents, the therapist's role in custody disputes, and so on?

This sampling of typical questions facing the child therapist demonstrates the exponential growth of factors to be considered when so many people are involved in the treatment situation.

To begin with, many of the questions listed have a deceptively practical tone, and to view these questions as primarily practical is to underestimate their complexity. They cannot be answered with a general rule and they cannot be answered in a vacuum. In fact there is something about the way they are always presented that makes them unanswerable, a certain naïveté that is out of keeping with the way we usually approach our work. Yet the questions raised are real and need to be dealt with if we are to proceed with our work.

I propose that it is only our search for understanding the dilemmas inherent in these simple questions that will lead us to a deeper and more comprehensive understanding of what we are really asking. We need to dig deeper in this area; we need to find ways of extending our considerable theoretical knowledge to cover the multifaceted and elusive relationship between child's parent and child's therapist. The therapeutic process always entails becoming aware of and making use of everything we know about the patient, everything we know about ourselves, and all we have learned of theory and technique. This knowledge must then be combined with the leavening agent, basic common sense, all in all a formidable piece of integration. The weaving together of this knowledge—the snowballing of knowledge as it augments with each new insight, experience, and encounter—this is our tool, our compass in finding out what we need to know, or what we perhaps cannot know but need to explore in ourselves and in our patients. All this is our familiar territory, what we live by every day in work with our child and adult patients, and this is what we all too often forget when the person facing us is the *parent* of one of the children we treat. This lapse in our professional role is at the root of the problem, *our* problem: to do justice to our work as child therapists we must approach parents with the same seriousness we invest in all other therapeutic endeavors.

This book is about the process we need to enter, over and over again, to keep this area of our work fresh and relevant to each situation and therapeutic moment. When you finish reading it, the questions listed earlier will have all been addressed in a way that will make them seem less categorical, less concrete, and less purely practical. That should make them a lot more interesting and will, I hope, provide the shift of perspective we need to make our work with parents as organic to the process of child treatment as is our work with the child. Only when this is in place can the working alliance with the child's parents be there as a reliable ballast, providing all the key participants in the child's life with working conditions that allow continuous adaptation to the vicissitudes of the therapeutic process.

2

Is This Parent a Patient? Working with Mrs. Adams[1]

Of all the questions listed in Chapter 1, question #2 is probably the most complex and the most elusive. It might even be the one most likely to cause disagreement and confusion among psychotherapists and to provoke heated discussions and debates. A question that arouses so much controversy must strike a deep chord in all of us; that in itself makes it interesting. Tackling it seems a good place to begin.

When the parent of a child in treatment is seen by his or her child's therapist, is that parent to be viewed as a patient or as something other than a patient?

This question raises a fundamental issue regarding the positioning of the child's therapist and the child's parent. If we can find a way of understanding how to think about this, we will already be ahead of where we were before we started. Perhaps if we examine a variety of situations we will have a better idea of

---

1. All clinical material in this book and all references to other therapists are either presented with the permission of these persons or so disguised as to be unrecognizable.

what we are struggling to understand when we ask: "Is the parent a patient?"

We might begin with a situation that appears pretty clear cut. Mrs. Adams is in a classical psychoanalysis. During the course of her treatment she recognizes that a deep-seated conflict, which throughout her life has been the cause of much suffering, is now hampering her ability to be a good mother to her son. She knows that the therapeutic process moves slowly and that her son's developmental needs cannot be put on hold. He has already developed disturbing symptoms: compulsive eating and a scapegoat position with his peers. She reacts to this with shame and anger and fully recognizes that her lack of empathy compounds the problem. Her husband is of no help since he too feels disappointed in their son and shares her disparaging attitude toward 6-year-old Timmy. Together they taunt him in ways too subtle to be readily apparent, thus making them doubly toxic. Mrs. Adams is horrified by her behavior but cannot stop herself and seeks out a child therapist with the hope that treatment will bolster her child's self-esteem and serve as an antidote to the unsupportive climate at home. She knows that he has become the object of her projections of archaic representations of a damaged self. She is distressed by this and particularly grieved that he plays this role so well, for he is shunned by his peers and only tolerated by his teachers.

The child therapist recommends treatment for Tim and regular meetings with the parents. The parents readily agree to the plan. Mrs. Adams is now going to take her son to see his therapist twice per week in addition to her own four weekly psychoanalytic appointments with her analyst. In addition, she is going to see Timmy's therapist on a weekly basis, sometimes with her husband and sometimes alone. Mr. Adams is also going to see his son's therapist weekly, sometimes with his wife and sometimes alone. Mr. Adams is not in treatment.

Back to our question: What do we call the relationship between the child's parents and the child's therapist? Is this mother a patient of her child's therapist? It's easy to jump to a quick "no" in this case because the mother has her own therapist. But that line of thinking would be based on the assumption that Mrs. Adams's relationship to her child's therapist is automatically more clear-cut than that of her husband's because Mrs. Adams has her own therapist and Mr. Adams does not. That type of assumption has no place in our work, for there is nothing linear or mathematical about the way we think about our patients. We cannot even say with certainty that the two and two we see equal four because we know that what we thought was a two could turn out to be a three or a four or a five. There are always new factors waiting to emerge, needing to be incorporated, and adding a new shading to what we already know. Since simple logic is often too narrow and too static to help us in our work, how do we proceed?

Perhaps we can begin to formulate a way of organizing our thinking by looking at what actually takes place in the situation with Tim's parents. To do that we need to observe these parents *and* the reactions they might evoke in us if we were their child's therapist.

Let's begin with Mrs. Adams. She is an intelligent and well-functioning woman who diagnostically fits the criteria of neurotic structure. Her lack of empathy for her son is ego dystonic and causes her anguish. She is not undifferentiated or indiscriminate. She knows who her therapist is and who her son's therapist is and does not blur these boundaries. She is an early childhood specialist and therefore has some sophistication regarding child development and child treatment. She is a naturally insightful person whose many years of analysis have further developed her sensitivity and self awareness. She is well aware of feeling some resentment towards her child's therapist. She even recognizes that it is she who has brought this about by placing her child's therapist in a position superior to her own, by imbuing the therapist with the power to save her child, and by expecting her to transform Tim into a narcissistically satisfied and satisfying boy.

Mr. Adams is also intelligent, worldly, successful at work, concerned about his son, ready to do the right thing, but rarely home. He reveals so little about himself that it is difficult to make a definitive diagnostic statement about him. His discomfort at having a child in treatment and at having regular meetings with his son's therapist is veiled by a humorous and slightly disparaging attitude about "mental healthers." He groups his wife, his wife's analyst, and his son's therapist as "the mental healthers," adding "not a rock group." He assigns to them the business of healing mind and spirit. They are the rulers of the inner world. In contrast, he describes himself as dealing with outer reality: order in our social structure, the production of goods, world governments, finance, and so on.

Mr. Adams rarely cancels sessions, always arriving five to ten minutes late with apology and the need to use his cellular phone for "just one minute." Mr. Adams is so nice, so amiable, that the therapist can't help but be slightly amused by his sigh of relief at each session's end. He's free at last, free to return to work, to his orderly law firm, to his partners, his clients, and the familiar environment he fits so well. And most of all he's free from having to think about Tim's troubles, which he willingly leaves in the hands of the therapist whom he gladly and gratefully entrusts with this responsibility. There is no contest to be fought here. At least it appears this way at present. Mr. Adams has arranged his world into two separate domains: the one where he is king, and that of the therapist. The domains coexist in peace and cooperation.

Surely Mr. Adams isn't a patient of Tim's therapist. What is he then? A concerned but distant ally? A father only too glad not to be confronted with the powerlessness of trying to help his son by entering into some mysterious, shapeless, and unfamiliar process? We don't really know what all this means to him or how it might develop. No, he isn't a patient in the familiar sense, but he is someplace on that continuum of parents who are not patients but are also not "not patients." What places him on that continuum has more to do with the way we approach him than anything he *consciously* asks of us. What he has subtly conveyed to us, what he wants from us is that his need for distance be respected. We understand that need of his diagnostically. We recognize it as a defense essential to his emotional equilibrium and we take it very seriously and accept his need for distance. We know that if there is to be any shift in this area, it will have to be initiated by him.

Mrs. Adams is the parent who brings Tim to his sessions, and she does so with unfailing promptness and regularity. Only significant illness causes cancellations. No alluring after-school activities, deliveries of furniture on the day of Tim's appointments, bad weather, doctor's appointments, or birthday parties are ever in competition with his sessions. The same meticulous promptness is manifested in her attendance at her own sessions with Tim's therapist and in the payment of the monthly bill.

Now let's take a look at what happens during some of her encounters with Tim's therapist. Sometimes she assumes a collegial tone and tells the therapist about a wonderful new play material she came across in one of the schools where she serves as consultant. She thinks this play material would be a useful addition to the therapist's repertoire of toys. Sometimes a slightly disapproving teacherish tone emerges as she asks why the therapist doesn't use paints during Tim's sessions, after all they are much more versatile than magic markers. And she's noticed that there are no magazines for children in the waiting room. Isn't that a strange omission for a child therapist? Also, why is the office kept so warm, in contrast to the waiting room where she sits for forty-five minutes with her coat on? Could something be done? When a cancellation for her son is not rescheduled and a charge for that missed session appears on the bill, she is surprised. After all, her Timmy had a fever. It wasn't resistance to the therapeutic process. It was a real honest-to-goodness flu. He's only six. How can his therapist be so inflexible? She deducts the fee for that session from the monthly bill, circling it in red ink.

We could try to argue that the question about the patient status of a parent doesn't even apply to Mrs. Adams; being the patient of her own analyst she cannot be that of her son's. How simple our life would be if the boundaries of patienthood were so clearly demarcated, but they are not. Unconscious forces are powerful and unruly and find expression in various ways, affects, and behavior as well as dreams and slips of the tongue. We know full well that transference manifestations are not restricted to the analyst–analysand dyad. The conflicts that became the core concern of Mrs. Adams's analytic exploration and caused her to recognize her limitations vis-à-vis her son were bound to find expression in the situation of her child's treatment. That Mrs. Adams designated her child's therapist as savior of her son automatically turned her into a serious rival. The treatment situation was colored by this wish–fear/hope–rage set of factors from the start.

There is always something like this at play in child treatment and that is a fact to be accepted and reckoned with without exception. It's hard for us as child therapists not to view this as a burden, especially since we do not feel free to interpret these often hostile communications (verbal and nonverbal) of the parents of our child patients. We must, especially when their own treatment is concurrent with their child's, leave that level of interpretive work to their own therapists. It *is* a burden to have to deal with their transference spillover to us and their acting out, but it's a particular kind of a burden. While not exactly analogous, we could compare it to unrecognized or unanalyzed countertransference. Both the acting out of parents and the therapist's countertransference are burdens when resisted. When they are acknowledged and accepted by the therapist, when they are pursued and explored with curiosity and energy, these unconscious dialogues become valuable sources of insight and serve us well.

The child treatment situation is always complicated by the ambiguous position of mother vis-à-vis therapist and father vis-à-vis therapist. It is a complication that is intrinsic to the process of treating a child. It is a dimension of the treatment, an organic part of what is to be treated. There are always too many people in the consulting room, too many currents to track and juggle. That we are unsure about the patient status of the parents is the tip of a formidable iceberg.

It is interesting that in social service agencies the term *client* rather than *patient* is used. I believe that *client* is meant to convey that we, the establishment, don't presume that there is something wrong with the person requiring help, in contrast with *patient*, which implies illness. A second reason for the preference for *client* is that it denotes a more equal and less polarizing positioning between the one who serves and the one who is served. This attempt at establishing an atmosphere of equality cannot work for two reasons. The more obvious reason is that one person is indeed dependent on the help of the other. The less obvious reason is that it disregards the unconscious. *Because of the power of the unconscious, it is far safer to view the child's parents as patients than to view them as anything else.* It helps us maintain our professional attitude and keeps us alert to their transference manifestations and to our reactions to their transference.

As we undertake the treatment of a child, before we have had sufficient time to know child and parents well, even the assumption that a parent, or the parents, are not going to be the primary patients, is precipitous. Before we make assumptions, we need to know the total situation really well. We need time to know what needs to be treated in child treatment. We need the time to gather information, to observe and to assess, before being able to determine where to place the parents on a patient to non-patient continuum. We need to remember that whatever a situation may look like, it might be quite different when we get to know it well.

In child treatment it is essential to extend the evaluation process until we have gathered sufficient information to know who and what in the family need to be treated. Just because we have been consulted about a child does not mean that the child must become the patient. The child might not need treatment or be ready for it at the time of the referral. Or the child might need treatment and be ready, even eager for it, but the parents might not be able to tolerate it for their child.

There is another not unusual situation that brings parents or one parent to the office of a child therapist. It is the parent's wish for treatment and inability to seek it directly for himself or herself. The wish is not necessarily conscious, nor is the action of presenting the child as the "patient elect" a conscious decoy. Some people have difficulty in seeking help for themselves and need a spouse or a child as the entry visa into their own treatment.

We need to be alert to all these and other possibilities and not confuse the manifest request with the underlying wish and aim. In many instances those initial consultations with parents remind us how readily some people turn into patients in any encounter with another person. When a parent reveals such a level of need during the initial sessions, this is significant diagnostic information that needs to be carefully explored. The child therapist has to track that parent's need to be a patient and consider which of the various possible directions to take. Is the parent seeking his[2] own treatment? Is a referral to a separate therapist indicated? Is this a situation where the parent cannot separate from her child and a tripartite approach to treatment might be considered? Should the therapist delay seeing the child and work with the parent only, and if appropriate eventually refer the child to another therapist?

Sometimes, after an initial consultation about a child during which the child is barely mentioned, a therapist might make the following comment to a colleague or supervisor:

> These parents came to see me about their child and in one hour I got almost no information about their daughter. The father talked nonstop about his early family life, the lost opportunities of his youth, his current frustration at work, and the difficulty in finding the time and quiet to play his beloved violin in a house with three noisy children. The mother sat quietly and looked sad.

The therapist might report this encounter in a critical tone of voice, frustrated that he hadn't gotten any information about the child. But why mind that? The therapist met a sad, angry man, and a sad, quiet woman. He witnessed their minimal interaction. His response was one of impatience rather than curiosity, empathy, or a variety of other possible responses. His main concern was that the daughter, the official prospective patient, was neglected. That's a lot to learn in one hour. It's a lot to learn about

---

2. He and she and his and her will be used interchangeably throughout the book to avoid the awkward sound of using both.

this family, but there's more, for it presents the therapist with a lot to learn about himself in having experienced such a strong and immediate countertransferential response to this father. Why did this father evoke so little empathy? Why did the therapist do so little to engage the mother, leaving her to be the forgotten person during the interview? Why was there such an identification with the unknown child? These are some of the questions the therapist needs to explore in himself. Of course this line of inquiry needs to take place with a benign attitude. If the therapist approaches this self-examination with a self-critical attitude the inquiry will not provide much further insight into this case. But if the therapist is able to question his responses in a spirit of openness, he might find that his quest will yield information at least as valuable as learning when the child walked, gave up her bottle, and slept through the night.

It's important to remember that while many paths are open to us, our purpose is to help the patient reach his destination. It's important to remember that we do not know who the patient is or what destination is sought. Often a parent doesn't know that he wants to become the patient, and nobody knows the sought-for destination, at least not for a long time. Most people don't even know how much better life can be. We learn that as we move along.

To return to Mrs. Adams and try to puzzle out how to view her, we could say that she is not *the* patient, but despite having her own analyst she is somewhere on that hypothetical patient to nonpatient continuum proposed earlier. It is hard to place her in a fixed place on that continuum because she changes all the time. There is good reason for her state of flux. She is, after all, an analysand. To understand Mrs. Adams we need to remind ourselves that psychoanalysis is a deeply intense process, one that at various times stirs up all levels of memories and affects, induces regressive-progressive states, and brings to daily life periods of emotional upheaval. If we then add the circumstance of having a child in treatment and consider how that must compound her states of disequilibrium, we might see her in a clearer light. This

could prove helpful in giving us insight into her ambivalence toward her son's therapist and help us be more accepting of her
acting out and occasional hostility. It also broadens our view and
helps us see Mrs. Adams in the larger context of her life. She is
after all not only the mother of Timmy, aged 6, whom she cannot
love so well. She is a person whose history and constitutional
makeup produced this adult, in her case, an adult who is trying
with all her might to grapple with her inner conflicts so as to grow,
do better, and eventually be more loving. To particularize her, to
see her as other than just Timmy's mother, helps us with our
countertransference. It reminds us that she is not our mother and
neither are we hers; it reminds us that the rivalry that is generated by our role in her life cannot be allowed expression from our
end.

    And what did Mr. Adams tell us about our role in his life? He
told us that he does not want to be a patient, is skeptical about
the legitimacy of our work, thinks we're a little weird, and thinks
that of his wife as well. He told us that he will cooperate because
his wife would be very angry if he refused. He told us that his
cooperation will be superficial because he doesn't want to disturb the equilibrium he maintains so well by avoiding, to a pre-
scribed degree, contact with his inner life. But he let us know as
well that one troubling factor that he cannot dispel, either through
humor or any other defensive maneuver, is his awareness that
Timmy is not a happy boy. He recognizes that and also recognizes
that he doesn't seem able to help him. He knows that perhaps we
can. He is ready to accept that possibility and it is in this psychic
corner that we stand a chance to engage or lose him, to form a
working alliance with him or a state of rivalry.

    Is Mr. Adams a patient? The degree of his patienthood will in
part depend on his son's therapist. Some therapists might take a
hard line with this father and insist that he come on time, leave
his portable phone at the office, and stop trying to amuse—in other
words, give up his customary armor. Some might decide that Mr.
Adams is so resistant to the process, so unwilling to become an
involved father, that it seems fruitless to have regular weekly ap-

pointments with him. Some will take a wait-and-see attitude and continue his weekly sessions, track the therapeutic work, accept him as he is, and place some weight on his willingness to come so faithfully. Is Mr. Adams a patient? Well, not exactly, but what is to develop is not yet known. We are still at the beginning period of his son's treatment and a lot could happen. But whatever the situation, we are always better off proceeding from our end as if he were a patient, or at least something like a patient.

It is always useful to view our work from a historical perspective; psychotherapy grew out of psychoanalysis. Psychoanalysis is both a treatment modality and a scientific theory. As a complex theory of human development it provides the clinician with a wide lens for understanding human behavior and imposes a disciplined approach for processing information. The scope of this mode of thinking is considerable and its applicability limitless. In discussing the patient status of parents of children in treatment our psychoanalytic training positions us in the best place possible for addressing this complicated question. Our training gives us the comfort to *not* know what cannot be known and to value whatever we do know, no matter how small it may be. It helps us tolerate the disorderly nature of the treatment situation and view the lack of orderliness as an intrinsic aspect of the work. It reminds us to view all aspects of this situation as we view all the material presented by our adult patients in psychoanalysis and psychoanalytic psychotherapy—as grist for the mill. It reminds us that complex questions can only be answered by an approach that respects rather than reduces the complexity of human development. And it reminds us that as we explore this and the other questions, we must examine the play of factors contributed by the parents *and* those contributed by the therapist, that is, the vicissitudes of transference and countertransference.

3

༚

Is This Patient a Parent? Working with Mrs. Kay

To thoroughly explore the many reasons that make work with parents so complicated, we will have to be vigilant and look into all aspects of this treatment situation. And we will have to question anything that we might take for granted, think unimportant, obvious, or irrelevant. In other words, anything and everything that crosses our path warrants our scrutiny.

One good direction to take is to review some of the assumptions that are generally made about parents, assumptions that often exist silently and unknowingly. For instance, the very word *parent* is rarely heard dispassionately; the same may be said for *mother* and *father*. These words set off an associative clang, rich with affect. When this visceral reaction fades and we can speak objectively, most of us would agree that parents are two adults, a mother and a father who together have a child, care for that child, and take care of that child. This basic, simple, and general definition would probably be agreed upon by a wide range of people including mental health professionals, correction officers, teachers, doctors, judges, and so on. In other words, even the people whose work exposes them to large numbers of inadequate and abusive parents hold on to this wished-for image. Indeed, it appears that on this subject our expectations remain curiously impervious to our daily experience with the actual parents we meet in our work and see in the world around us.

It is relevant to our exploration to note how stubbornly we cling to equating parents with an image of a man and a woman living together for a long time and in harmony. The familiar family of our childhood picture books remains so real to most of us that we are slow to revise it to fit the growing incidence of one-parent households and single-gender couples.

Over and over again we attribute to the word *parents* care and caring. These embellish their literal definition: (1) a mother or father (2) a progenitor or ancestor (3) any animal, organism or plant in relation to its offspring. . . . (*Webster's New World Dictionary*, p. 982). Similarly we confuse *mother* and *father,* which, like *parent,* have a primarily biological and relational-generational meaning, with the ideal of *motherly* and *fatherly,*[1] which refer to such traits as care, kindness, wisdom, and nurturance. And we do this despite our exposure to child abuse of every sort becoming a common occurrence, and despite our only moderate number of encounters with parents who fit our wished-for image. I believe that here lies the beginning of insight into the root of our problem. Since most of us hold on to our ego ideal of parent, then of course we are going to have difficulty in maintaining our customary neutrality when the parent in our consulting room does not fit our expectations. This shift from our usual therapeutic attitude of interest and curiosity combined with objectivity is certain to cause some professional disequilibrium and affect the way we work.

As responsible professionals let us stay with a definition of parent that is bare and realistic. A parent is a person biologically involved in producing a child, or a parent is a person who plays

---

1. Chiland (1982) "proposes the word 'fathering' for the role played by father in the upbringing of the child." She distinguishes it from "fatherliness," which she reserves for "the changes that take place in a man who becomes a father and *exercises* (italics added) his developing fathering qualities" (p. 370). Mothering and motherliness could be understood the same way.

no role in the biological production of a child but adopts a child. There are no adjectives in these definitions and no promises either. In fact, such definitions are hard to accept because an almost universal sense of protectiveness about children causes us to wish parents to have those characteristics that we associate with parenting: love, devotion, patience, and guidance. When these are seriously lacking we become uncomfortable, and perhaps also anxious. This is not surprising since the severe mistreatment of children is bound to elicit sadness and pain in everyone. Psychotherapists are not exempt from this reaction.

But our tendency to overidentify with children is not only evoked by our regressive reaction in the face of horrible circumstances. Even those parents who love their children and take care of them reasonably well have shortcomings that often arouse our criticism and disapproval. We tend to get angry at their lateness in bringing their child to therapy appointments, at vacations taken just as the child's treatment deepens, at home rules too lax or perhaps too strict, at bills paid late, demands that treatment be hurried along, and so on. When we feel our annoyance at these "infractions," when we are angered that these parents do not fit our ego ideal of parent, we must recognize that our therapeutic role will be compromised unless we analyze our negative reactions and deal with them to deepen our insight into what is going on between us and those parents. This is sometimes difficult to accomplish, but unless we succeed we are as much a saboteur of treatment as is the uncooperative parent.

To return to the question discussed in Chapter 2 regarding the parent's status as patient or nonpatient, whatever our answer may be, that parent must be viewed from a professional perspective. As mentioned earlier, it is essential that parents be assessed with the same care and thoroughness that we apply to the evaluation of any of our primary patients. A careful assessment of the strengths and vulnerabilities of parents is essential to our being able to do our work, but it is more than that. It is also an action on our part that delineates and formalizes the *professional* nature of our relationship with that person.

Some therapists might find this objectionable on the grounds that the parents are not the "real" patients, and on the grounds that to assess is to classify, distance, and perhaps even take a superior position. But such an attitude, besides being counter-productive, misses the point. When we take on the treatment of a child we automatically accept a role vis-à-vis the parents of that child. We must do all we can to carry out that role as well as we can, and that includes forming a working alliance with the parents.

I propose that it is rare for a therapist to be able to treat a child without having a working alliance (Greenson 1967) with at least one of the child's parents (Geleerd 1967, Siskind 1992) and in order to bring that about, an assessment of the parents is an indispensable safeguard. We must learn to understand how the parents of the children we treat perceive themselves, their child, each other, our role in their lives; how they perceive their past and its impact on the present and so on. If we consider these questions with care and make no assumptions, we will at least have a fair chance of understanding their difficulties in parenting and might, for instance, gain insight into their lack of cooperation in their child's treatment. This in turn could enable us to work constructively with parental ambivalence as well as our own. Not only is it our right to assess all family members, it is our job to do so, and this action on our part helps to transform "parent" into a person in his own right. That is an invaluable shift of focus for the child therapist.

Parenthood, in the full sense of the word, is a developmental stage (Benedek 1959) that is attained when all that precedes it has produced a reasonably reliable level of psychic stability. When this readiness is in place, the experience of parenthood, in turn, affords new opportunities for growth and development. How does this come about?

From birth on the infant passes through stage after stage of growth and reorganization. For instance, Mahler (Mahler et al. 1975) discusses, in exquisite detail, the infant's journey through the parallel and interconnected processes of separation and individuation. Her time table describes the infant's first three years of life as he moves through the stages of autism, symbiosis, differentiation, practicing, rapprochement, and finally, when things go well, arrives at what she calls *psychological birth*. When this is in place, his sense of specificity and awareness of separateness have been more or less established. One of the most dramatic achievements of this process is the "attainment of unified whole self and object representations" (Edward et al. 1991, p. 344); a state wherein the child can retain mental representations of self and object regardless of the object's physical presence. We generally refer to this as *object constancy*.

Simultaneous to and inextricably intertwined with the separation-individuation process is the child's passage through the psychosexual stages. As with all development, the more adequate the resolution of one phase, the better the foundation for the next. Conversely, the greater the difficulty at each pivotal point of development, the more likelihood for skewed development in the next stage. The state of parenthood places enormous demands on psychic resources and when an adult has reached the stage of "generativity" (Erikson 1950) all levels of development have converged to form a readiness not only to meet these demands, but to welcome and embrace them and to enjoy caring for one's child. This fortunate synchronicity of developmental attainment with developmental challenge bodes well for both parent and child. As mentioned earlier, when the demands of caring for a child can be reasonably well met, this experience affords the parent renewed opportunities for furthering development. But when these demands exceed the emotional resources of an individual, the sense of failure can be devastating.

The following vignette will illustrate the frustration and sense of failure of a mother who feels unequal to her job. The mother is talking to her therapist. The therapist works in an agency for children located in a working-class, urban neighborhood. The children are generally referred by someone in their schools. Although the child is the primary patient, parents are expected to participate by attending weekly sessions. In this agency it is generally mothers who attend these sessions. Fathers are encouraged to participate but very rarely are willing to attend regular sessions. The purpose of the sessions with parents is to help them better understand their child, to learn improved ways of handling the child's problems, and to be responsive to his developmental needs and stages. In other words, this is a pretty typical situation.[2]

This mother is young, pretty, and overwhelmed at having two children. Her older child, Annie, a first grader, is the designated patient. Annie's rebelliousness at school precipitated the referral. The mother, Mrs. Kay, readily accepted the referral, explaining that Annie questioned and challenged everything at home and that she certainly could use some help in handling her since she was at her wit's end.

Mrs. Kay is constant in her attendance at the child guidance sessions, but they can best be characterized as monotonous, repetitive, and generally unproductive. She spends her time complaining in an agitated manner. She complains that her daughter doesn't listen to her at home any more than she listens to her teacher at school. She complains that she brings her to her social worker every week and nothing changes because her daughter is bad, was born bad, has always been bad, and will always be bad. Now her two-year-old son is getting to be the same way.

Mrs. Kay tells the following story about her son Danny, age two. She told him to clean up his room five times and he didn't listen. She asked him with a "please" the first two times. She took a sharper tone the next two times, and finally she yelled and threw him into his room, slammed the door, and left him there for an hour. When she opened the door she found the room the same mess it had been earlier. None of her efforts worked; they never do. There he was, fast asleep on the floor, thumb in mouth, and the room as messy as ever. She stated with despair and anger that no matter how hard she tries nothing ever helps, not with him, not with her daughter, and not with her husband, who is as messy as the children. What was she to do, clean up everybody's messes?

---

2. I thank Ellen Wald for allowing me to use the material about Mrs. Kay, which she provided during her supervision with me.

Why was it her job to clean up other people's messes? And what was her social worker doing to help her? Nothing at all!

This young woman is a mother. She has two young children and she is responsible for them and she takes care of them as best she can, but when that evocative word *mother* comes up, she doesn't fit our picture very well. In order to be useful to this young woman we will have to put away our idealized notion of mother and get to know the person in that chair facing us, how to listen and hear what she has to say, and how to work towards helping her.

Mrs. Kay probably does not seem unusual to people who work in child guidance clinics. There are many young women who become mothers because of biological maturation and not because of emotional readiness. This is not to suggest that Mrs. Kay would necessarily have been ready to mother children ten or even twenty years later. Some people are not equipped for parenthood at any age because their early history was too stunting to allow adequate development of a character structure suited to being a parent.

What happened along the way to hamper the development of so many of the parents we meet and limit their ability to care for their children? We know that many of them have had terrible home situations and were themselves abused and neglected children, but while that knowledge might make us more sympathetic, it won't help us know how to work with them. Only through the thorough study of human development do we, as psychotherapists, begin to equip ourselves with the theoretical tools needed to unravel and understand the early failures that derailed the development of our patient population. This, of course, includes the parents of the children we treat. We need to know what went wrong in their psychological development: where they got stuck, how that impeded their ego development, their object relationships, and their mode of dealing with anxiety. Furthermore, we need to understand what form of pathological adaptation took place and what their internal life is like now.

What I am describing does not necessarily require lengthy and intensive interviews with these parents because when psychoanalytic developmental theory is well understood, the listening mode becomes fine tuned and the therapist is alert to recognizing key communications. This aids the process of selection and affords the therapist some clarity about what to explore and what to leave alone, what expectations are appropriate or might be beyond that person's psychological capacity. For instance, if a mother reveals that she cannot say "no" to her three-year-old, two possibilities immediately come to mind. One is that this mother is so undifferentiated from her child that to say "no" would feel too separate and cause unbearable anxiety over loss and abandonment. Another could be that this mother is very angry at her child and her indulgence is a reaction formation over this unwelcome affect. With these two possibilities in mind, the therapist would be in a position to explore with some focus and it would be relatively easy to discover whether either of these possibilities had merit, and if so which of the two fit the situation. The approach to the undifferentiated mother would differ from the approach to the mother whose anxiety stemmed from fear of loss of love, that is, anger at her child.

In the above example, the therapist's mode of thinking in response to this type of parental overpermissiveness rests on aspects of classical psychoanalytic theory that have been expanded to include preoedipal development. For instance, Freud's formulation regarding the relationship between anxiety states and the psychosexual stage is used diagnostically to gain insight into the parent who can't say "no."

Freud (1905, 1926, 1933) speculated that each psychosexual stage has a corresponding anxiety level. The anxiety of the oral phase is fear of loss of the object; at the anal phase, fear of the object's love; at the phallic phase, fear of castration; at the oedipal phase, fear of the superego. The psychosexual stage that corresponds to the focus of anxiety yields valuable information about the parent in our consulting room and gives direction to the way we might approach our work with her. For instance, in the example of the mother who can't say "no" to her three-year-old, two possibilities for this difficulty were considered. In the undifferentiated mother the anxiety most likely corresponds to a regression or fixation at the oral phase. Consistent with the affective state of this early phase is her inability to experience herself and her child as two separate people. When oral phase anxiety predominates, "no" represents loss and abandonment. To understand this mother and how to talk to her it is essential to be clear about the significance of the word "no" from a developmental point of view (Spitz 1959).

The young child's ability to say "no" indicates that a level of separateness has been attained and with it comes some capacity for autonomous action. Many people who are more or less able to function as adults were derailed at various pivotal points in their early development. We can sometimes reconstruct the origin of their derailment by observing their vulnerable areas as parents. For instance, difficulties during separation-individuation and failure to reach or maintain the state of dawning autonomy that in normal development begins to be apparent at around eighteen months when children discover the power of "no," could be manifested in the adult's difficulty with that word. This could be symptomatic of a primitive psychic structure and consequently these poorly differentiated adults would most likely function at the oral level, which would cause them to be further handicapped by their limited repertoire of defense mechanisms.

In talking to the undifferentiated mother about her three-year-old you might get a description of a child who goes to sleep whenever and wherever sleep overcomes him, and so is it with food, dressing, and all other daily routines. If you question this mother about her acceptance of the child centeredness and lack of structure in her home, she might get dreamy and tell you of her belief in self-expression, of her disinclination to say or do anything that might make Brian unhappy. She might talk of his creativity, his original mind, and of his lack of patience with the ordinary play and interests of other children his age. If you see this child in your consulting room he might overturn your wastebasket, and before you have a chance to intervene, pull a handful of journals off your shelf. You might be surprised when his mother, comfortably seated in one of your chairs, offers the prideful explanation that Brian is a virtual little scientist, so filled with curiosity that he must inspect anything in his path.

You had learned over the phone, when this mother, let us call her Ms. Lake, phoned for an appointment, that she was calling at the suggestion of the school. She was vague about the reason the school made this request. Her call was followed the next day by a telephone message from the director of the school. The message stated that Brian is so wild and unmanageable that Ms. Lake was told that unless she was willing to have an evaluation and accept the recommendations that follow, Brian would have to leave his school.

That Brian has a mother who can't say "no" to him is a serious obstacle to his growth and development. How is he to identify with a "no"-saying parent and eventually develop the ability to say "no" to himself, an important aspect of self-regulation? When asked about her marital status Ms. Lake, a single mother, stated that as long as she had Brian she neither needed nor wanted anyone else. Consequently there is nobody else at home to intrude on and dilute the close and exclusive tie between this mother and her child. The impact of an emotional climate that is paradoxically both intrusive and distant, that gratifies but doesn't hold or contain, doesn't bode well for Brian's development. A lot rests on the talent of the therapist who has now entered the picture. She has a difficult challenge ahead. To begin with, her appearance on the scene was not at the mother's request. If she is to have any impact, she will have to disturb the carefully guarded homeostasis of the mother–child pair. Much will be required of the therapist: exquisite tact, timing, insight, and more. Her diagnostic skills will have to extend to tracking the mother's shifting affective states as they are altered by what transpires in the consulting room.

The therapist will need her theoretical grounding. She will be well served by taking into account Freud's ladder of anxiety states, Mahler's separation-individuation schema, Spitz's (1959) organizers of the psyche with particular attention to the importance of the "no" in development. Anna Freud's (1946) classification of defense mechanisms will also help her assess and organize her thinking about Ms. Lake. Ideally, the excellent grounding provided by her knowledge of psychoanalytic developmental theory will allow her the freedom to proceed in an open-minded, exploratory manner, always curious and interested, and taking nothing for granted.

Psychoanalytic thinking is not linear. Its marvelous circularity allows for limitless arrangement and application. The more we know, the more we learn, the better we hear, the more we know, the more we learn, and so on. When the integration of some of our basic theoretical principles becomes part of what we know, in other words really ours, then we can listen to the patient's verbal and nonverbal communications and process what we hear in a really productive way. Although Freud's famous advice to physicians to listen to the patient with "evenly suspended attention" (Freud 1912b) was designated as a principle of the technique of listening to the free associations of patients in psychoanalysis, it is a listening mode that is applicable in a variety of other therapeutic situations. It is invaluable in all aspects of our work for it requires the therapist to listen in a state of complete openness, dispensing with customary logic, anticipation of where the material is going, or judgments and conclusions of any sort. This attitude of receptivity with no advance agenda is also very useful in consultation and in our work with people who are not seen frequently or regularly, such as the parents of our child patients. Even with these not-quite patients, such disciplined listening gives depth to our insight, and focus to our interventions.

Later in this book, in Chapter 10, I will discuss the treatment of a mother who also had difficulty in saying "no" to her child, but who presented a different diagnostic picture than the one presented by Ms. Lake, and in Chapter 7 I will describe a consultation with a mother whose difficulty with "no" had yet another set of underlying dynamics.

For now, let us return to Mrs. Kay and concentrate on the vignette about her little boy and his messy room presented earlier in this chapter. If we gather the information she gives us about herself in this brief encounter we will find that we can learn about her on multiple levels. For instance, it is startling that a mother would expect her two-year-old to go into his messy room and clean it up all by himself. It tells us that Mrs. Kay's perception of her two-year-old is not based on what she sees but on some quite unrealistic notion about her son's capabilities. When he fails to comply she does not question her expectation of him. Rather, she experiences his noncompliance as intentional and as an indicator of "badness." She has made up a story about her little boy and she believes her story with angry passion. Not even the sight of her child asleep on the floor of his still messy room evokes any feeling in her other than despair and hopelessness at her position in the family as the one who is not heard. He went to sleep on her, he turned a deaf ear, more evidence that no matter what she does, nobody listens and nobody hears.

Among the many things we learn is that her story startles us. It is vital to note that we are startled. It serves as a dramatic signal that our response to her story about her little boy differs so much from her perception of what happened. Mrs. Kay's expectations of her child, her handling of him, her explanation of his behavior, her anger at him, and her despair over her own plight are almost hard to comprehend, so drastically do they differ from our view of what transpired between this mother and child. When we organize all the information and insight we have gathered about Mrs. Kay this difference in perception should rank high on our list of significant factors to consider in our work with this mother.

Keeping this in mind, imagine the futility of telling Mrs. Kay that two-year-old children are not capable of cleaning their rooms by themselves, her expectation that her little boy do so is unrealistic, and she needs to match her expectations to his capabilities. No matter how kindly stated, this intervention would probably result in Mrs. Kay's feeling criticized. She would experience the therapist as being more concerned with her two-year-old son than with her. Most likely this would confirm that the therapist is part of that omnipresent "nobody," no different from all the other people who don't listen and don't hear. She would be quite right in her perception because the therapist's educational information about two-year-olds would have been offered at the wrong time in Mrs. Kay's psychic development. The therapist would not be seeing and addressing this adult as she is but as she "should" be to fit the therapist's image of parental behavior. Thus while much less obvious in its inappropriateness, an educational intervention at this point would be analogous to Mrs. Kay's misplaced expectation that her two-year-old clean up his room. If really listening, the therapist would have learned that Mrs. Kay needs the experience of being heard. She said so, and a response directed at anything other than her urgent need to be heard would confirm that even the therapist has unattuned ears.

To understand Mrs. Kay's communication more fully, let us go back to the beginning of life, to early infancy, that time when some of us are lucky and some of us are not, and the consequence of our luck, or lack of it, is more profound and irreversible than at any other time of life. At the beginning of life an infant has very limited resources for communicating need. Crying, of course, is the usual signal announcing such uncomfortable states as hunger, cold, indigestion, and other states of unpleasure that most mothers and fathers try to allay and transform into states of well-being. When the infant's caretaker is good at giving care and the infant has repeated experiences of crying bringing about the relief of discomfort, then eventually that infant's unfolding ego lays down memory traces of states of satisfaction. Gradually the satisfaction becomes linked to what at first is only a hazy perception of a force outside the self that provides comfort. In the early months, the infant cannot yet form an image of a person. That will come later. At this early stage the lucky infant perceives a vague presence that provides food and well-being. These repeated good experiences of being responded to build in the infant an affective state that Therese Benedek (1938) calls "confident expectation." The fortunate infant expects to be listened to because over and over again he has had this experience; being heard and satisfied becomes something he can remember and count on. By three or four months he already remembers that footsteps in response to his cry will be followed by a greeting, a face, a way of being held, a familiar smell, food, warmth—whatever is needed. Because good memories allow him to anticipate a response to his cry, footsteps and a familiar voice grow to be enough to stop the cry. These sounds are recognized as a signal that help is on its way. Gradually the infant's cry will lose urgency and become a sort of calling, something purposeful, the beginning of a dialogue with the caretaking other.

Here I am talking about something that happens, or fails to happen, at the earliest stage of life and sets down an immutable mark on all that is to follow in the development of a person. This earliest preverbal time (Blanck and Blanck 1994) can obviously not be remembered consciously, nor can it be forgotten, as it is preserved in the unconscious. Not knowing this unrememberable piece of history the patient cannot tell us in words but does tell us in other ways. For instance, Mrs. Kay reveals her expectation that nobody will listen and nobody will hear her. She conveys her repeated experience that no matter how hard she tries it's all in vain. In listening to the vignette about her little boy it is easy to be distracted by her unrealistic expectations and her lack of empathy for her son. It is difficult not to focus concern on that little boy who fell asleep on the floor after being yelled at and thrown into his room. Furthermore, Mrs. Kay's diatribe against her six-year-old daughter, whom she dismisses and condemns to "badness," has the quality of a bizarre tale, a horror story about a bad seed with a will of its own. This, of course, can be very off-putting, but as professionals we can derive a great deal of diagnostic information from these extreme communications.[3] Understanding and putting to use this information, including our visceral reaction to her behavior and affect, is the first step towards forming a working relationship with Mrs. Kay. This important step opens the path to helping her and ultimately helping her children.

---

3. The term *diagnostic* is being used to denote an assessment of development. It is not used in the *DSM-IV* sense of listing symptoms for purposes of categorization.

The application of psychoanalytic concepts adds scope and depth to our work, and this is equally true whether the patient is viewed as primary or adjunct. There is no doubt that some exceptionally gifted practitioners who do not have any psychoanalytic training might find a way of working with Mrs. Kay to help her and her children. Some people are profoundly talented and are able to hear themes of another story behind the manifest content of a patient's statements. By hearing these other themes, even in their vague and incomplete state, a very creative and intuitive therapist might find a way to connect with Mrs. Kay. Many of us can do that at certain times and with some patients, but not always or with everyone. Most of us have areas of strength as well as blind spots. We are not all equally effective with all of our patients, parents or other, or equally alert at all times. Most of us need a theoretical framework to organize our thinking and keep us on target, a structure with which to harness and shape intuition and transform it into effective interventions, tools that allow for a union of creativity and professional discipline.

As mentioned earlier, the infant develops confident expectation out of repeated experiences of being heard and responded to by the caretaking person. This good early experience affects all developmental lines. Such early ego functions as memory and anticipation become operative and spark secondary process thinking in the infant, for example, cry → footsteps → caretaker → feeding → satisfaction. This ego activity paves the way for the next ego function, intentionality. An indicator that this has taken place could be that change in the infant's signal, a call rather than a cry to summon the caretaker. This in turn sets off a "reciprocal dialogue" (Hartmann 1958) since the caretaker will register the alteration in the infant's way of communicating and will be likely to respond with warm affect to this friendly call. The infant who feels heard and who can summon his caretaker with intentionality does not experience the unimaginable anxieties of those infants whose cries go unheeded and who consequently are not able to develop, in the same straightforward way, the ego functioning, secondary process thinking, or confident expectation in their caretakers. Furthermore, the lucky baby with a mental representation of a good presence outside the self also experiences a good something inside. The baby is not yet sufficiently formed and differentiated to have a mental representation of a whole person outside the self or of a representation of a whole self. Edith Jacobson (1964) suggested using the terms *object representation* and *self representation* to find a precise way of discussing these theoretical constructs.[4] She distinguishes self representation from self, and object representation from object, self and object both being more concrete concepts that refer to the actual self and the actual object as located in time and space. Jacobson's contribution is helpful in understanding the evolution of object relations and identity formation. For an illustration of how this might work let us return to the satisfied infant. The affect of satisfaction becomes stored in the infant's memory as an embryonic representation of satisfied self and satisfying part object. This psychobiological experience fuels and is fueled by ego development. Simultaneously the mother's[5] experiences of satisfying her infant are stored as representations of good-mother, good-infant, and good-mother–infant pair. These self-enhancing experiences fuel her confidence in her mothering ability and in the "excellence" of the infant she produced, and further promotes her capacity to "fit together" (Hartmann 1958) with her infant. The experiences of fitting together, a form of primary adaptation, are also stored in memory as aspects of self and object representations.

It is useful to the clinician to think of psychic structures building out of these minuscule experiences. It allows us to understand that when our patients speak of Mother, Father, Sister, Brother, and so on, they are talking about representations of these im-

---

4. Jacobson (1964) defines self representation as the "unconscious, preconscious and conscious endopsychic representation of the bodily and mental self in the system ego" (p. 19). Object representation is defined the same way with the word object replacing the word self.

5. Mother is used to denote the primary caretaker.

portant others. These representations are aggregates of images and experiences that date back to infancy, images that convey the climate of early life but also contain distortions about early objects. In other words, it cautions us to allow for a measure of distortion in our patients' descriptions of members of their primary family and in the pictures presented of themselves as children and adults.

The previous paragraph presents an aspect of fundamental psychoanalytic knowledge basic to our work with adult patients. Unfortunately, many of us forget to consider this knowledge as equally relevant in our work with the parents of the children we treat. This, then, is a reminder. We must balance what we hear with what we perceive in the transference–countertransference manifestations that take place in our consulting room. We must do this regardless of whether the person in that chair is a patient or someone whose status in that regard is not yet known, such as the parent of a child patient. We must be attentive to what this parent reveals of his view of us, of our total person: our appearance, our attitudes and values, our voice and accent, our style of dressing, our taste in furniture, and so forth. We must carefully note any such communications and the responses they evoke in us and know that we are witness to different realities and differing realities.

This leads right into one of Freud's (1912a, 1915) fundamental psychoanalytic discoveries, that of transference and its corollary, countertransference. Freud observed that patients reexperience with the analyst many of the feelings, fantasies, and attitudes they experienced with their early caretakers and that the repetition of these affects is largely unconscious. Through the analysis of the transference, much of the past is rediscovered and some of the infantile distortions are uncovered and revised. The concepts of self and object representation are enormously useful in understanding the aggregate nature of these affective experiences with significant objects dating back far into childhood and the reenactment of these in the psychotherapy of adult patients. In turn, the psychotherapist also has unconscious responses to the patient and these countertransferential responses date back to early experiences in the life of the psychotherapist. Since these are also largely unconscious, the therapist might remain unaware of them.

Freud saw countertransference as an obstruction to the treatment process because it caused the analyst to have blind spots in regard to the patient. The combination of sound training and personal psychoanalysis has been viewed as essential in helping clinicians observe in themselves countertransferential manifestations through the derivative signals they produce. For instance, we might find ourselves consistently sleepy with a particular patient, or feeling very protective, angry, filled with rescue fantasies, highly critical, and so on. If we analyze these reactions we often find that the patient evoked in us something in our own past, and unless we analyze it we risk allowing a major obstacle to block the treatment.

While this basic description of countertransference is still considered fundamental to psychoanalytic theory and technique, the concept of countertransference has passed through a gradual evolutionary enrichment and expansion. In the process of change, the strictly negative view has given way to one that considers analyzed countertransference to have the potential of communicating a dimension not accessible in any other way. This expansion is part of a trend to distinguish between different kinds of countertransference. For instance, Casement (1991) states that we should "distinguish that part of a therapist's responses which offer clues to the patient's unconscious communications from that which is personal to the therapist" (p. 67). He goes on to suggest that we call the first "a diagnostic response" and the second "a personal countertransference." Along similar lines, Sandler (1976) suggests that among the many facets of transference is the patient's casting of the analyst into a particular role. When the analyst unconsciously complies and accepts the role assigned to him he aids the patient in actualizing some element of an infantile relationship. Sandler suggests that in some of these situations the countertransferential response can, when examined by the analyst, yield important information about the patient's unconscious communications as well as information about the analyst's unconscious compliance to the role casting imposed by the patient. In short, when we succeed in analyzing our countertransference we stand to learn something illuminating about ourselves, our patients, and the interaction.

A woman like Mrs. Kay is bound to evoke a range of reactions, including countertransference. She sits and complains about her little children. There is nothing motherly in her tone. Many a therapist listening to her would at times feel frustration, hopelessness, indignation, identification with her children, and the wish to rescue them from this condemning and unattuned mother. Furthermore, despite our best efforts, her insistence that we are useless to her, not listening, not hearing, and not helping when we were quite certain that we were trying very hard to find a way to help, would perhaps make us begin to doubt our efforts. In fact we might begin to feel not so dissimilar to the way Mrs. Kay feels: helpless, hopeless, and unheard. The drama in the room may shift with this insight. Yes, this young woman is supposed to be here to find improved ways of mothering her children, but she can't do it, at least not yet. How do we bring her closer to this goal?

We could begin by examining our reaction to Mrs. Kay's complaints that nobody listens. We are beginning to feel a bit the way Mrs. Kay feels. After all we are listening, we are doing our best, and to no avail. But are we? Obviously not, since nothing has changed for her. Could it be that we have been cast into a particular role and have accepted that role? One problem is that despite all that she has said to us we are still viewing her as a 26-year-old woman with two children who is here to refine her mothering skills, and she is not letting us do our job. It's time to analyze our countertransference. Does Mrs. Kay evoke some archaic object representation in our own past, one of an unattuned and uncaring parental figure? If that is so, who are we? Are we the whiny child who isn't listened to, or the unlistening adult who feels reproached by the whining child, or both? Something countertransferential must be serving as a serious obstruction because otherwise we would hear the distress behind the complaining and feel empathy.

The tragic consequence of being one of the unfortunate infants who repeatedly waited too long for food, received little comfort, had no basis for establishing confident expectation, is that the very lack of expectation often generates defeat. Think of the difference between Mrs. Kay's quest for help and that of Mrs. Jones, who arrives in our office and says, "I feel nervous about being here, but I also feel a sense of relief. I've run into a situation I can't deal with and I'm very upset. Now that I'm here I at last feel the hope that you can help sort things out. That will make me feel less anxious and confused." Both women are revealing something of their preverbal experience, and clearly Mrs. Jones expects the therapist to continue a familiar pattern of being heard and helped while Mrs. Kay's pessimism is an expression of a world deaf to her needs. The problem is that it is easy to be drawn to Mrs. Jones, who will probably make good use of our help, and to be put off by Mrs. Kay, who relegates us to an unhelpful role. Mrs. Jones creates the satisfied baby=good mother equation transposed into satisfied patient=good therapist. Mrs. Kay is the opposite: frustrated baby=bad mother, updated to frustrated patient=bad therapist. Here is another good reason we need to do careful assessments.

Mrs. Kay's ability to adapt to another person is impaired. We see this in her inability to fit together with her two-year-old. She is unable to adapt to his needs and developmental level as demonstrated in the vignette about the cleaning of his room. As we listen to her week after week, we learn that all her object relations are fraught with difficulty. Her husband ignores her, her daughter defies her, her sister criticizes her, her neighbor snubs her, her daughter's teacher thinks badly of her, and her father and mother show no interest in her. Of course Mrs. Kay's perception of people's indifference extends to the therapist. The therapist is perceived as cold, indifferent, and ineffective.

The rigidity of attitude we witnessed in Mrs. Kay when she described the messy room incident with two-year-old Danny, her lack of accommodation to her little boy, gave us important information about her. Rigidity and lack of accommodation to another person are not simply descriptive terms. We shouldn't worry about sounding judgmental by applying such adjectives to a person who comes to us for help. These describe characteristics indicative of severe developmental deficits and if we do not name them we might silently react to them in a diffuse manner. In fact, that is what had been taking place in the therapeutic situation and took the form of discomfort and apathy (Seinfeld 1991) in the therapist, a form of countertransference that tuned out the meaning of what Mrs. Kay was saying. The therapist had to overcome this obstacle in order to become receptive to Mrs. Kay's communications.

A person who is not accustomed to being heard naturally has difficulty communicating, in recognizing her own affective states, and in recognizing when she is being listened to and heard. A therapist needs to be a creative linguist in working with such a person, for the words we often hear with such patients are not the words we know. "Leave me alone" could mean "Please listen to me," and "I don't want to come here any more" could mean "Please don't send me away." In turn, the therapist's language must also change to fit, and it is not suitable to say to such a person: "It's difficult for you to accept help," or: "You describe how critical you feel about the people around you, but you are your own harshest critic." This is not language that can help the patient. Both interventions can easily be heard as criticism. It is language that pushes the patient away under the pretext of making an offering. No, this language only serves the therapist's need to express frustration.

In a situation like this the therapist can serve the patient best by offering hope in a way that is unintrusive and does not expose the patient's state of need. With this principle in mind, the therapist uses words that have become de-mystified to express this therapeutic attitude. The therapist can say something very simple like: "We haven't yet figured out how to work on this together, but with time we will."

What we strive for is that this therapeutic opportunity and the empathy it may tap in the therapist will, in time, spark Mrs. Kay's growth. Hopefully she will be able to travel developmentally and arrive at a point where no longer the frustrated child, she can stop being the frustrator of her children. She will need to become a patient in her own right to achieve this goal. She has a long way to go and the main thing that she has going for her is her consistent attendance at her sessions. That, too, can be viewed as a preverbal communication; she has not completely given up hope.

For Mrs. Kay and many other mothers and fathers, nothing in their lives prepared them for parenthood. If our expectations for this patient population take this into account and if we are given the time and training we need, we can have an impact. Then, with no other agenda in mind, we can demonstrate to Mrs. Kay that we are ready to listen and mean it. Sometimes this is difficult to accomplish because, as mentioned, Mrs. Kay's expectation of being unheard makes it difficult for her to recognize when she *is* being listened to. However, once we understand what we are dealing with in our patients and in ourselves, it is amazing how attuned we become to even the smallest therapeutic opportunities.

Here is a brief description of how the initially futile sessions with Mrs. Kay were transformed into something meaningful. To begin with, the therapist became consciously aware of her own apprehension prior to and during her appointments with Mrs. Kay and of her generally feeling useless to this person. The analysis of this insight and a careful assessment of Mrs. Kay made it clear that "child guidance" was an unrealistic treatment plan and that Mrs. Kay needed to be viewed as a patient in her own right. With increased sensitivity to this patient, the therapist recognized that Mrs. Kay began many sessions by complaining about how hard it was to get to the agency on time: there was traffic, weather, chores at home, the phone rang, and so on. In the past, this litany of complaints presented in a whiny tone of voice had caused the kind of role responsive "actualization" in the countertransference de-

scribed by Sandler (1976): the therapist had accepted the assigned role of listening without hearing. Now the therapist responded to the scheduling complaint with interest. After some
discussion she offered to move the appointment to fifteen minutes later, allowing for the leeway this patient felt was lacking.
Mrs. Kay responded with relief and appreciation, which rapidly
gave way to concern that she was too much trouble and worry
that her complaints had been offensive. This then became the
theme of the therapeutic work: that being heard and responded
to could cause such relief and worry at the same time.

Mrs. Kay responded to the shift in focus with unexpected ease
and spontaneously began to talk about herself, her past, and her
childhood. Over time, and with her therapist's help, she began to
see connections between her past and present difficulties. At
around the same time she reported for the first time some positive behavior on the part of her children as well as some nice interaction with them, and seemed pleased to able to share this with
her therapist. The therapist noted this sign that the working alliance was stabilizing, an indicator of the important psychic growth
that now allowed her patient to have a measure of trust and a
glimmer of hope that help was possible.

4

The Professional Attitude[1]

$\mathcal{M}$rs. Adams and Mrs. Kay were presented in earlier chapters to illustrate some of the problems and therapeutic issues typically encountered in work with parents, and to further address the question posed earlier regarding the place of parents on a patient to non-patient continuum.

Mrs. Adams was presented as an example of a sophisticated parent, well educated, an accomplished professional in the related field of early childhood development, a reflective and psychologically aware person, a woman who fitted the diagnostic criteria of neurotic structure and was undergoing a classical analysis. Despite her many accomplishments and what appeared to be a secure and comfortable style of life, Mrs. Adams was a dissatisfied and unhappy person.

Mrs. Kay was presented as an example of an unsophisticated parent, not well educated, and not possessing any particular accomplishments in or out of the home. She was impulsive, impatient, not reflective or interested in self exploration. Diagnostically she presented features of a borderline personality struc-

---

1. Winnicott (1960), in his paper "Counter-transference," reminds us that the analyst (or psychotherapist) during working hours is "in a special state, that is, *his attitude is professional*" (p. 161). This attitude requires that he "must remain vulnerable, and yet retain his professional role . . ." (p. 160).

ture. The sole area of commonality between Mrs. Kay and Mrs. Adams was that both were predominantly dissatisfied and unhappy people.

While the demands of working with these two mothers were very different, it would be hard to say that one mother was easier or more difficult to work with than the other. More to the point is that they presented very different technical challenges to the therapists who worked with them. A brief narrative of Mrs. Kay's treatment was presented in Chapter 3 and conveyed the general tone of her treatment during the early phase when her therapist was faltering, followed by a description of the change of direction that occurred when her therapist gained clearer insight into the dynamics of the case, and with that a more solid footing. Some aspects of work with Mrs. Adams and the issues regarding technique they raised were described in Chapter 2, but these were left unresolved and will be further elaborated in the pages that follow.

Mrs. Adams, despite her impressive credentials, her breadth of knowledge about early development, and her many strengths in other areas of life, had a difficult time being motherly to her child. She was more than adequate in the practical realm, providing good physical care, an orderly, predictable home, and ample stimulation of an educational nature. She was, however, not able to be a full-fledged "good enough" mother. There was about her a coldness towards her son, an insufficiency of libidinal cathexis, if you will. Consequently, no matter how hard she tried, and she tried very hard, she seemed to not have within her that love, that spark of delight born out of love that Spitz (1965) so eloquently describes as having the effect of quickening the infant's development. Perhaps that paucity of love, a failing exhibited by the boy's father as well, had the cruel effect of making their child less than appealing. And so his absence of liveliness, of charm, of playfulness (normally such natural traits in a six-year-old), resulted in *not* gaining him the admiration and affirmation of the people in his environment.

The snowballing of bad fortune to such a hapless end is not always the case. Some children who are not wonderfully loved by their parents nonetheless have within them great sending power. Consequently other people in their environment are drawn to them, enjoy them, and through this interest and attention provide them with much needed narcissistic supplies. And some children have within them a particular ego strength that Mahler (1968) refers to as "the capacity to extract," a talent for being able to derive the most from any situation that comes their way, whether in response to the kindness of a stranger, to aesthetic or intellectually stimulating experience, or even from the opportunity to do something useful on their own. Some children are endowed with this quality of being able to grow and flourish even when the emotional supplies in their lives are rather meager. But Tim was not so lucky. He was a heavy, somber child who took in little and gave forth even less. His unresponsiveness was striking and constant. This quality of personality, so unfailingly present, was felt, particularly by his mother, as an inescapable reminder of her shortcomings, an ever-present reproach.

I would like to concentrate on this aspect of the Adams family: the mother's and father's obvious shortcomings as parents and the lackluster personality of their son, in order to illustrate the particular demands on Tim's therapist generated by these circumstances. These were demands of a very delicate and challenging nature and they played an important role in the work with Tim and with each of his parents.

I refer here to a situation in which the therapist is required to deal professionally with what appears to be an ongoing deficiency in the affective connection between the parents (or parent) and child and must find a way to work with the insufficiency. My stress on the need for a *professional* approach to such a problem is to emphasize that the therapist's dealing with the insufficiency by taking on the role of becoming a better and more loving parent to the child would *not* be a professional solution.

In the case of Tim, the parents were aware of the limits of their love for their child, were very ashamed of this shortcoming in themselves, and felt guilt at being embarrassed by him. Their shame and guilt became a significant factor in their relationship with their son's therapist.

At first they both hoped that the therapist wouldn't notice these shortcomings of theirs. Mrs. Adams tried to cover them up by being ultra-cooperative, by always remembering to telephone Tim's therapist to report any important events in his life, by being on time for Tim's sessions, paying his bills promptly, and so forth. Mr. Adams hid behind humor and an exaggerated show of confidence in the therapist's expertise with emotions and their vicissitudes.

Eventually they both confessed in their characteristic ways. Mrs. Adams with great sorrow shared her realization that she lacked the love and pride that so many other mothers naturally possess. Mr. Adams mentioned, with an attempt to be casual that quickly shifted to uncommon solemnity, that he has no natural inclination to do the fatherly stuff like play ball with his son or do hobbies, model planes, and such. He added that lack of talent for being a good dad must run in the family since his dad had the same failing.

Here is our dilemma as the child's therapist. We might assume that we are being asked by these parents to provide what they cannot, asked to compensate for their pale love by providing a richer and more nourishing version. But is that what we are trained to do? Is it our job to be the better parent? Of course not. Yet it happens in cases like this that a therapist, in a state of unrecognized countertransference, possessively takes the child on with the zeal of a missionary.

When the child's therapist takes on the role of being a better parent, the case may play out in many ways but what will have been set in motion is not psychotherapy. It is something else that has nothing to do with our training and purpose.

What is the purpose of our work with Tim and Tim's parents? We have to get to know Tim deeply, develop a working diagnosis of him so as to understand his limited affect and general constriction. We have to use our professional knowledge in getting to know him, and in the process help him become more self-aware, and ultimately (developmentally) closer to what a boy of his age and stage is like. To put it very simply, we hope to make it possible for Tim to become a more ordinary boy who fits in and is accepted and enjoyed by parents and peers and can in turn enjoy them. Of course this only sounds simple. It is a very serious undertaking. If we do not succeed Tim will remain an outsider and with the passing months and years will, at best, develop a defensive armor that will distance him farther and farther from the object world. A lot rests on our commitment to doing our job thoroughly. The seriousness of our commitment will be conveyed in our attitude and sooner or later recognized by Tim and his parents. Our attitude must differ from that of any other person in Tim's life or in the life of his parents. Whether with Tim or with his parents, whatever the moment, whether solemn, puzzling, flat, uncomfortable, or humorous, our response will always be different from that of any other person in their lives. To maintain this difference is our job, an essential aspect of our work.

What do I mean by maintaining this difference? I mean something we all know, something very familiar in our daily work. It is the way we place ourselves vis-à-vis the patient so that we can allow our affective response to exist without losing our power to observe and think. We may feel sad, amused, bored, but we don't just feel these affects as we might feel them when not working. We feel and observe what we feel, and think about what is happening. We do this with children and with their parents, and with our adult patients. This is our role, and this is what Tim and his parents will ultimately recognize about us. This evenness about us, this disciplined but not unfeeling professional stance, conveys our competence and creates a climate of safety; it can go a long way in firming up the working alliance. This professional attitude of unwavering dependability can ultimately become one of the mutative factors that sets a case onto a productive course.

Compare this approach of observing, responding, and processing with one that focuses primarily on the shortcomings of family members, or on their hidden agendas, or on imagining that we are complying with the roles the parents assign to us to compensate for their own deficiencies. And on this last point most of us know that whichever way they would want it to go it wouldn't work because the root of the problem is elsewhere. And although obvious, still it should be mentioned that the parents of our young patients are not always conscious of the wishes and fantasies they have about our role in their child's life, nor are these wishes and fantasies constant. Since we are dealing with unconscious factors here, this is a murky area where the rules of logic change from moment to moment. We can be perceived as the good mother one day and the rivalrous sibling the next. Mrs. Adams might be very appreciative of our dedicated work with Tim and also have periods during which her shame at her failings as a mother might be projected onto Tim's therapist and experienced as criticism.

There is another point that must be made here. Just because we can identify a quality of coldness in Mrs. Adams and a level of distance and lack of interest in Mr. Adams, should we assume that these are the reasons that Tim is lacking in the liveliness and energy that are so typical of six-year-old children? Of course not! It's bad enough that the parents believe this to be the whole story. It would be doubly unfortunate if their child's therapist joined in this belief. I mentioned before that some children can make the most out of very little and are good at finding ways of being nurtured by anyone, including people other than their parents. Another child born to Mr. and Mrs. Adams, a child with a dissimilar endowment, would have developed very differently from Tim. This dissimilarity would have been the result of differences in basic temperament and ego apparatus. For instance, a very lively, smiling, and responsive baby might have fared very differently in the Adams home, and might have roused responses in these parents that their stolid, somber infant failed to evoke. Had that been the case, it most likely would have changed the course of all that was to follow.

As Tim's therapist gets to know him it will become clearer why he is the way he is. There are reasons for these inhibitions of affect that go beyond the emotional climate created by his parents. We understand the interplay of forces and their circularity in the formation of an emotional climate; a child with a limited affective range can dampen that climate and cause his parents to feel rejected, which in turn could precipitate their withdrawal. Conversely, a lively baby could rouse the responsiveness of depressed parents, or, if met with constant indifference, that same baby could eventually wilt, sink into apathy, and become part of the lifeless climate. The predominant affective tone is not the work of one person but rather the sum total of all the harmony and discord, the enriching connections and the painful dislocations of the principal players. With a child like Tim, it is likely that his therapist will also experience feelings of rejection and a sense of being superfluous. Tim's therapist will be able to track this response in herself and use it in his treatment. She will, for instance, find opportunities during her sessions with Tim to reflect out loud on the effect of his inscrutability. And she will also use this aspect of her experience of being with Tim for understanding what it must be like for his parents to be held off by him, to be so continually subjected to his indifference.

Given what has just been speculated about the therapist's experience with Tim, we can consider anew the descriptions of Mrs. Adams's encounters with Tim's therapist presented in Chapter 2, her sense of defeat, and the transferential themes that emerged and placed the therapist in the position of rival.

How would we, as her son's therapist, respond to these powerful currents? Since she is not the primary patient we cannot interpret the transference. This limitation can make our task more difficult but it is a condition of our work that cannot be changed. That doesn't mean that in extreme circumstances we might not say to a parent that she is misperceiving us in a way that might do harm to the treatment of her child. If that parent is in her own separate treatment, we might suggest that she discuss this with her own therapist. If she doesn't have a therapist of her own, it sometimes makes sense to recommend that she consider treatment for herself. But in general our best approach with parents is to remain objective, quietly attentive and interested—in other words, to maintain our professional attitude. We have to have our feet evenly planted and be clear about our own role. That way whatever role parents might assign to us will be considered information that will help us to get to know them better.

Objectivity and neutrality are not qualities that go hand in hand with coolness or a withholding manner. This needs to be mentioned because it is so often misunderstood, particularly by beginners who are trying to act like experienced therapists and think this is the way to do it.

For instance, when Mrs. Adams complains about our use of magic markers rather than paint, we might tell her that we find magic markers easier to use because they require less preparation and are easier to clean up. We say that since painting is primarily a prop for the work of therapy, magic markers are simply more practical. We can agree that of course paints offer a great deal more from an artistic point of view and are the preferred material from that perspective. We talk as two adults, both professionals in related fields, discussing the different merits of these art materials and how a particular situation might affect the choice of one over the other.

When Mrs. Adams complains about being cold in the waiting room, we carefully check the temperature and if it is indeed cold, we apologize and buy an electric heater. In this situation we are a host or hostess who should provide an adequate environment and correct the situation when we learn that we are not providing a comfortable setting. If we discover that it is not at all cold, we tell her that we are sorry that the waiting room is not more comfortable. We don't interpret that she might feel left out in the cold. We don't need to explore her feelings of exclusion or her rivalry, but we do need to be aware of them, and consider this important information about how she might be experiencing her son's treatment. We need to think about these lonely times in the waiting room and what this might stir up from her past about being displaced, excluded, rejected, and so forth. This way of thinking helps us feel more connected to her, supports our alliance, and aids us in letting her know in quiet, unintrusive ways, and at opportune moments, that we understand that having a child in treatment is hard work on every level. It is hard work from the most practical aspect of time spent chauffeuring and waiting to the most deeply felt emotions that this experience cannot fail to stir and awaken. Both she and Tim's therapist need to have this simple truth stated now and then so it doesn't fade in importance or become relegated to the status of something trivial and annoying. We need to hear that it's cold in the waiting room even when it's not, to be reminded that the mother (or father) sits out there waiting; we need to hear this lest we become complacent about the hardship of the parents' situation. This awareness on our part will further our work with them and with Tim.

In our work with Mr. and Mrs. Adams we let them know that we have observed and experienced Tim's tendency to distance the adult, to make the adult feel extraneous and unwanted. We tell them that we know firsthand what it's like being dismissed by him, and that we understand this quality of his to be detrimental to his relationships with everyone. We let them know that it is an important issue in his treatment. We might also tell the parents that as we gain insight into how to deal with Tim's inaccessibility we will share these insights with the parents and of course do this without compromising Tim's confidentiality.

To return to our contrasting and comparing Mrs. Kay and Mrs. Adams, it is always interesting to discover and rediscover that in our field a patient's diagnosis tells us very little about how treatable that person will be. One exception would be the severe character disorders, a diagnostic category known not to be generally amenable to treatment. But whether a patient is diagnosed as a high-functioning neurotic or as a person with very primitive structure tells us very little about his response to treatment. In medicine, barring the elusive common cold, a diagnosis does hold prognostic value. Less so in our field. This is equally true of work with parents. I believe that the cases of Mrs. Kay and Mrs. Adams are illustrative of this point. Mrs. Kay was described because she was so clearly representative of a large portion of our population, young women unprepared for motherhood. This unreadiness was obvious and totally understandable in light of her own history of neglect. Mrs. Adams was also unprepared for motherhood but in a much more uneven and oblique way, and probably on balance was the more difficult parent because the quality of her turmoil was more diffuse and more elusive. Another way of viewing the relative difficulties presented by these mothers is to consider how they both might affect the particular vulnerabilities in their children's therapists. Some therapists might have a more difficult time in dealing with the type of apathy in the countertransference that occurred in the work with Mrs. Kay, while others might find more difficult the ambitendence of rivalry with longing for help expressed by Mrs. Adams.

These cases also raise the issue of a common difficulty for child therapists: the need to remain neutral and objective in the face of parental neglect. There was a measure of neglect in both cases, dressed in different guises. The therapist's response to neglect is one of those factors that can lead to a judgmental attitude toward the parents and evoke rescue fantasies about the child. Either of these reactions constitutes a serious departure from the professional attitude so vital to our work. But it must also be stated that there is a difference between neglect and abuse, especially severe abuse. Severe abuse requires the therapist to step outside of the customary treatment conditions wherein confidentially is sacred and call outside agencies for help. Neglect has to be worked with; that is part of what we do, part of the therapeutic task. Severe abuse requires intervention beyond our role as psychotherapist.

It is important to remember that we also see many people whose abilities as parents are well developed and who consult us about their children for a variety of reasons. These can range from consultation about a mild transient developmental disturbance, to a request for assistance in finding ways of helping their child deal with the death of a family member or a divorce situation, and to such serious conditions as childhood autism. There can be requests for child treatment for many reasons unrelated to parental limitations. In fact, many particularly devoted and even gifted parents consult child therapists for what some would dismiss as minor problems. Many of these super-responsible parents are either in our field and/or people who have benefited from psychotherapy or psychoanalysis. Often these cases are short-term and serve as examples of effective primary prevention.

There has been a tendency in our field to readily blame parents for anything and everything that goes wrong in the lives of their children. This trend is equally true of therapists who treat adults and those who treat children. This is a really dangerous trend. It grows out of blind countertransference, obscures the real picture, and consequently limits the effectiveness of the therapist. We must remember that life is not that simple; some children are constitutionally more vulnerable than others, or more uneven in their development, or have been exposed to traumatic circumstances that were beyond the control of anyone.

There are also circumstances where parent and child are poorly matched and from the beginning bring out the worst in each other. A good example of this would be a depressed mother and an extremely passive infant. The depressed mother might not be sufficiently roused by her infant to respond, with the sad consequence that the passive infant would fail to receive much needed stimulation. The reciprocal dialogue described by Hartmann (1958) so long ago as an early form of adaptation and a precursor to object relations would be curtailed in such a case or fail to develop altogether. However, if the mother's depression is mild and the infant is not too passive, that infant might succeed in rousing the mother out of her depressed mood, engaging her in a reciprocal dialogue. It is awesome to consider that these small differences in temperament and mood can play such a pivotal part in shaping the tone of the early mother–child dyad and all that follows.

It is essential that child therapists not oversimplify all the forces that meet and combine in the process of becoming and being a parent. Our understanding of this is one of the factors that might curb a tendency that contributes to one of the common pitfalls of child treatment: the therapist's overidentification with the child. Such overidentification can cause serious difficulties for the child and is certainly likely to work against the formation of a working alliance with the child's parents. This is very troublesome since the child's treatment depends on the parents' cooperation, which includes willingness to bring the child to sessions and pay for his treatment. The need for parental cooperation makes the working alliance imperative, an essential safeguard to the continuity of the child's treatment.

The relationship we have with the parents of our child patients differs in so many ways from our relationship with the adults who are in treatment with us about themselves. Take, for instance, the obvious difference between consulting a therapist about oneself and consulting a therapist about one's child. In the former the topic is the patient, the person in the room. In the latter the cast of characters immediately swells. We have the child, his parents, siblings if any, sometimes teachers, baby sitters, and other significant people in the life of the child. The therapist wants to learn about the current situation, the presenting problem, the child's early development, school functioning, friends, some background on the parents, their marriage, and so forth. In some cases teachers, pediatricians, and baby sitters are actually interviewed to round out the picture. All this collateral activity is not uncommon in child treatment and stands in sharp contrast to work with an adult and its consistent one-to-one contact.

The initial sessions in child cases also present very wide variations in response. Some parents approach the initial consultations with an urgent wish for advice and guidance. Others find providing the early history very difficult because they don't remember the early years. Some find providing this information annoying and irrelevant to the present problem and just want the child's treatment to begin. Other parents enjoy remembering the early months and years of their child's life, and the experience of remembering and sharing these memories with the therapist fills them with pleasant affects. Still other parents welcome the initial sessions without the child present as a time to ask questions and to assess whether the therapist is to their liking. There are various ways of beginning and even more reactions to this process, which is so much less tidy than beginning with an adult patient. The skills required to do this well can be quite formidable, and, although they are not discussed in books on technique, the same theoretical grounding that applies to all other aspects of our work applies here as well. The difference is that we have to work out our own way of adapting our theoretical knowledge to this situation even though it presents us with conditions that differ in many ways from the conditions we find in the typical one-to-one treatment situations.

For instance, a common complication that arises out of the interdependence of therapist and parent, a condition that in and of itself habitually precipitates transference and countertransference reactions, is the following. Many parents feel that their need for a therapist's help with their child places the therapist in a position of greater stature and authority than their authority as adults and parents. This reduced status is experienced as humiliation by some parents and combines with narcissistic mortification at having a child in need of treatment. Consequently, parents sometimes feel antagonistic to the very help they seek. A regressive state of "badness" is then replayed, with the parent becoming the bad child of the bad therapist. In this state of negativity the parents often undermine the treatment by such acting out as missing appointments, arriving late, and so on. In turn, the therapist's resentment at dependence on parental cooperation may heighten identification with the child, whose treatment is now in jeopardy. Combined with growing frustration with parental hostility, this can precipitate a regression in the therapist to feeling like the bad child of the bad, frustrating parent. Unless the therapist can resolve this countertransference and take charge of the situation the case will either limp along or collapse.

It takes a great deal of maturity, tact, and determination to establish and maintain a reasonable working alliance with initially hostile parents. Sometimes parental pathology is such that the case is doomed no matter how wise and skilled the therapist. We need to have working conditions that allow us to make full use of our skills and knowledge. If parental hostility invades the therapeutic climate and is impervious to our interventions, then we sometimes have to accept defeat and not subject ourselves to destructive conditions. Our commitment to our patients need not eclipse our concern for our own comfort and well-being. Perhaps some of the therapists who limit or give up working with children do so because they did not sufficiently protect the climate in which they worked.

The more we talk about the challenges of this work the clearer it becomes that the child therapist needs to be very well trained in theory and technique and well analyzed as well. These are the safeguards for not allowing countertransference to upset the treatment of a child because of festering issues with the parents. Our knowledge, insight, and empathy are the vital factors that will allow the precarious yet essential alliance between parents and child therapist to stabilize, and in this situation the therapist will often have to do the lion's share of the work.

With all this stated I believe that it grows clearer and clearer that the parent must be regarded as a patient. There is no other sensible way to view a situation where one person is afforded the enormous leeway a parent has as a player in his child's treatment while the therapist must find and hold a position of absolute groundedness and at the same time maintain an attitude of flexibility and adaptability—in other words, demonstrate basic attributes of the professional attitude.

The Dynamics of Referrals

The referral of patients, particularly when the patients are children, can be a complex process that can lead to surprising complications. There are many factors that contribute to these complications and I will describe some in this chapter. Of course many referrals are made and received in a straightforward manner. Still, this subject merits attention, particularly in a book on working with the parents of child patients. After all, parents are the ones who on their own or on the advice of someone outside the family initiate the referral process for their child. They are the ones who generally interview and select the therapist who is to treat their child. And while the role of parents in this first step into treatment is appropriate and in fact requisite, their involvement may nonetheless increase the likelihood of complications as early in the treatment process as the referral telephone call. As I present some clinical material, the themes that emerge will be so familiar that the only surprise will be to see them in such concentration and so boldly stated in print.

On some occasions in the treatment of adults or children it is the way a referral is made that has an intrusive tone. While that tone may sometimes be dispelled after the initial consultation, there are situations when it remains and its presence lingers throughout the treatment process, an unwelcome distraction, a strain that doesn't go away. Sometimes these initial strains do not stem from the way a referral is made but rather from the way it is received, or from something in the relationship between the one who makes the referral and the recipient.

I will present some vignettes that will illustrate points of difference as well as points of similarity in the referral of children and that of adults. The following three examples illustrate typical adult referrals. The first is a straightforward exchange between two professionals. The two that follow are examples of varying ways that strains can be set in motion by this opening move into the treatment process.

ADULT REFERRAL 1

Referring Therapist (on the phone): I'm calling to find out whether you have time in your schedule for a consultation that might lead to treatment. The patient is a woman in her fifties, a relative of one of my patients. I don't know anything about her except that she asked my patient to find a therapist for her. I'm hoping that you might see her and find out what's needed. . . . Oh, good, I'll give my patient your name and telephone number and when this woman calls you she'll mention my name. If she needs treatment and you find that you can't see her for reasons of schedule, fee, or whatever, please feel free to refer her to someone you feel to be suitable, or if you would rather not, call me and I'll find someone else for her. Of course I would be pleased if it works out that you can see her.

What makes this an unencumbered referral is the professional manner of the referring therapist. He is courteous and straightforward. He divulges nothing about his patient except that the referral request originates with his patient for a relative, a woman. By informing his colleague that he knows nothing about this woman he is both absolving himself of any responsibility should this be an inappropriate referral and alerting his colleague to such a possibility. Therapists vary in how much they like to know about a perspective patient. Some of us like some information while others are more casual about having knowledge in advance. The referring therapist is also very clear about the limits of his involvement in regard to exchange of information on any level including name, age, profession, or any other identifying information. The confidentiality of his patient and the perspective patient is respected, as is the autonomy of both therapists. The referring therapist wants to place a prospective patient in the hands of a trusted colleague. The colleague accepts the request. No hidden agendas appear in this exchange.

The next example presents a common situation that highlights the potential impact of professional rank on the referral process.

ADULT REFERRAL 2

Mr. Ames, a young therapist who works for a social service agency and is concurrently developing a private practice, receives a referral from his supervisor. This action evokes a variety of feelings in Mr. Ames. He feels pleased and flattered by this show of confidence, especially so since the referral comes from a professional who knows the quality of his work firsthand and over time. The initial good feelings persist but gradually a mild unease develops, a gnawing worry that he might not measure up to the supervisor's standards. He wonders whether the supervisor might now expect him to present this case for supervision. He begins to feel an uncomfortable resentment at suddenly feeling small in comparison to his supervisor, a particularly unpleasant development at this turning point in his professional life when he was feeling big.

This example illustrates that receiving a referral, even in the most benign manner and from a respected and admired colleague and mentor, may evoke a variety of conscious and unconscious responses that cover the whole range of developmental hurdles, from issues around autonomy to oedipal rivalries.

Now let's consider a less benign situation, one where control rather than rank is the manifest issue.

ADULT REFERRAL 3

Mr. Ames is offered a second referral. This one comes from Mr. Bard, a colleague and former classmate at an advanced training institute from which they both graduated. Mr. Bard is calling to refer the husband of one of his patients. He says that he sees his patient, Roberta Grey, twice per week at such and such a fee and that he expects Mr. Ames to follow suit with Joseph Grey, her husband, regarding both the fee and the frequency of appointments. He adds that he strongly believes this case requires ongoing communication between therapists and that he would want regular weekly telephone discussions with Mr. Ames. He goes on to offer his diagnosis of Joseph, whom he has never met. Joseph is a borderline patient with narcissistic features and a propensity for extremely childish behavior. He states that in contrast to Joseph, his patient Roberta has a neurotic structure. In fact Roberta is a perfect candidate for a full analysis but has not yet agreed to use of the couch and the more frequent appointments this would require. Mr. Bard suspects that her current demand that her husband enter treatment is a form of resistance to her own analysis. She insists that her husband have equal time with his own therapist. Mr. Bard makes it clear that he considers the husband's entry into treatment nothing more than an obstacle to Roberta's analysis. He adds that Joseph is clearly not a candidate for analysis. He concludes with the advice that Joseph needs a firm approach or the marriage is bound to fail.

This referral might sound extreme to some readers; if so, they are lucky, young in the field, or perhaps my putting it down on paper highlights the offensive manner in which this referral is made and emphasizes the referring therapist's hostility and demand for control.

Note that in this last referral the full names of patients are disclosed. This common breach of confidentiality mimics the medical model wherein the neurologist calls the neurosurgeon or the dentist calls the oral surgeon to introduce the patient and the patient's condition. But in our field there is never a need to divulge names, particularly since not all referral requests result in a phone call from the actual patient-to-be. If and when the patient calls he can provide his name and that of the referring person and that will suffice.

Mr. Bard's referral to Mr. Ames might strike a familiar note in some readers who have been at the receiving end of situations in which the referring person's countertransference is revealed in his blatant overidentification with his patient. Sometimes such overidentification is exhibited in hostility towards the patient's spouse, parents, children, or others. In this example, Mr. Bard's general bossiness suggests that his hostility to his patient's husband now extends to Mr. Ames. In fact it appears as if Mr. Ames is being handed this referral with a "firm hand." It's easy to see how the potential for tension between therapists can be set in motion before the initial contact with the prospective patient ever takes place.

There is more to ponder about this referral for it raises some ethical questions as well as issues about our theory and technique. Most obviously inappropriate is the assumption that two therapists, each treating a member of a couple, should automatically discuss the treatment of these patients. If this is done without the patients' permission, a breach of confidentiality is taking place. But if the therapists do hold their discussions of the treatment with the permission of their patients, what is being conveyed to these patients in requesting permission that they be discussed? What aspect of our theory supports such an approach? What does it do to the privacy of the treatment situation and to the expression of intense feelings that the assurance of such privacy facilitates? We cannot underestimate the force of the therapeutic dyad, its synergistic impact on therapist, patient, and therefore treatment process. Since some of that force is generated by the promise of exclusivity, an inviolate aspect of the therapeutic relationship, to discuss patients is a transgression that is likely to dilute the intensity of treatment and distance therapist from patient and patient from therapist.

For two therapists to hold regular discussions of spouses they are treating in individual treatment sounds, at best, parental. This turning of our patients into quasi-children is the antithesis of what treatment strives to achieve. After all, our aim is to enable our patients to discover and develop autonomy, identity, and self-determination. It is not to infantilize them and increase their dependence on authority figures. Certainly extreme situations such as the threat of suicide, severe psychosis, or other life-threatening conditions might arise and warrant collegial consultation. But outside of these catastrophic conditions, or the supervision of therapists in training, there are rarely reasons for planned ongoing contact between therapists of ambulatory adults.

Finally, if we probe even slightly into the "practical" requests made by the referring therapist, what may we speculate? Here I place in parentheses what the latent content of these conditions might be: frequency of sessions (not more than me), fee (not more than me), treatment technique (firm approach=you should not be better loved and your patient should not be better loved=not more than me), and the goal of saving the marriage (behave yourself, be good to me, don't leave me or try to get or have more than me). The referring therapist is either very poorly trained or his countertransference is so extreme that his response to his patient and the total treatment situation has deviated from our professional stance, which holds that neutrality and respect for the autonomy of others (patients and colleagues included) are paramount. To accept such a referral without serious discussion and refusal to accept such conditions is likely to undermine the treatment and lead to one of those collegial feuds that develop in our field when our professional ego ideal is seriously compromised.

The first example was a referral with no extraneous factors. In the second, the focus was on the transferential response of the receiving therapist. In the third, the referring therapist was out of bounds in every direction. One could speculate that he was driven by powerful but unanalyzed countertransferential forces that caused him to turn his colleague (as well as his patient's husband) into a rival. In some people these unresolved issues are all too ready to surface and the only possibility of change lies in their having an analysis that reaches deeply enough and effectively enough to accomplish it. But even those of us who have reached an adequate level of self-awareness need to be vigilant in tracking transference–countertransference currents as early in the treatment process as the making and receiving of referrals. Generally, most of us can handle that well enough in our work with adults.

As mentioned earlier, the referral of child patients is often more complicated than that of adults for the same reasons that all aspects of child therapy are more complicated than that of adults. For one thing, it is the nature of child therapy that more people are involved in the treatment situation. More people equals a greater coming together of affects and agendas. More people means more apprehension, more rivalry, more frustration, more confusion, and so forth. There is occasionally unease on the part of the referring person about what is going to transpire in that room between that therapist and that child. Is the therapist really competent? In referring adults we at least have the illusion that an adult can, to a degree, evaluate a therapist and decide whether to stay or leave. But how is a four-year-old or a ten-year-old to know whether the therapist is competent? And how are parents to evaluate whether they have placed their child in good hands?

> *A mother asks over the phone:* Who are you? It took me two weeks to find you. My pediatrician didn't know anyone who worked with a child as young as my son. She asked around and got your name, but she doesn't know you. Who are you and how do I know you're any good?
>
> *I answer:* Come and see me. We'll talk about your little boy and you'll get a sense of who I am and how I work.

We make an appointment. The odds that she'll cancel are 50/50. Had the pediatrician known me, the likelihood of the appointment being kept would have increased. Had the referral come from her therapist, the likelihood of our actually meeting would have been high, but this meeting would have created the potential for complications particular to the formation of a new triangle: the patient, her therapist, and I. Later in this chapter I will give an example of this problem so common in child treatment.

There is no question that to most people, making a child referral feels like a bigger responsibility than making an adult referral. When the referring person is a therapist, the full extent of this responsibility is often recognized from an even broader and more sophisticated perspective. For some of us, the uneasiness we feel in referring a child for treatment rests not so much with concern that the therapist do a good job with the child, but that the therapist have the skill and tact to work well with the parents. It is not unusual for strains with the parent who calls for an appointment to appear during that initial phone call.

Let's start with the ideal referral and move along a continuum to the tricky ones, the ones that take great skill and forbearance, impose uncomfortable working conditions on the child's therapist, and raise ethical issues regarding confidentiality.

CHILD REFERRAL 1

Telephone message: This is J.G., I'm a therapist practicing in Chicago. I was given your name by our mutual colleague, W.W. An extremely shy eight-year-old boy who has been in treatment with me for a few months is moving to New York next fall and will need to continue treatment. His parents will be in New York City in a few weeks to prepare for their move. May I give them your name and telephone number so they can meet with you for a consultation? Please call me to let me know whether you have the time to see them.

CHILD REFERRAL 2

Referring therapist (on the phone): One of my patients asked me for a referral for his niece. She's four and keeps waking during the night and resists going back to sleep. Her parents are exhausted and worried and want a consultation. Can you do it?

CHILD REFERRAL 3

School principal (on the phone): We have a second grade girl who cries very easily and is hard to comfort. She is teased for it by the other children, which makes her cry all the more. The teacher and

I have met with the parents and it's a very puzzling situation because the parents say that she's characteristically cheerful at home and rarely cries. The parents could hardly believe our observations. Then they came to see her at school and were shocked at the accuracy of our report. They're eager for a consultation. Will you see them?

CHILD REFERRAL 4

Matrimonial lawyer (on the phone): I represent a father who was just granted custody of his two sons ages six and three. Their mother is an alcoholic who ran off to the midwest with an unsavory drifter type guy; the drifter might have been abusive to the two little boys. The father flew out to get them and just returned with his sons. They're going to live with him and his new wife. The father is overwhelmed at what lies ahead and wants to consult a child specialist. Would you see him?

In each of these referrals the presenting problem is different and the people making the referral vary as to professional background and knowledge of the therapist, but they are very similar in their tone of respect regarding both the family being referred and the person who is being asked to take on the referral. In each case they present information in a manner that is succinct and to the point. They describe the essence of the case without becoming indiscreet. They make no conditions or intrusive remarks of any sort, nor do they assume that the referral need necessarily result in treatment. In each case the referral is for consultation, leaving the actual management of the case to the discretion of the person whose assistance they requested. In short, in each of these examples, the referring person is truly transferring the responsibility for whatever decisions need to be made to the therapist.

Next is an example of the other extreme, a referral to a child therapist that fills the room with a chorus of voices, each expressing its allegiances, its special agendas and its territorial imperatives.

In the case that follows, I will be the recipient of the referral. The referring person, Therapist X, will be a long-time acquaintance and a colleague who received her training at the same time and place as I did.

CHILD REFERRAL 5

Therapist X: "Well hello, you picked up. Good, I'm glad I got you in person and not your machine. I only have a couple of minutes before my next patient. Can you talk? . . . Good. I'm calling to refer a child to you and I want you to know that this is a wonderful case. You're in for a treat. It's a five-year-old girl. Her mother's in analysis with me. The child is basically a healthy child. She's shy around strangers and the mother worries that she's a little anxious, but this is a bright, creative, and quite delightful little girl. Her mother would like her to be a bit more assertive, especially now since soon they'll be thrust into the typical New York City race to get Angie into a good private school. I don't have to tell you what a toll this school competition takes on parents. Anyway, the mother wants Angie, that's the child's name, to be evaluated by an experienced child therapist, and that's you. I hope you have time to see them, for their sake of course, but really for your sake as well. I don't imagine that there are many opportunities to see such a well-endowed child and such cooperative parents. They have a good marriage. The father is able to be successful *and* interested in his family. He's in analysis too. His analyst is M., not my favorite person, but . . . anyway. Don't let me forget to mention that the mother has recently entered the field and is going through the program at XYZ, our old institute. Believe me, it's only because she's in the field and knows so much and is a particularly sensitive mother that she's having her child evaluated. By the way, she's able to deal analytically with whatever narcissistic hurt this evaluation represents and to place her child's well-being as top priority. You'll see for yourself when you meet her and Angie. That is if you're willing and have the time, and I hope you do. I imagine that children with such minor issues as Angie rarely see therapists.

The more I talk to you this way the more unsure I become about my reason for making this referral. I wonder whether one is really warranted. The reasons I gave you sound almost frivolous. But my patient was insistent and I guess I felt that I had to respect her wish to proceed. Maybe I should have explored the situation more fully. One last thing—my bell just rang. I see the mother four times a week and she's a very scheduled young woman, what with a part-time job, starting her private practice, attending the institute, and taking care of home and child. I hope your schedules will mesh. Oh, but I know you. You'll be flexible for a future colleague.

I almost forgot this most important concern. I know you'll need to see the mother at the beginning, but if it turns out that Angie needs a little treatment, I hope you won't need to see the mother regularly. I don't have to tell you what that does to the transference. Just tell me quickly, may I give her your name? . . . Oh good, you'll really enjoy this one.

Later that day:

Angie's mother: Oh hello, my name is Joan Case. I believe you spoke to my analyst, Mrs. X, earlier today. She spoke very highly of you, and then this afternoon I mentioned your name to Don Doyle who's at my institute with me, and he said that he had been in supervision with you. He was very enthusiastic about you. I feel very good about this referral, and I should add that having you so highly recommended by two people is going to help me convince my husband that we should proceed with seeing you. Brad, my husband, is in analysis and his analyst had somebody else in mind, somebody not acceptable to my analyst. My husband's analyst never heard of you so he can't very well be against—oh, I'm sorry, that sounds awful. I don't mean against you, you know what I mean. You've probably run into these situations before, you know, where everyone becomes territorial about whose recommendation should be the last word. Anyway, I'm pretty sure I can get my husband to come. My daughter Angie is five, she's a little shy, and I would like her evaluated to help her be more assertive. How much should I tell you on the phone? I'm in the field but I work with adults and all this is out of my sphere. . . . Oh, okay, I'll tell you what you need to know when I see you. . . . Yes, we do need to work out a time to meet. . . . Oh that's a good idea. I'll write down the times you have available next week. . . . Oh, for a full hour? All right, that makes a lot of sense. . . . And you would like my husband to be there as well.

That sounds good. . . . Both the times you mentioned are possible for me and as soon I clear this with my husband I'll call
you back. Better yet, I'll have him call you back to confirm. He
might as well take equal responsibility in doing this from the start.
His name is Brad Bond. . . . Yes, I do need your address, thank
you. I'm really looking forward to meeting you.

The next morning:

Angie's father: Hello, is this Mrs. Siskind? . . . Hi, I'm Brad Bond.
My wife Joan asked me to call you regarding an appointment about
our daughter Angie. I'm calling to confirm one of the times you
gave Joan. Six-fifteen on Thursday is a definite possibility but it
would be better for me if it were half an hour later. . . . You can't.
Well, being in analysis myself I know how tightly scheduled shrinks
are. Believe me I know how hard it is to change an appointment.
I'll be there at 6:15. If I'm a couple of minutes late, please start
without me. Incidentally, my analyst, M., would love to talk with
you. Is that okay with you? . . . Oh, you prefer to wait until you've
completed the evaluation? I think he wanted to give you some
background on me. . . . Yes, I can understand that. I'll tell him that
you like to gather whatever information you need directly from the
parents. . . . Yes, that's fine with me. I'll tell you anything you want
to know. By the way, Angie is a great kid. Wait till you meet her.
See you next week, Thursday at 6:15. One more question, how's
the parking up there near your office, just in case I take the car?
. . . So-so? Well, thanks, I'll figure it out.

The following week:

Therapist X: Thanks for calling right back. One of the fringe bene-
fits of sharing a case is that we'll get to talk to each other more often.
Of course I'm dying to hear what you thought of Joan, Brad, and
little Angie. By the way, Joan told me that you only have the *New
Yorker* in your waiting room and she told me that she asked you
why you restricted waiting room material to only one magazine.
She's such a curious young woman, very talented I think. Why do
you just have the *New Yorker?* She said you weren't very forthcoming with an answer. . . . Because you like to keep that part of
your life simple. I guess that's as good a reason as any. So what

about Angie? Is she everything I said she would be? . . . I can't believe my ears. What do you mean "she's an attractive little girl but you'd rather not discuss your impressions at this point?" . . . Yes, I can understand that you want to complete the consultation process before venturing an opinion, but I'm not asking you to reveal state secrets, and I'm not going to hold you to anything if you change your mind. . . . Well, I'm disappointed, but of course I'll have to wait if that's the way you feel. I must say that you're alarming me. Is there something wrong with Angie? I really need to know that because if she's not as her mother thinks she is I should know about it so we can address it in her treatment. . . . Look, it's all well and good to tell me that you see no cause for alarm, and I understand that you like to gather all your information and observations before making a statement but I don't understand all this insistence on formality. . . . Yes I know your bell rang. I heard it over the phone. It's a very loud bell. I hope you'll find the time to call me when you're ready to talk.

Three weeks later:

Telephone message from Dr. M., Angie's father's analyst: Hello Mrs. Siskind. This is Joe Moss. My patient, Brad Bond, has been keeping me abreast of the evaluation of his daughter Angie and I understand that you're about to meet with him and his wife Joan to report your observations. I was told at the onset that you preferred not discussing the case with me until you completed the evaluation process. May I assume that we can talk now? I would like to hear your findings and recommendations before they're presented to the parents so that I can have some input on how this is to be done. Thank you.

The reader will have to indulge me and accept that the above example, while at the extreme end, does not fall off the hypothetical continuum I've constructed for referral process complications. I have, of course, for the purpose of confidentiality, disguised the referral of Angie. The disguise relates to specific facts only. The spirit of the exchanges is quite accurate and I believe it captures the territorial zeal, anxiety, and rivalry that sometimes appear in our actual practices. These types of exchanges are not limited to, but seem most common, when a child is referred by the therapist of one of the parents. They illustrate behavior not at all in keeping with our training as therapists. This "anything goes" attitude among professionals seems particularly prevalent when a *child's* treatment is the object of attention.

At the root of what is wrong with almost everything about the referral of Angie is the insidious note of disrespect that permeates the entire situation. This is a familiar kind of disrespect, one not uncommonly accorded to children by their parents, their teachers, their doctors, and many other adults. It is a disrespect that places them in a category somewhere between person and pet. Sometimes members of the psychoanalytic community are not exempt from taking on this role. In the referral of Angie it is exhibited by the therapists of both parents, and not only in their attitude toward Angie, but toward Angie's therapist and Angie's parents as well. In this not so uncommon development in child treatment, the therapists of the adult patients have appointed themselves as the two parents, and all the others are, to varying degrees, children. For instance, Therapist X and Dr. M. expect Angie's therapist to answer all their questions. She can either join in their disregard of confidentiality and be one of them or she can hold firm and refuse. When she refuses, Therapist X gets pretty angry at her and talks to her as if she were a stubborn child. Dr. M. wants to hear the results of the evaluation before the parents do so he "can have some input on how this is to be done." He is going to tell Angie's therapist how and how much to tell his patient? What is that about? The reader can well understand that Angie's therapist is burdened from the start by these demands and intrusions. And, you might wonder, what happened to the observing egos of these two therapists who have taken on the role of parent, teacher, and supervisor? Has their ability to observe gone to sleep altogether? Countertransference must be a powerful factor here, for how else could such blind spots exist in well-trained and supposedly well-analyzed professionals?

In the child referrals described so far, I have focused on what the child's therapist is handed by the referring person, from the most uncluttered situation to the most encumbered. The complications encountered also need to be viewed from the perspective of the referring therapist, and might explain, but not justify, some of the apprehensiveness and possessiveness that are so striking in the referral of Angie.

Here we need to backtrack a bit and explore some of the factors present when a therapist refers the child of her patient for an evaluation. How does this come about? Two possibilities come to mind. In one, the evaluation is initiated by the patient and in the other, by the therapist. There is nothing simple about either situation, for in both cases an extra-analytic factor is now going to intrude on the treatment process.

Let us backtrack even more and investigate more fully how these referrals might come about. Here's a common situation. An adult patient in treatment repeatedly expresses concern about his child and describes the areas of concern. At the extreme of classical psychoanalytic orthodoxy some analysts might confine their attention to exploring and analyzing the patient's need to talk about his child and would investigate the root of the anxiety he experiences in regard to that child. These analysts might view their patient's concern as resistance to the analytic process. A referral to a child therapist would most likely not be made by this group of analysts even if the patient described a great deal of worry about his child.

Now let's look at another approach to the same situation. During a period of treatment the patient repeatedly expresses concern about his child. The therapist considers the role that resistance might have in the patient's shift of attention from himself to his child. This is explored, but the therapist pursues this inquiry without taking the position that resistance is the only factor here. There are many reasons for talking about one's child and resistance is not the only one. This therapist listens to many themes simultaneously and is therefore also able to pay attention to his patient and yet learn something about the state of mind of his patient's child. If a referral seems warranted, and desired by the parent, a referral is made. The nature of the child's problem or the degree of anxiety experienced by the parent vis-à-vis the child's problem are both factors that might warrant a referral. Sometimes a child does not present a very worrisome picture but parental anxiety about the child is so intense and the parent's treatment process so slow that the child is bound to be adversely affected by the anxiety-ridden climate and needs the steadying presence of a therapist.

The case of Angie illustrates another situation. The child was described as only mildly anxious, and yet Therapist X was quick to make a referral, admitting that she wasn't sure why. During the referral call she described her reason as "frivolous," and to a lesser degree the parents in their initial calls to the therapist sounded pretty lighthearted about the matter. The referral of Angie is puzzling and one must wonder what really was going on and why Therapist X was so willing to gratify her patient's request for a referral without first thoroughly analyzing what in fact was being requested.

Let's consider yet another common situation in the treatment of adults who are also parents. The patient does not ask for a referral but constantly reports disturbing behavior on the part of his child, or refers to what we would view as alarming symptoms. The patient might convey this information by complaining about the child rather than showing concern or considering that the child is in need of help. Here again is a situation that would evoke a varied range of responses from therapists. At one extreme the therapist would confine the child's problems to a background position limited to playing the role of providing grist for the mill of the adult's treatment. At the other extreme the therapist might arrange to actually see the child to ascertain whether treatment is warranted, and then possibly take on the treatment of the child as well as the parent. A more balanced therapeutic approach would be to explore the information offered by the patient about the child and the patient's apparent lack of concern about the child. In fact it is difficult to imagine not addressing and exploring as basic and central an issue as a patient's lack of concern about his child. No matter what such lack of concern signifies about that patient, the therapist does not have to join the patient in this form of neglect.

The pitfalls of the extreme positions are obvious. At one end the child could be in serious need of help and then the therapist's inaction amounts to abdication of responsibility justified by a concrete and misguided view about the boundaries of the therapeutic dyad. At the other extreme, the therapist's countertransference muddies and alters the nature of the treatment by inviting the child into the therapy room, rather than referring the child to a colleague. This is not to say that to see the child of a patient is always and in all situations a therapeutic blunder. But one would have to have a very compelling reason for taking such a step. More often than not such a plan is a mistake, one most likely powered by such factors as the therapist's rescue fantasies, omnipotent needs, wish to be idealized by the patient, and so forth.

If we leave behind the extremes of rigidity and those of overgratification and confine ourselves to a well-examined, sound, informed, and rational decision on the part of a therapist to refer the child of a patient to a colleague for evaluation and possibly for treatment, we find that even under these optimal conditions this is no simple matter. This action on our part adds an extraneous factor to the treatment of our adult patients and we need to be prepared to deal with the complications that so often follow.

As mentioned at the beginning of this chapter, there is a greater sense of responsibility in making a child referral than in referring an adult for treatment. There are many reasons for this fact. Most obvious is that children are not equipped to judge the competence of their therapists. While we assume that their parents are more able to make such judgments, this is true to a limited degree. For one thing many parents are ambivalent about seeking help for their children. Their wish to see their child in a better emotional place is juxtaposed with their narcissistic hurt at needing the help of an outsider, a professional expert. Often their fear, anger, and guilt make them perceive the therapist as a rival rather than a potential source of help. Their confusion is exacerbated by the likelihood that their child's therapist may become the object of their transference, or if they are in their own treatment, this might be viewed as transference displacement from their own therapist to that of their child.

For parents who are undergoing their own treatment, the role of their child's therapist is particularly complicated because of the transference spillover. The child's therapist might become a perfect decoy for all the hostile feelings the parent is afraid to express in his own treatment. Or, conversely, hostile feelings might be expressed towards his own therapist by presenting the child's therapist as vastly superior to his.

Let's take these possibilities further and see how they might actually be expressed in the adult's treatment. One way might be for the adult patient to complain to his own therapist about the child's therapist: to report her unanswered phone calls, her lateness in starting sessions, her unwillingness to speak to the child's teacher, her rigid rule that the child not ever be allowed to bring home any toys from the therapy sessions, her secrecy about the content of the child's sessions, her cold and formal manner, and even the messy, overflowing wastepaper basket in the bathroom. All these criticisms are evidence of her worthlessness. True, in the past, this patient complained about his wife in much the same whiny tone as he now complains about his daughter's therapist. True, this complaining mode needs to be explored, interpreted, and, finally, understood. But sometimes it's hard not to be a little concerned about what is really going on between one's colleague and one's patient and his daughter. Is it only the patient's transference now split between two therapists or is it also that one's colleague is doing something that doesn't sound quite right? How does one really know?

I particularly remember a situation I had a long time ago in which I felt uncomfortable about a referral I had made. The patient in question was in analysis with me and I had referred his four-year-old son to a trusted colleague. I had made this referral at the father's request and felt that the reason for the child's treatment was sound and wise. Both my patient and his wife were committed to the child's treatment and understood that they too had a part to play. They were cooperative in all the usual ways. They faithfully kept appointments, brought the boy on time, provided the information requested by Mrs. Lotte (the child's therapist), and of course paid their bills on time. They were also most eager to learn from Mrs. Lotte's observations of their son anything that might help them be more in tune with his needs.

My patient often talked of his encounters with his son's therapist, and much as he tried to like Mrs. Lotte he often felt bruised and bewildered by her remarks. For instance, she sounded surprised that they cared about receiving insurance reimbursements for her fee. My patient said she acted as if it were quite beneath her to bother with anything so mundane as money. Once, apropos of something else, when my patient described his son walking around the parents' bedroom in his mother's high-heeled shoes, Mrs. Lotte said that it sounded as if the boy had transvestite tendencies. Another time, along a similar vein, when the mother described their frustrating search for the boy's shoes on a rushed school morning and their discovery that he had hidden them to avoid going to school, Mrs. Lotte's comment was that this was not the first evidence of their son's delinquent tendencies.

I remember feeling a shock of discomfort at my colleague's use of such dire terms in regard to some pretty unremarkable behavior in a child of four. I wondered what was going on between her and these parents whom she treated with condescension sprinkled with these occasional alarming statements. Was this behavior triggered by these parents, by their child, or could it be the object of displacements of transferential feelings about me? I knew that my patient was reporting Mrs. Lotte's tone of condescension and her jabbing comments accurately since I had met her on a couple of occasions at professional meetings and she had inappropriately commented about this family, including telling me about her provocative and sadistic statements about the boy's dressing up and hiding shoes, and did so in a disdainful tone.

As the reader can imagine, I was distressed at having made this referral. Furthermore the whole situation became an intrusion on the analytic work with my patient. I tried to work with this material as best I could by exploring, among other issues, why my patient was accepting an unsatisfactory therapist for his child. Eventually the child was withdrawn from treatment and I never referred a patient to Mrs. Lotte again. I wish I could say that this was an unusual situation, but I can't. Child therapists reading this will be able to think of many situations in their practice when a colleague seriously mishandled the parents of a child in treatment.

So how do we really know whether the complaints of our adult patients about their contact with their child's therapist are fact or distortion? Of course there is no single answer to this question. So many factors have to be considered. But even the most disciplined, well-analyzed, and well-trained therapist, one who is able to view all these complaints as possibly other than an accurate description of the real situation, might still wonder and worry about the referral choice that was made. The degree of worry would rise and fall in response to the quality and content of the complaints and would be modulated by the overall opinion and subjective feelings about the therapist in question.

How can a therapist ever predict what forces will be activated upon referring a patient's child to a colleague? The entire approach to the child and to the child's parents is bound to reflect on the referring therapist. When things go badly it is likely that the adult patient will view this as the fault of his therapist because she made the referral. But even when things go well in the child's treatment and the adult's therapist is "wonderful" for having made such a marvelous referral, even that circumstance creates a set of problems. The point is that no matter how things go in reality, rivalries of all sorts are often activated in all the participants.

The potential for transference and countertransference begins with that first telephone contact. A message on an answering machine as well as a person-to-person phone call is enough to trigger a chain reaction, one that grows incrementally more complicated as the cast of characters expands. The drama is not necessarily confined to the patient–therapist pair; it may at times, as the case examples clearly illustrate, extend to the participating

therapists. The revival of early and painful self and object representations may be activated when the climate becomes toxic enough
and reawakens old fears, frustrations, and insecurities. When the
participating therapists succumb to childish rivalries they are in
dangerous waters. Countertransference[1] of this sort must inform
our work, not blindly lead it. The child's therapist must be resolute in this regard, a difficult task at times, but there is no choice
if we are to do our job.

---

1. The term *countertransference* is used here to include the spillover
of the therapist's unconscious response to the patient (child and parents) to the other therapists treating members of the patient's family.

The Child Therapist as Consultant on Transient Childhood Problems

Consultations with Parents Who Need Help in Dealing with Commonplace Childhood Problems

There is no circumstance in the treatment situation in which the initial rapport between patient and therapist plays as critical a role as when a parent seeks help because he cannot cope with some very ordinary childrearing situation. I make a distinction between parents who seek help for a child with pervasive developmental problems that affect his life and that of his family in a profound way, and parents of a child who is developing well but gets stuck at a particular point and is unable to take the kind of step that is usually helped along by parental rather than professional intervention.

Of course any initial contact between patient and therapist holds great importance. It sets the course for what is to develop in regard to those aspects of the treatment relationship that we divide into three basic categories: (1) the working alliance, (2) the transference, and (3) the countertransference. However, when an adult seeks treatment for himself, the initial meeting does not necessarily determine the outcome of the case. Even initial strong negative affects in the patient, in the therapist, or in both do not preclude the possibility of productive treatment. But I suggest that the possibility of productive work rising out of negative feelings generated in the first meeting is not likely if the patient is the parent of a young child who is experiencing a transient developmental difficulty.

The reason the initial rapport is so much more crucial to the outcome in this circumstance over all others is neither complicated nor mysterious. It rests on several factors, the most obvious being the brief nature of this therapeutic encounter. Since many of these consultations require as little as one and no more than a dozen sessions, there isn't time for the gradual formation of a working alliance, that essential alliance between patient and therapist that endures and weathers some of the storms inevitably encountered during the therapeutic process. In brief consultations something akin to the working alliance must ignite right away. The initial phone call must set a receptive attitude, one that at least provides the anticipation of rapport. How else are the parents of a well-developing child going to feel comfortable enough to expose their problem to this stranger, this person in the field of mental illness?

I remember being told of a conversation that illustrates the embarrassment parents often feel at exposing the difficulties they are having with their child. This conversation was repeated to me by one of the teachers in a nursery school where I was a consultant. The teacher had accidentally discovered that Polly, one of her very perky and precocious three-year-olds, was still being nursed. It happened one day when Polly's mother had unexpectedly come into the classroom mid-morning to bring Polly's warm jacket as the weather had turned cold and she wanted Polly dressed warmly for the outdoor period at school. Mrs. P. sat down for a minute to rest and Polly ran up to her, climbed into her lap, and tugged at her breast demanding "mommy milk." Polly's mother was visibly embarrassed and talked Polly into returning to her block building project. Some time later, during a parent–teacher conference, Polly's mother and her teacher discussed the situation. Polly's mother said that she didn't know what to do about this protracted breast feeding. She knew that she must stop, that it was a foolish thing to continue doing, but when her daughter climbed into her lap and demanded "mommy milk" she felt helpless, found herself unable to say "no," and complied. Polly wouldn't drink milk from a glass or bottle. It was "mommy milk" or no milk at all, and that too made it difficult to deny her. Besides, it was hard to be clear about what possible harm could be done by something they both enjoyed so much. The teacher asked what her pediatrician had to say about it. The nursing mother looked at her incredulously and said, "Are you serious? Do you think I'd tell him that I still nurse Polly? I think I'd die of shame. I love my pediatrician and he's always so complimentary about Polly . . . I know he considers me a good mother. I would never tell him that I'm still nursing a three-year-old child. Why, he'd think I was crazy and lose all respect for me."

Polly's mother so perfectly illustrates the conflicting forces that parents often experience about seeking help: the embarrassment at having to admit to being unable to handle an ordinary childhood situation, the wish for help, the reluctance to seek help because they fear being humiliated by exposing their difficulty. The consulting therapist must, of course, be aware of the shame and embarrassment that parents often feel when unable to do what most parents do as a matter of course. The obvious, the surface layer, is a good place to start, as long as we remember that it's only the beginning of the story.

We must wonder why Polly's mother is still nursing. She knows that she should stop; she knows the pediatrician would advise her to stop, but she avoids discussing it with him. Her relationship with her pediatrician has grown into something complicated. Perhaps he has become an idealized figure, an object of transference. Clearly her embarrassment with him specifically is part of the story. After all, if Polly's mother really wanted help in stopping nursing she could consult one of us, strangers who would help her with this problem, but she doesn't come to us either. Most likely she finds nursing Polly so gratifying that she is unwilling to give it up, at least at present. Eventually, of course, she will stop. Here is what might happen. Her conflict and the discomfort she feels over nursing might be primarily intrapsychic in nature. If that is the case, then whatever gratification she experiences will be mixed with anxiety and guilt. Superego and ego factors will place pressure on her to stop nursing. Libidinal gratification will be relinquished in favor of living up to her ego ideal of being a good and responsible parent. Or perhaps her discomfort over nursing might be experienced more as an external conflict, one between her wish to nurse and her fear of arousing the criticism of other mothers, Polly's teachers, family members, her pediatrician, and so on. If this second possibility is a more accurate description of the source of her discomfort she will stop nursing in order to retain the good opinion of others. Perhaps a combination of these forces will be at play and will help her to stop. She will stop when her discomfort overrides the gratification that nursing provides. Or she might find herself unable to stop despite her discomfort and come to one of us for help. But she will not stop until she experiences psychic discomfort caused by conflict, whatever its source.

There is so much to consider in thinking about the embarrassment of parents who come to us for help with these "simple" problems. After all, embarrassment itself is no simple matter. It's one of those overly familiar generic words, like "boredom" or "laziness" that simultaneously conveys and obscures. It describes an uncomfortable affect but behind this affect lie multiple layers. I refer here to the latent content of the request for help, the unconscious motivation. I propose that the success of the outcome of these brief consultations depends to a great extent on the therapist's attunement to the motivation of the parents seeking our help and particularly to the latent content of their request.

Our awareness of the importance of the patient's motivation dates all the way back to early Freud. The basis for his famous abstinence rule was to preserve the patient's motivation to do the analytic work. He wrote: "I shall state it as a fundamental principle that the patient's need and longing should be allowed to persist in her, in order that they may serve as forces impelling her to do work and make changes" (1915, p. 165).

Of course Freud was referring to psychoanalytic treatment, a deep, intense, and long-term therapeutic approach, and we are discussing short-term consultations with parents. Yet, as we so often find, Freud's theory has a range of applicability that is much greater than psychoanalysis proper.

Keeping the principle of motivation in mind, we find it helpful at this point to approach our parent consultations with the question "Why is this mother in our office? What brought her here? And what about this father? What brought him to this appointment? What need and longing are operating in him, and what does he want help with?" Of course the patient generally believes that his conscious reason for coming to see us is the whole reason. It is up to us to be alert to that other more elusive theme, the unconscious wish.

We are well aware of the existence of unconscious motivation in adult patients who consult us about themselves. In fact we take for granted this dimension of treatment. But how easy it is to forget that unconscious motivation operates equally when a parent consults us about his child.

Consultation with parents is most likely to be effective when we approach it with unfailing awareness that the parent's latent motivation is a powerful force. This awareness on our part is helpful on several counts. It organizes our listening mode and allows us to be interested in the factual without becoming overly involved and in the process losing sight of deeper levels of meaning. Of course the presenting problem is important, family history relevant, developmental landmarks significant (more so if they fall outside the normal), and current circumstances noteworthy, but the question of *what these parents want* must be held in the mind of the therapist throughout the consultation process. It is needed to light our way, much as we need the light of a full moon on a dark night, for we are truly in the dark until we understand this dimension. We need it to keep us aware of the patient's multilayered agenda and to prevent us from imposing our own. It's so easy to be misled in these situations. After all, the request for help in these "simple" consultations is always very clear: "Johnny refuses to sleep in his own bed," "Annie won't be potty trained," "Frankie won't let any kids play with his toys and hits them when they try," and so on. There is no question that parents sincerely want our help with these impasse situations. That is a given, but then we must ask: What is hampering these parents from dealing with this problem on their own, and what roles have they assigned us? Where and how do we fit in their picture?

A slight digression, a detour with a purpose, follows. A long time ago I treated a psychotic child. Over the years she became more socially "appropriate," more normal in her general behavior. Did her psychotic core really change? It's hard to say, but she did appear to be less fragmented and increasingly aware of ordinary things in the world around her, particularly of the difference between normal children and the disturbed children at her "special school." She began to express the wish to be more like those "regular" girls who played with dolls, fussed with their hair, and pretended to be grown-up women rather than chess-playing robots, flying cars, and giant eagles, the world of "make believe" that Emmy was more accustomed to.

In working with psychotic children, therapists often find themselves taking on roles that normally belong to parents. This is so because in addition to relying on the therapist for their child's treatment, these parents also need help with other aspects of the child's life such as school, leisure activities, and other practical matters. This need for extra help from the therapist is twofold. In part it stems from the heavy demands of life with such a child and the state of depletion it creates in the parents. But also it stems from the fact that it is frequently more difficult to assess the needs of these baffling and often uncommunicative children, and the therapist, being less vulnerable than the parent, is more able to deal with this aspect of care and communication. It was therefore not unusual for me as the therapist to see Emmy's interest in normality both as material for our work together and also as a signal that she was ready for some environmental changes.

At the time that Emmy expressed a wish for normalcy I knew of a very interesting small summer camp for normal children. This camp allowed and encouraged a great deal of individuality in both campers and counselors and did so in a warm, supportive atmosphere. I thought that perhaps my young patient would thrive in such a place. I decided to call the camp and discuss this notion with the director before approaching Emmy's parents with my idea. I did not want to present these parents with what I thought was an appealing prospect without having made sure that they had at least an even chance of seeing their daughter accepted. When I felt satisfied that the camp director and his senior staff understood the challenge of taking Emmy into the camp and the difficulties that they might encounter, and when I listened to their reason for wishing to meet her and their hope that they could offer her a place, only then did I present my idea to Emmy's parents. They were cautiously enthusiastic and immediately applied to the camp. What followed was a typical camp director's visit to the family home, a slide show of the camp, and some time spent chatting and responding to questions. When Emmy was accepted we were all a little anxious but mainly pleased. I found out later that our pleasure stemmed from very different reasons. It was Emmy's mother's response that has prompted me to tell this story in the context of this chapter.

Emmy's mother was an austere woman who wasted no words. In discussing her reaction to Emmy's acceptance into this camp she shed the first tears I ever witnessed. She said that calling a camp for normal children to request an application and being visited in her home by a director who showed slides of happy children having a good time, playing with animals, swimming, cooking outdoors and such, why this was the best thing that had ever happened to her. It made her feel like a regular parent of a regular child and she never thought that she would experience anything so plain and simple, so typical of the real world of parents and children, and so lacking in what she was accustomed to: psychiatric interviews, psychological tests, neurological examinations, assessments, evaluations, and treatment plans. Since Emmy was two the mother had been subjected to a diet of psychiatric language, a sterile language that never lets you forget that your child is crazy. Her current experience was an antidote to all this and she found herself playing back the camp director's visit and all the simple ordinary things he told them: that the water they swim in is very cold and that it takes time to get used to it, that after dinner they always sing around a fire and toast marshmallows for a second dessert, that among the animals there are two pigs, a goat, two horses, three cats, and he wasn't sure how many dogs because puppies were expected before the opening of camp. Emmy's mother never mentioned her daughter's reactions to the director's visit or to the idea of camp. She refused to discuss any apprehension she felt about Emmy going to camp, and being away from home for eight weeks. All she could talk about was the experience of being treated like a normal parent. This must have satisfied a hunger hitherto unexpressed by her and perhaps not even known consciously.

It would be unfair to the reader to stick so closely to my point as to leave out that, yes, camp was a success for Emmy, and that Emmy's parents both experienced with pleasure a normal visiting weekend in a regular (though outstanding) camp. But the reason for this digression has more to do with the surprising twist this case took and the insight provided by this experience.

Of course I had the satisfaction of having come up with a plan that worked well for everyone. Emmy did well at camp. Being exposed to normal children who recognized that she was different from them but who in the very benign climate of that camp were accepting and responsive was a good experience for her. It was probably also good for these campers to have the opportunity of meeting a child so different from them, yet being able to feel safe enough to react to the unfamiliar with interest and curiosity rather than with fear. They had been able to welcome rather than shun this young stranger. For Emmy's father the camp experience served as an indicator that Emmy's world could broaden beyond special education schools, psychotherapy, and social isolation at home. But it was vis-à-vis Emmy's mother that I experienced deep and illuminating insight. Without realizing that this could happen, I felt that I had provided a form of care to a woman whose most prominent quality in the past had been her rejection of any help, concern, and care. Before the summer camp experience Emmy's mother really felt that there was nothing that anyone could give her. She had a crazy child and that was that. It would be so forever, so what could she want? Did she know how much she longed for a normal child? I believe not. I believe that she was so defended against any longings as to be totally out of touch with herself. Yet the longing was there, stored in the unconscious, probably a remnant of memory traces of the symbiotic stage she herself experienced with her own mother and the wish to reexperience this with her own child, a wish that most mothers are granted, but she was not. As an infant Emmy did not respond to voice and touch as normal infants do, and her mother was particularly untalented at wooing an unresponsive infant. This tragic mismatch triggered failure upon failure at every developmental step. The many professionals who were involved with this family at various times were able to have some impact on Emmy and her father, but Emmy's mother eluded any attempts we made in trying to connect with her, until the camp incident.

There was something poignant about playing a part in igniting a spark of pleasure in such a stark and rejecting countenance. True, Emmy was still a psychotic and the mother's brush with normality was in part illusory, for it was no more than a brush. Nonetheless it opened an affective door for her, let in some light, and gave her some warm moments. This episode became an eloquent reminder for me that everyone longs for something. Some will not let on, at least not for a long time, and some, as if their life depended on it, not ever. But however repressed it may be, the affect of longing is preserved. It is retained and stored in our self and object representations.

Normally, the experience of becoming a parent reawakens those early longings and when things go well, gives them new life and the opportunity of being transformed into an updated version. When Hartmann (1958) talks of "fitting together" he refers to an adaptive regression in the parent of a young infant that quickens empathy and fosters intuitive insight into the infant's primitive psychic state. This form of adaptation, this capacity for attunement to one's infant, hinges on what Kris (1952) calls "regression in the service of the ego." The parent regresses to meet the coenesthetic, the visceral needs of the infant. The symbiotic closeness is reexperienced with the parent now at the other end of the dyad, as the caregiver. But satisfaction of these early needs is not always possible. In some unfortunate circumstances, as in the case of Emmy's mother, the infant stays in a quasi-autistic state and is not awakened by the mother's affective overtures. The mother finds no partner in her infant, no opportunity to play out and satisfy the closeness anticipated during the nine long months of pregnancy. For Emmy's mother, becoming a parent was a crushing disappointment, a source of devastating pain.

One reason for this lengthy detour is to emphasize some of the marked differences in work with the parents of severely disturbed children and parents of "normal" children who are experiencing a transient problem. For instance, I have found that parents of severely disturbed children often do not experience the kind of rivalry with the therapist that is typical of parents of more normally developing children. There is good reason for these differences. Parents of psychotic children generally are desperate for help. They are exhausted by their children, baffled by their behavior, and often at their wit's end. These parents are understandably only too willing to hand their child over to a professional; in fact a professional takeover is often what they want. Whatever fantasies they might have once had about being good parents and giving their child all the things they wished for when they were children and received or failed to receive, those wishes and hopes are dashed by the time they arrive in our offices, often leaving no trace at all that they ever existed. Their longings appear to have been erased by the daily emotional storms and destructive behavior of their children and by social isolation, a consequence of being avoided by other parents. These parents live in a nightmare world with no relief in sight. The embarrassment described by Polly's mother about nursing a three-year-old might seem like a frivolous matter to the parents of a psychotic child. Parents of psychotic children are front-line fighters, with survival as their goal. Such had been the life of Emmy's mother and understandably she had been only too willing to hand her daughter to the specialist. Therefore when a woman as emotionally defended as Emmy's mother experiences the longing to be an ordinary good mother, that is an epiphany, a dramatic lesson about the power of longing and its immutability, no matter how tightly repressed or for how long.

Ours is a strange field. Throughout its history we have learned about normal development and "average" human behavior by studying pathological development and extreme behavior. When we approach things this way we use pathology as a magnifying glass that blows up the picture, allows us to see the details, and highlights the contrasts between the ordinary and the extreme. The detour into the world of Emmy and her mother in a chapter on consultation with parents of normally developing children follows this trend. I took it because it seemed to me that a woman who appeared to lack any traits of motherliness or interest in being maternal, and then unexpectedly exhibited these very affects would be most useful in illustrating the immutability of the symbiotic experience. Symbiotic affects and the longing they create are surely the precursor of motherliness and fatherliness. It is not always simple to assess whether they are lacking or defended against. We know that their true absence is a most dramatic indicator of severe pathology, but we cannot always distinguish between what may never have existed and what has been severely repressed.

We must use caution in relying on the pathological to help us better understand the normal. This approach only works up to a point. The severely pathological is not really an extreme version of the normal; it is more than just that. There is a difference in the quality of the personality in psychotic structure, a profound difference that alters that person's relationship to self, others, and reality. Despite this core difference, and perhaps because of it as well, moving between pathology and normality sharpens our awareness of the difference and structures our observations.

We know surprisingly little about the inner world of normal adults as they go about their lives. We know surprisingly little about their experience as parents, how parenthood impacts on their core and influences delicate psychic balances. We know something about this in our analytic patients who are or become parents while in treatment, but this has not been an area of psychoanalytic investigation per se, although that too is changing as psychoanalysts become interested in the growing field of infant, and parent–infant observation.

Right now, as things stand in our current knowledge, brief consultation with parents on ordinary problems of childhood is not a treatment modality that has a theoretical base or that has a body of literature that offers technical application of existing theories of human development. It holds a catch-as-catch-can position reminiscent of the place held by psychotherapy fifty years ago before ego psychology was developed and allowed psychoanalytic psychotherapy to become a specific treatment modality. Right now we must learn by using whatever we find helpful in our theory, our practice, our experience in the world, and our powers of observation. For instance, what we can learn from our detour into the desolate world of Emmy's mother and the much sunnier world of Polly's mother who can't stop nursing, is that they do share the profound wish to be a good mother.

The most reliable tool available to the therapist in this area of our work is the ability to observe with interest and curiosity and patience. I assume, of course, that the therapist is well trained in psychoanalytic (classical and updated) theory and technique. This basic training will give direction to the curiosity, scope to the observations, and objectivity to the interest. Anticipatory excitement and the therapist's confident expectation that the "not yet known" will gradually give way to emerging insights and meaningful connections will tame our impatience and sense of urgency. Even in brief consultation this attitude of taking our time is a vital aspect of what we do.

There is no reason to suppose that such a therapeutic attitude need ever be altered. It is intrinsic to all aspects of our work, whether it be the well-established modality of psychoanalysis proper, or the fledgling attempts to provide consultation to parents. What we must avoid is falling into a very diluted and questionable therapeutic role, that of not exploring, not particularizing, but simply giving advice.

CHAPTER

7

❧

Consultation about a Sleep Problem

$\mathcal{W}$hy do they call, the parents who come to see us? What is it they need? What can we learn if we listen carefully from the first moment, from the initial phone call, or the telephone message so plain and simple on the answering machine?

> My two-year-old daughter Bonnie won't sleep and one of the nurses at the hospital where I work said to call you, she said you would know what to do. My husband and I both have the day off from work in four weeks, on X holiday. I hope that you can see us that day. My number is. . . .

I call back in the evening and the husband answers. When I identify myself he recognizes my name and tells me that they have been waiting for my call. I hear him yell to his wife, "It's Diana Siskind calling you back."

Since I'm not available on X holiday as Mrs. B. had hoped, a long discussion follows during which I learn that she and her best friend Nadine both work at the same hospital, Nadine a five-day week and Mrs. B. a three-day week. On Mondays and Fridays, the two days that she doesn't work, she takes care of Nadine's four-year-old daughter Rachel. She will have to get her sitter to work a fourth day and take care of Bonnie and Rachel in order to come to see me. Since her best sitter has classes in the morning and early afternoon on Mondays and Fridays, a late afternoon appointment on either of those days would be best and also work into her husband's work schedule. She discusses possible back-ups for a sitter in case Claire, the sitter she has in mind, is not available. Mrs. B. then talks about travel considerations in getting to my office and previous commitments (a christening and her nephew's birthday party) that eliminate some of the times I offer. It takes four more telephone conversations over the next two weeks before a firm appointment is made. This is very time consuming but it's part of a process. It certainly yields valuable information about this mother; it highlights her ambivalence about the consultation and her expectation that I pretty much accommodate to her schedule. It also yields interesting information about my response to her, for I find that she has drawn me in very nicely and I'm willing to accommodate to her schedule and to her leisurely pace over the phone. There is nothing imperious in her attitude about taking up my time and requiring so much attention. Rather, she's dutiful in the way she goes into detail, and her tone is friendly. She's like a little girl showing off her life, introducing me to her people by name, telling me about her important events; I'm her audience. Her ingenuousness is appealing and I find myself interested and curious about what is to unfold. We are starting off well.

It's early evening and the time of our appointment. Bonnie's parents arrive together and on time. They are one of the parent couples I want to write about because they illustrate some of the features particular to brief consultation. These two parents sit in my office and tell me that their two-year-old will not go to sleep at a reasonable time and then will not stay asleep, and that this goes on day after day with no exception, to the point that nighttime has become a dreaded time in their lives. They add that this is so despite their best efforts, consultations with friends, relatives and the pediatrician; and all their reading of books on this very subject. They explain that they have had no difficulty with Bonnie in any other regard, that she is an intelligent and engaging little girl, in all other ways the joy of their lives.

Mr. and Mrs. B. present me with a typical example of a situation that normally does not require professional intervention. After all, in the ordinary course of life parents are able to put their two-year-old child to sleep and expect her to stay asleep through the night. But here they are in my office assuring me that Bonnie will just not go to bed and stay asleep despite their best efforts.

Bonnie's parents go on to describe their own state of exhaustion at never sleeping more than an hour or two without being awakened by little Bonnie who wants juice, milk, a story, a video, or a move into the parents' bed. As I listen to this tale of frantic evenings and disrupted nights I wonder (silently) why putting Bonnie to sleep should be so hard. I begin to wonder too at something else. In the first few minutes I thought I perceived a tone of desperation in the way Bonnie's parents spoke about their chronic exhaustion and the difficulty of getting their child to sleep. Could this be a misperception on my part? Is it possible that I've projected the frustration I would feel at such prolonged bedtimes and disturbed nights? Here is something to pay close attention to, something that lies at the heart of our work: to recognize and accept what we don't know. I don't know these parents. I have to allow their story to unfold as it will and not assume anything until I know more about them. Also, Bonnie's parents are two distinct people; naturally their reactions to the sleep problem are going to differ. I remind myself that Bonnie's mother took her time in coming to see me. She certainly sounded anything but desperate on the phone, and yet it was her idea to arrange for the consultation. Her husband, on the other hand, sounds as if he might feel more urgency about this problem, but I don't know this for sure; it's just a possibility. I will learn more about the differing perspectives of these parents as the consultation continues.

Now Bonnie's mother is speaking again. Her voice is soft and kind as she goes on to assure me that she has tried everything, including letting Bonnie cry for a few minutes, but to no avail. She speaks very gently to me, very kindly, as if to reassure me in some way. I am momentarily puzzled by her manner until it occurs to me that she is letting me know that what she has described is a problem without solution. This raises an interesting question and makes me wonder whether a problem without solution is what she wishes. It certainly seems so at this moment. Did she come to have professional confirmation that Bonnie is different from other two-year-olds, and that indeed normal ordinary nights are not her destiny? It's fifteen minutes into the hour-long consultation when I am struck by this possibility. There will be time to check it out. There is no limit on the fantasies (conscious and unconscious) that parents have about their children, and plenty of variations exist on the fantasy of having a "special" child. A child who doesn't sleep might fit the fantasy of specialness.

Now the father speaks and he, too, is intense, sincere, and very invested in what he wants to tell me. He did not want to come. He admits this a bit bashfully. It's nothing against me. I probably do my work well, but he doesn't expect this meeting to be any different from any other discussion on the subject of Bonnie's sleep, and none of the other people they've spoken to have helped. The pediatrician said that when Bonnie, who is tall for her age, reaches a height of 5' 8", she'll sleep so well they'll have trouble waking her. That's amusing up to a point, but it's a little hard to be amused when you're tired and Bonnie is only a little over two feet tall. It's hard to laugh if it's really true that it's out of their hands and that only an undetermined period of time will correct the situation. Right now it feels to him as if they've been sentenced to a life without sleep.

The father's overt frustration, his agitation as he talks, is in striking contrast to the mother's calm manner. He states with some bitterness that he looks forward to the train ride to work, a sixty-minute sleep that can be counted on.

What happened to these parents? In their house a two-year-old runs the show. Exhaustion (in part) brings them to the office of a therapist. If I can help them, they will be able to sleep, but they will also know that their problem was not without solution. There is a trick here. Since most two-year-olds go to sleep at a predictable time and stay asleep all night unless they are ill or frightened by some noise or such, is there something wrong with Bonnie, who does not sleep like the other two-year-olds? Or is there something wrong with Bonnie's parents because they have been unable to establish an ordinary sleep routine with their two-year-old? I'm in a delicate area here, and this consultation is taking shape very nicely.

The mother describes a popular sleep book that suggests, as a final step when all else has failed, keeping a child who will not sleep confined to her room.

"How do you do that?" she asks. "How do you prevent her from just opening the door and coming out? Do you put a bolt on the outside of the door so that she's locked in? Do you tie her to her bed with ropes?"

Is that what she's supposed to do to her child—lock her up, restrain her like a prisoner, a criminal? Her eyes sparkle as she speaks; her tone is impassioned. No way will she resort to such barbaric action. I look at the father to note his reaction to this, and see that he is looking away. He seems pained; something unbearable is causing him to withdraw. I wonder whether Mrs. B.'s angry passion is directed at her husband. Is she implying that he is capable of "barbaric" action? The situation is beginning to take shape. I have a tentative hypothesis, but it had better be very tentative or it will narrow my field of observation. It seems possible that the mother wants this to be a problem without solution while the father does not. I must check this out.

I ask Mr. B. what he would do if it were all up to him. His attention returns and he talks willingly, eagerly, looking at me and not at his wife. He explains that his wife, a very fine nurse, is by education and profession much more qualified to make childrearing decisions than he is, and he always reminds himself of that and follows her lead. However, since I have asked what he thinks, he must answer fully, or why bother? He and his wife have very dissimilar views about raising children, probably based on their different backgrounds. His family is African-American and his father was a porter. His working class parents were strict; he was not raised with the kind of delicacy and sensitivity that is being offered to his daughter. In his home children had to toe the line and he doesn't see that it hurt him or his sisters to do what they were told even when they didn't like it. His wife comes from a Jewish middle-class family in which the children were catered to by the parents. He recognizes that he is more direct than his wife, and has noticed that Bonnie listens to him more readily than she listens to her mother. There is no question that he would take a tougher line on the sleep business, but his wife is so horrified at the thought of Bonnie being unhappy that he hasn't acted on it. After all, maybe he's wrong to think it all right to be more strict. What if his judgment is blinded by his wish to sleep, to have quiet evenings? What if his wife is right and it would do Bonnie harm were he to take a tougher line with her?

Now, in addition to the earlier tricky question (Is there something wrong with Bonnie or is there something wrong with her parents?) I seem to have another dilemma: there is the implication that a choice must be made between Bonnie's welfare and sleep for the parents. Am I, the therapist, on the side of the barbarians (Could it be that this is the role the father was assigned and accepted?) who would lock Bonnie up in her room or tie her to her bed with ropes, or will I join the mother and patiently accept the edict that sleep is inaccessible? This request for help regarding a "simple" problem is heating up, as these consultations always do, and typically what appeared simple and commonplace at the beginning turns out to be unique, complex, and very interesting as the hidden agendas begin to emerge.

I decide to shift away from the mounting tension in the room to get some more information. I ask the parents a question that I have learned to ask at some point during any and all of these brief consultations. Whatever the problem may be, my question is directed at whether the parents have clearly and directly demanded that their child do the very thing that she is not doing and that they are therefore consulting me about. In Bonnie's case what she is not doing is going to sleep and staying asleep.

I ask the question of Bonnie's parents in the following way:

> Have you ever told Bonnie that you want her to go to sleep after
> her bedtime stories and stay asleep all night until morning . . .
> that you don't want her to get up and come to your room, or ask
> for food, drink or anything else during the night . . . that night is
> for sleeping and that's what you expect her to do from now on?

They look at each other and at me in surprise. They have never
said that to her. It never occurred to them to do so. The father
looks a bit sheepish and the mother looks annoyed and asks why
I think she would listen to them. I softly say that I think that she
might listen to them because they are her parents.

The father is interested. He says that he could definitely do
that; it sounds in line with his upbringing to just tell a child what's
expected. It feels natural to him to take charge. He has always
held back because of his wife's unhappiness with what she calls
a "dictatorship" approach.

I suggest that we return to this later and discuss it more fully.
Before we do that I would like to know more about Bonnie outside the sleep problem. An abbreviated developmental history
sounds unremarkable. Bonnie sounds like an intelligent, friendly,
and energetic two-year-old who likes people, play, food, and accepts the ordinary routines of life such as baths, dressing, excur-
sions to friends and family, and all normal aspects of life. I establish in my mind that Bonnie is a well-developing child with an
intense sleep disturbance. This symptom is what brought her
parents to my office. Sleep problems are a fortunate site for trouble
because sleeplessness is inescapable and can only be tolerated
so long before it moves into the unendurable, a realm requiring
that help be sought. Of course there are exceptions. Some families do without normal sleep for years, and while the underlying
problem goes unrecognized it grows and festers, but when that is
the case we know that we are dealing with more serious pathology.
Such acceptance of hardship is in fact pathognomonic; that would
place the problem outside the domain of brief intervention.

As this consultation continues I come to believe that Bonnie's mother called me not to bring about a solution of the sleep disturbance but to have me impress upon her husband that no such solution exists, at least not without the price of doing damage to their child. Bonnie's sleeplessness and theirs have a special meaning to her. I can speculate that some fantasy of "specialness" plays a part here, a fantasy of Bonnie being different from regular, ordinary two-year-old children who are expected to sleep, and I can speculate that the sleep disturbance has other unconscious determinants. I can also speculate that the busy, frantic nights could be symptomatic of something amiss in the marriage. These speculations are useful in keeping me properly aware of the complexities inherent in such a situation and in navigating with this in mind. It's about thirty minutes into the consultation with Bonnie's parents and I'm almost ready to address the sleep problem, but first I ask the mother what she would do if Bonnie threw bits and pieces of her dinner on the floor. Mrs. B. says that Bonnie does that sometimes and she talks to her something like this:

> Bonnie, honey, Mommy loves you so much . . . and thinks you're the best girl in the whole world, but honey, if you don't want your peas and chicken, just leave them on your plate and Mommy will get you something else to eat. Okay?

I ask her what would she say or do if Bonnie were to continue to throw her food on the floor. Mrs. B. explains that her operating principle is to assure her that she loves her but that she doesn't like what she's doing. She would therefore coax her to stop throwing food on the floor while reminding her of her love for her. I ask her whether it's possible that Bonnie knows that she is not supposed to throw food on the floor and is doing so because she wants to break the rules. Mrs. B. looks startled by this possibility. I explain that Bonnie sounds much too bright to *not* know such a thing. If I am correct on this would she still be so cautious, gentle, and apologetic in her approach? Mrs. B. looks confused and unhappy.

I propose that if Bonnie has in mind to find out who is the stronger, she or her mom, is it not much better for her to find out that her mom is stronger? After all, it is pretty awesome to be two years old and to be the one in charge. Bonnie's safety depends on her parents being in charge for they can take care of her. She really can't take care of anyone, and she knows that. Bonnie's mother is nodding sadly. I continue to talk to them and say something like this:

> You all need to sleep, all *three* of you. You know that; that's why you came to see me. I believe that something has gotten in your way of taking charge. That's what I hear in what you've told me so far. I don't claim to know what's blocking you, and of course whatever it is, it's different for each of you, but I'm certain this difficulty you each have in taking charge is at the heart of the problem. I can tell you from my knowledge of children that Bonnie sounds like a well-developing little girl in every other way. You must feel the same way about her since I'm basing my opinion on the very positive picture you have given of your daughter. If she is indeed as you describe her, there is no reason for her not to sleep, providing that you make your expectation that she do so clear and non-negotiable.

Now Bonnie's mother becomes upset and interrupts me. She doesn't understand what I'm saying. Yes, she understands that Bonnie could just be told that she must go to sleep and stay asleep, and then what's going to happen? What's going to keep her from getting up? She has two legs and a mind of her own. Bonnie will just get up and run around as she always does, and she is not tying her to her bed.

I tell Mrs. B. that a firm tone of voice should be enough to keep Bonnie in bed. I agree with her that locks and ropes are out of the question. Not only are they barbaric as she had suggested, but their use undermines parental authority. By using ropes to tie a child up, a parent expresses weakness and cruelty at the same time. The cruelty is obvious, the weakness less so; I see it as subtly being conveyed by the need to rely on a prop. By using a prop you are saying to your child that you are lacking in the ability to make use of your strength and authority as a parent and that therefore you need to rely on an inanimate piece of equipment—ropes, locks, straps for spanking and such—to execute a parental demand.

I go on to tell her that if she really believed she had the right to demand that Bonnie stay in bed, and if she believed that this was for Bonnie's welfare as well as for the sake of all three of them, her tone would reflect this conviction. I believe that would be enough to keep Bonnie in bed. I go on to say that from what I have learned so far it appears to me that she doesn't believe she has the right to make that demand or to allow her husband to do so, and this is at the heart of the problem. I suggest that if we viewed Bonnie's sleeplessness as a riddle that had two possible answers, they would be as follows: (1) Bonnie doesn't sleep because there is something wrong with her. (2) Bonnie doesn't sleep because there is something wrong in her parents' expectation that she go to sleep and stay asleep like other two-year-olds. Only one answer can be correct and I am assuming that it's answer #2. If I am wrong my recommendations will not work and then I would need to see Bonnie in person and figure out how to proceed. But if the problem is in their undefined expectations of her, then perhaps we could place more of the responsibility for conveying these expectations with Bonnie's father, who is less conflicted about taking a firm position about the sleep problem. Would they agree to such an approach?

Mrs. B. nods sadly and whispers "okay." Mr. B. agrees to take over bedtime until Bonnie's sleep pattern normalizes. He tries not to look too pleased that his more authoritarian approach has been supported by a "professional."

As we talk about specifics around bedtime I notice the sad manner in which Bonnie's mother listens. I remark on it and she tells me that going back to work when Bonnie was six months old had been very difficult for her. Even though it was for three days a week and not for five it broke her heart to have to leave her, but they needed the money, so she did. She suspects that leaving her at such a young age probably contributed to the current difficulties. She always tries to compensate for her absence by making Bonnie happy, and can't bear to see her unhappy about anything. I respond by saying that I could hear in her tone of voice how close she feels to her little girl. It must be so frustrating to leave her on those mornings and go to work. Of course it isn't surprising that she would feel reluctant to cause her any unhappiness or frustration. Mrs. B. nods and wholeheartedly agrees, adding that the passage of time has not allayed the grief she feels at each morning's parting. Why even leaving her today to come to see me was hard. And her work days are long and difficult and she comes home tired, has her chores to do, dinner to prepare, and so little time to relax and just be companionable. The idea of also being a disciplinarian seems awful to her. She adds that it took them ten years to conceive and that due to medical complications they will not be able to have any more children. Bonnie will be their only child. At first she wasn't going to even mention this fact since she didn't think it had anything to do with the situation around sleep but perhaps it does and so it is best for me to know.

I respond by saying that it is best for me to know since it is another indication of the depth of her investment in her child. To have waited so many years to have a child is bound to have a profound effect. I suggest that we consider whether there might not be a way to satisfy her loving feelings, her wish to nurture Bonnie, and still have age-appropriate expectations of her. I express my concern about the current situation, which clearly is detrimental to everyone. There is the serious problem of lack of sleep for all of them, the pattern of chaotic evenings, the lack of structure, and the tension between her and her husband. That is the obvious part of how Bonnie's sleeplessness affects the family. Then there is the other part of the problem that is less obvious and particularly worrisome to me, and is as follows. The current situation is detrimental to Bonnie's development because in regard to the sleep problem Bonnie is not experiencing her parents as powerful and protective figures, at least not around bedtime. Bonnie needs an image of parental strength, for that is her most solid assurance of being safe and well cared for.

I tell Mrs. B. that she has done too good a job of convincing her husband not to play the role of a powerful dad. This is something for her to reconsider. After all, her husband's strength is a good thing for all three of them. It is good for Bonnie to have a strong dad, it is good for Mrs. B. to have a strong husband, and it is good for her husband to use his strength rather than to suppress it. I talk some more to the two of them and they listen quietly. I say that there are differences between fathers and mothers at all stages of life. Mothers often have more difficulty in separating from their children during the early years than do fathers. Perhaps it's because of the long pregnancy during which they indeed are not separate at all. Then there are the early months during which nursing perpetuates a state of great intimacy. Because of this, the role of a father in early childhood typically entails helping the mother around issues of separation (Abelin 1971) and dealing with her tendency to baby her child past a time when that is growth promoting. In their case, Mr. B. has been reluctant to assume this role forcefully for fear of displeasing his wife, and probably having waited so long for this child and being unable to have more children contribute to his reluctance. Perhaps he will feel more able to assume his role now that we all have a better understanding of what has been going wrong in their lives.

Mrs. B. says that if this will really help Bonnie develop well, sleep better, and allow them to have better evenings and nights, she is willing to let her husband take the lead. At that point in the consultation I think it's possible that my interventions have finally reached her, at least on the surface, but to a sufficient degree to let the father get the necessary foothold. That is often enough in a brief intervention such as this. If Bonnie's mother has, as I suspect, an unconscious fantasy that operates around the idea of a "special" child, this is not something I can tackle directly. But I can help the father avoid buying into it by not playing the part of second-class parent. My interventions are directed at: (1) the mother's reaction formation against sadistic impulses, revealed by her references to barbaric-style discipline such as locking Bonnie up or tying her with ropes to keep her in bed, (2) her difficulty around letting her child individuate, as exemplified in her unawareness that in throwing food on the floor Bonnie is expressing her rebelliousness and ability to act autonomously, (3) a narcissistic component that leads Mrs. B. to believe that she has to choose between her needs and those of her daughter, an unbearable choice. Mrs. B. is unable to perceive the mutuality of their needs as far as sleep is concerned.

In the last few minutes of the session Bonnie's father and I discuss the installation of a new regime in the home. He suggests that bedtime would be from 8:00 to 8:30—time enough for Bonnie's bottle and two stories. After that, lights go out and it's goodnight until morning.

I make the suggestion that the new rules be spelled out and that Bonnie be told that from 8:30 at night when her parents kiss her goodnight until morning when her parents have to get up, she must stay in her bed and sleep. If she wakes she must find a way to put herself back to sleep. No food or drink or stories are allowed during the night. These are the new rules to make sure that everyone gets the sleep they need.

The father is comfortable with the plan he designed and with my suggestion that it be spelled out to Bonnie, but Mrs. B. once again becomes visibly upset and bursts out with "But, that's ridiculous. We've tried all that a million times and it doesn't work. She'll get right up. With all that you're saying I still don't understand what's going to keep her in her bed."

I try again. I say that I am pretty sure that I now understand what is in her way. Perhaps it seems inconceivable to her that Bonnie could be induced in a loving way to go sleep and stay asleep. I, on the other hand, am convinced that this can be done, and that to do it kindly and firmly is the only right way. Because she doesn't believe that it can work while her husband does, he is the one who should set up the new regime at the beginning. She would then see Bonnie not only accept the new order of things, but find comfort in the new structure and derive pleasure from having a strong dad, from being in her cozy safe bed, and from going to sleep when tired rather than running around feeling scared and silly and out of control.

I tell her that Bonnie will eventually identify with these expectations, take them in and own them, and when that happens they will become her standards. Through this she will learn to be clearer and less capricious in her general demands and expectations. Going to sleep will become a warm and utterly predictable time, a time of feeling safe, of feeling close to and cared for by her parents.

I tell Mrs. B. that in these months of daily frustration and disturbed sleep she has lost sight of something very simple and I am going to remind her. She forgot that her little girl cares about pleasing her and must feel worried when her mother is displeased. Could she have forgotten how important that is to Bonnie? After all, isn't the awareness of another person's pleasure and displeasure the basis on which caring and concern for others grow and develop? Mrs. B. is an expressive person and the fluctuation of her pleasure and displeasure have been apparent during this consultation, both in tone of voice and facial expressions. These responses are apparent to her daughter, and as Bonnie grows and learns to use them as a barometer, a guide, so to speak, to another person's emotional states, she will be the stronger for it. It will firm up her understanding of cause and effect and of relationships. For instance, when Bonnie evokes a tone of helplessness in her mother and finds that her mother surrenders to her will, *this must be a big worry to her. It's enough to get Bonnie out of bed to check out that her mother is all right.* But if Bonnie's mother sounds strong and sure, then Bonnie feels safe and can stay in bed and go to sleep because she feels confident that her mother is fine.

Mrs. B. listens quietly, looking teary, and nodding. She says that she can hear my words, and while what I say makes good sense, she has trouble retaining their meaning. She hears me but it doesn't penetrate. She is more affected by my tone. I sound so sure of what I am saying, so confident, and that is helpful. And yet she feels as if she is being asked to give up something precious and that's what makes her feel so sad. She is ready to go ahead with the plan but will do so on faith. Perhaps insight will follow. I ask her if she is sure she can do this. Should we meet again and talk further . . . ? We don't have to rush. If she needs more time, we can wait a while longer and talk some more. She assures me that time won't help her, that it would be best to get this over with now.

Just before we say goodbye I suggest that Mr. and Mrs. B. call me if they need my help, but even if they don't, I would like a follow up call in three or four days. The father calls four days later. He reports that everything worked out much more smoothly than either of them had thought possible. As he describes what happened I find myself impressed that he so effectively convinced Bonnie that a new set of rules was in effect, that even on the first night Bonnie slept right through to morning. The going to sleep process took thirty minutes, and since it ended at 8:30, as we had planned, the parents now had their evening *and* night to themselves. Bonnie's father reminds me that he was the one who didn't want to come to see me. He was so sure that I would tell him, as had the others, that some children don't sleep and that there is nothing to be done about it, it's just one of these things that happens to some people for no special reason. Well, he never believed it and how glad he was that I had felt the same way.

Mr. B. said that he and his wife both considered the change in their lives nothing short of a miracle, but I knew that to be the wrong word. Something important did take place, but it was no miracle.

What did happen in our consultation to allow for the change? I believe that an important field of perception shifted in these parents. The shift was slight, but that's all it took to allow them to view their role as parents differently. I only saw Mr. and Mrs. B. once and therefore have very limited knowledge of them but I learned just enough to make certain assumptions that allowed me to intervene effectively.

Why did they come to see me; what was their motivation? It appeared on the surface that Mr. B. mainly came to appease his

wife who was very angry at him, perhaps for not living up to her
ideal image of husband-father. What emerged was how thoroughly
he had joined his wife in devaluing himself, and how he had sur-
rendered to her will in regard to Bonnie and the sleep problem.
He had become too frightened or too guilty to be able to do anything to change matters, yet he was intensely distressed by the
situation at home and wanted Bonnie to sleep in a normal way.
He clearly did not want anything to be "wrong" with Bonnie.
Whatever had gone awry between him and his wife, and whatever his wife had come to represent had blocked him from being
resolute in his dealing with the excessive closeness between his
wife and his daughter that was manifested by the sleep disturbance. Although Mr. B. was the parent who did not want to come,
he quickly became the agent of change, a powerful force in bringing about order in all their lives.

The more delicate work was with Bonnie's mother, who did
convey a latent wish that there be something "wrong" with Bonnie,
rather than with the approach taken by her parents. Mrs. B. came
to see me with the purpose of having me convince her husband
that Bonnie was "special" and could not be expected to sleep as
did other two-year-old children. Perhaps both Bonnie and Mrs. B.
were "special," not "ordinary" like Mr. B.

These themes are indicators that alert us to the presence of
elaborate unconscious fantasies. As this case illustrates, these
fantasies not only play a powerful role in what is occurring on
various psychic levels but also influence daily behavior. As mentioned earlier in this chapter, it is important to note these trends
even in a brief consultation such as this, but obviously we can't
do much with them in such a short time. It is actually surprising
that we can use our awareness of this dimension at all, but as you
see, we can and I did. I addressed the surface layer of the fantasy
very directly through the intervention, using the riddle:

(1) Bonnie doesn't sleep because there's something wrong with
her, or (2) Bonnie doesn't sleep because there is something wrong
in her parents' expectation that she go to sleep and stay asleep
like other two-year-olds.

This is the kind of intervention that just barely brushes preconscious awareness of the fantasy, but it does so just enough to bring reality to the foreground. What (sane) mother would really prefer to have something wrong with her child? The intervention gave a gentle jolt to the system ego and sparked it into action. It served as an appeal to logic and to mobilizing the person's highest level of functioning.

If we pay careful attention to all that Mrs. B. conveyed during the four telephone contacts and the sixty-minute consultation, we see that we can learn quite a lot about her in a short time. During that first telephone conversation she imparted her need to describe minute aspects of her life, such as the schedules of her sitter, her social engagements, and so forth, thus revealing her wish to draw me in, to establish a connection prior to our first meeting. As mentioned earlier, Mrs. B.'s chattiness was engaging and she succeeded in drawing me in very nicely. If we think of this initial exchange in terms of a preverbal dialogue, we would be able to say that Mrs. B. expressed confident expectation that her needs would be met. Thinking along the lines of the preverbal dimension is diagnostically useful and holds interesting implications for the outcome of the consultation. I will return to this point later.

It is very useful to pay attention to these early communications. Of course this is time consuming, and can be irritating if one is in a hurry and the anticipated two-minute telephone call for the purpose of making an appointment stretches into a ten-minute conversation. But if we consider this as part of the consultation, rather than something extraneous to it, we allow the time and carefully register the early diagnostic impressions that begin to form from the first telephone contact. The other important reason for allowing for a leisurely pace in these situations is to establish some rapport prior to the first meeting. I have stressed the importance of rapport in these brief consultations and I think that the case of Bonnie's parents demonstrates its critical role. I believe that my willingness to adapt to Mrs. B.'s pace during our telephone conversations contributed to her arriving at my office feeling welcome. Perhaps this feeling of being well received by me made it possible for her to tolerate my *not* giving her what she came for, *not* confirming that there was something wrong with her child, that Bonnie was special in some way that made her mother special as well.

I did not get to know Mrs. B. well enough to understand her fantasies or the nature of her anger at her husband. I did, however, rely on my impression that she was not a disturbed woman but rather a woman in the throes of something difficult, a regressive state perhaps, a period of disequilibrium. It was during the telephone contacts that I initially formed the diagnostic impression of basic solidity. During the consultation her psychic distress became apparent, rounding out a picture, however cursory, of what I had to work with.

We know that the developmental stages that children pass through evoke particular affective states in their parents (Benedek 1959). For example, mothers and fathers who cope very adequately with early infancy and the extraordinary dependency of their baby, who have a fairly easy time helping their child become weaned and toilet trained, may be quite unequal to dealing with the anger and jealousy aroused in the toddler when a sibling is born. There are countless variations on the theme of the good enough parents suddenly running into a problem that renders them not good enough to deal with a particular stage in their child's development. If only one parent flounders while the other can cope, the situation has a hope of not causing a significant problem, providing that the parent who feels stronger takes charge. Sometimes both parents are vulnerable in their reaction to the same stage in their child's development. Then, what would normally be a transient developmental problem could turn into something more complicated and skew future development. The case of Max in Chapter 10 illustrates the role of consultation in primary prevention of more serious pathology.

Combining the valuable theoretical formulation offered by Benedek with my impressions of Mrs. B., I wondered what had been stirred up during the long years of infertility, by not being able to have more than one child, and then by the too early physical separation from Bonnie. Could there be something about this particular developmental stage in Bonnie's life that might reverberate to a particularly painful stage in Mrs. B.'s own past? If so, it would mean that whatever was operating in her was powered by the unrememberable, by sorrow, by grandiosity, and by narcissistic hurt and anger. This, of course, was an assumption on my part. I didn't know Mrs. B.'s history well enough to really know whether this was so, but my intervention was based on the speculation that she was partly operating in the dark, led by unconscious forces.

I felt that I had to proceed on my belief that no mother in her right mind really wants something to be wrong with her child. It was my job to represent reality and to assume that if the choices were clearly defined for her she would choose being an ordinary good mother to her daughter. It was my job to *not* give her what she came for because what she came for was powered by fantasy, by desperation, and by guilt rather than by reason. Had she not felt welcomed in my office, had not some good feeling been established prior to our face-to-face meeting, I might have lost her upon not giving her what she wanted (or thought she wanted). She might have dismissed me rather than allowed me to become an auxiliary ego for her, for that is what happened towards the end of the consultation. I became someone whose judgment she was able to accept on faith and out of recognition that she had encountered a blind spot in herself, one that clouded her own judgment and caused her to blur the line between mothering as a complex adult role and the belated gratification of infantile needs.

I had some other clues about the degree of distress that Mrs. B. was laboring under. As close as she felt to Bonnie, she did not perceive her realistically. She alternated between overestimating and underestimating her. She gave her enormous executive rights while at the same time failing to realize that throwing peas on the floor was not out of ignorance or lack of etiquette but out of rebelliousness and testing limits. Because I sensed a core solidity in Mrs. B. and believed that she was much too aware a person to misperceive such obvious rebelliousness in her child, I proceeded as if her distress must be very great to cause such confusion in her. Had my diagnostic impressions of Mrs. B. been wrong, the consultation would have been extended and I would have taken a different approach.

Having gotten my bearings with these parents, it was clear that Mr. B. was going to have to do the job he wanted to do but felt unable to tackle. Although he did not share his wife's vulnerability to his daughter's current developmental stage, he nonetheless felt unequal to take charge for other reasons. It appeared that the obstacle to his effectiveness lay more in his reaction to his wife's attitude of dismissal of him. What Mr. B. wanted from me was something I could offer. He wanted to be a good father *and* a good husband. He didn't want to choose one over the other, and I was able to give him the foothold he needed to accomplish this objective.

One goal of these brief consultations is to set back on track that aspect of the child's development that has gotten derailed, or to spark development when a delay is keeping the child from being on track. In Bonnie's case a developmental delay was expressed by her inability to fall asleep and stay asleep on her own. Falling asleep involves regression in the service of the ego and the ability to self-soothe and self-regulate. It is not a minor achievement. As we well know, many adults have failed to master these developmental steps and experience sleeping disturbances all of their lives. Another goal of these brief consultations is to enable *the parents* to do the reparative work directly with their child, thereby setting the progression of their development as parents back on track.

The wish to be a good parent is universal. Except in the most extreme pathology it is something we can count on, a given, an attribute of being human. When parents experience failure in satisfying this wish the disappointment is painful. Generally, the parents who consult us because they have run into a commonplace childhood problem that has rendered them unable to help their child want our help in restoring their ability to take care of the problem on their own. Only this outcome fulfills their wish to be good and competent parents. As we work with the specific characteristics of each parent and with the particularity of each parent pair and also consider their conscious and unconscious motivations, that is the one common denominator that is the key to our understanding of them: the wish to be a good parent.

We can talk so clearly about the purpose of psychoanalysis and psychoanalytic psychotherapy. We know that the goals there take years to reach and pertain to the resolution of neurotic conflict and the firming up of a sense of identity. We know that in child treatment we aim at restoring development to its age-appropriate place and pace. I propose that the purpose of brief consultations with parents of well-developing children who have run into a stubborn developmental hurdle is to restore parental effectiveness and, concomitantly, parental self esteem: to help these parents fulfill their wish—to be good parents.

8

~

The Consultant
as Auxiliary Ego

*I*n the preceding chapter I described a single-session consultation with the parents of Bonnie, a little girl who had a sleeping
problem. It must be stressed that there had been no way of knowing in advance that one session would be enough to alleviate the
problem that had brought Bonnie's parents to my office.

Among the many unforeseeable aspects of consultations with
parents is their duration; another is the identity of the primary
patient. These unknown factors make certain demands on the
consultant that differ somewhat from those in the more customary situations we encounter in our practices. For instance, since
clinical decisions are by necessity made within minutes of beginning a consultation, these decisions rest on limited information.
Thus, the consultant must take certain risks in choosing interventions, risks that affect the focus and direction of the interview.
These risks are not wild, nor are they random in nature. As with
any interventions that are not purely interpretive, they consist of
questions and observations that reflect the therapist's clinical
thinking based on an ongoing assessment of all that is unfolding
in the consulting room. Since this does not sound so different from
the way we normally work, why refer to these interventions as
carrying a greater risk factor than usual? The answer is that the

word risk reminds us of the speculative nature of these interventions, a factor that cannot be overstressed given the fact that the interventions are offered despite our limited knowledge of the parents who come to us in our capacity as consultants and of their child, the subject of the consultation, who is not even present.

One safeguard to keeping these interventions as close to being on track as possible is to present them in a provisional manner; another is to ensure that they have exploratory value. Sometimes it is even useful to share the use of these two elements with the parents by drawing attention to them in a question, a statement, or an observation. That way the therapist's effort to maximize the usefulness of any information gained is enhanced by involving the parents in this exploratory process. For instance, the parents could be told that we will try a particular approach and if it works we will know thus and such, but if instead we discover X, we will know that we took an approach that won't work, and will try another. Or we might preface a question we are about to ask by explaining to the parents what alerted us to thinking this might have relevance to our understanding of Mary's fear of the bath or Jimmy's diet of peanut butter and jelly and practically nothing else.

Engaging parents in the process of looking for solutions to the problems they bring us can sometimes, but not always, work out well, or it can work well with one parent and not the other. In the case of Bonnie, for instance, I expressed my impression that based on what they had told me, Bonnie was a well-developing child whose sleeping difficulty was the result of her parents' inability to state their expectations of her in a firm and clear manner. I presented this as my premise and added that if my assessment of the problem proved to be wrong, I would want to see Bonnie in my office, reevaluate and deepen my understanding of the problem, and then try a different approach. Mr. B. was immediately receptive to my assessment of what was causing the problem and eager to discuss a remedy and to assume responsibility for initiating a different approach to Bonnie's sleep problem and routine. In contrast to her husband's receptivity, Mrs. B. was skeptical.

She didn't think a change of approach would work, nor was she willing to actively participate in trying it out. But she was willing to let her husband assume responsibility and carry out the changes we discussed.

In Bonnie's case it was enough to have the full participation of one parent because the other parent was willing to allow the necessary work to take place. I believe that it is a mistake to automatically demand or even expect equal participation of both parents. That we have to accept things as they are and work with what is before us is basic to our work. We have no difficulty in understanding this as a normal condition for beginning treatment when it concerns our adult or our child patients; we consider our assessment of the situation before us to be the basis of our diagnostic understanding. But where work with parents is concerned, even experienced therapists sometimes falter in this regard, disregard the real people in the room, and make demands that cannot be met, thereby jeopardizing any chance of a successful outcome. When such distortion and rigidity on the part of the therapist goes unrecognized it serves as yet another example of unobserved countertransference manifestations, a phenomenon that is unfortunately too often evoked and left unexamined in work with parents. In Chapter 11 the case of Gus will serve as an example of a consultation in which the therapist fails to sufficiently integrate her diagnostic impressions of the parents into her approach to helping them better understand their child. The erosion of our professional role holds particular significance in these consultations to parents since their brevity precludes the opportunity of developing a working alliance. This factor in our more leisurely cases sometimes mitigates against the occasional lapses of maintaining this role.

Despite the divergent attitudes of Bonnie's parents toward the root of the problem and its solution, the consultation moved along nicely. I believe that my relaxed attitude about taking a particular direction, but my willingness to take another should I prove to be wrong, worked out well for them both. It perhaps created a holding space for them and deflected some of the "life and death" quality with which they experienced their situation. And because I found the case of Bonnie pretty clear cut and felt fairly confident that I had assessed the situation correctly, I felt that I could take a fairly definitive stand. This is not always the case, and in fact it is unusual to be able to arrive at such a clear picture so quickly.

I believe that it is very important for us to have and maintain an unhurried and open-minded attitude throughout consultations and to convey this attitude to the parents in the way we express our interest in their situation, our curiosity about what is going on in their child's world, and our confidence that together we will gain the necessary understanding to move things back on track. A welcoming and receptive climate can go a long way towards drawing the parents into the consultation process and making use of the information they provide, rather than having them experience their information as being of limited use and even viewed as burdensome, as if it were baggage to be discarded and disowned. I refer here to the attitude that parents so often have about the problem that precipitated the referral. Their distress may take many forms, but it invariably limits their ability to think about their problem constructively or to believe that the information they provide could hold the key to its cause *and* solution. They are often so caught up in their distress (or in denying that a problem exists) that they have difficulty in observing what is happening in front of them and inside them.

A short detour into some theory will help us understand where we need to go and take the parents in order to get them back on track. As we know, synchronicity between the work of the observing ego and that of the experiencing ego is as fundamental a part of the analysand's work as is free association. The analysand develops this ability gradually over the course of an analysis, at first with help from the analyst and later, independently. The analyst fosters this ability in his patient because it is essential to the analytic work. But the analyst also continually develops and refines this ability in himself.

Gradually and over time, this skill in the analyst, this ability to observe and experience simultaneously becomes so inherent to his work that we might regard it as the analyst's basic therapeutic tool, his "work ego,"[1] a component of what Winnicott (1960) refers to as "the special state" that the analyst resides in during work hours. But this work ego is not reserved for analysts doing classical analysis. It is as vital to psychotherapists engaged in psychotherapy or consultation, an organic dimension in all aspects of our work. Whatever the therapeutic modality, the existence and use of our work ego is what distinguishes us from the lay public and makes the therapeutic encounter different from any other social or professional interchange. Whatever professional situation presents itself, it's essential to maintain that special state that is the product of our work ego.

When the person before us is not a patient coming to us for help, but a parent coming to us for help with her child, it is all too easy to feel somewhat confused about our role and fail to assume our customary professional attitude. Too often the fact that the person before us is not directly requesting help for herself throws us off balance. Then our work ego loses its fullness and dimension and our listening mode becomes more concrete. It is a pity when that happens because in order to do our work as psychoanalysts, psychoanalytic psychotherapists, and psychoanalytic consultants, whether engaged in long-term or in briefer treatment situations, we must rely on the blending of what we experience with what we observe.

I propose that whatever the situation before us, the therapist's work ego functions effectively only when blending information gained by listening to and observing the patient with information gained by observing our responses to the patient. If we add to these

---

1. I am borrowing this term, coined by Robert Fliess (1942), and using it in a somewhat different context.

two key sources of knowledge the body of theory basic to our work, we complete the trio of elements that serve as our foundation. It is our job to integrate this vital knowledge and to find a way to convey our findings to the parents who consult us; this is the skill that we have to offer to them, the skill of making use of our full knowledge. And this skill is exactly what worried parents are lacking. Parents have their special knowledge, but when we see them in our offices, their anxiety often clouds their ability to trust their perceptions and common sense.

We know that anxiety has a regressive effect, one that curtails the range of resources available to the ego. Parents generally find themselves in a state not only of anxiety, but also helplessness when they call us. It often takes a lot of failure and frustration to prompt their initial phone call; we can assume that by the time they contact us they've had a pretty bad time, even though their distress is often veiled. Sometimes when we enter their world, our presence alone stirs hope and the expectation that help is possible. When that happens, when our presence sparks optimism, that is in itself an important diagnostic indicator. It suggests something positive about their past experiences in being helped. It is often a sign that a good working alliance is likely. When the consultation begins with either one or both parents feeling a surge of hope that help is on the way, that can have an ameliorative impact on the parents' state of anxiety and helplessness and allow them to begin to mobilize their resources.

I am referring to something very simple here, a form of instant transference based on the expectation that help is possible, that it exists and will materialize. If the consultation begins in a transferential mood of confident expectation, it is important for the therapist to accept this role and the idealization it confers. It is not helpful to the parents to be subjected to listening to our more modest version of our effectiveness, or to our more "realistic" understanding of what our work together will entail. If we can bear it, it is best to leave their confidence in us untarnished. It has a useful side, such as having the immediate effect of allaying some of their anxiety. With reduced anxiety and with the sense of help being on the way, these parents might move closer to rediscovering their own resources. That is just the direction towards which we strive since one of our goals is to eliminate their need for us.

Very often in these brief therapeutic encounters the consultant plays a role akin to that of auxiliary ego. Although, strictly speaking, this term generally describes a role assumed by the caretaker of an infant to protect the infant's ego from being overwhelmed by stimuli (Edward et al. 1991), or from having to develop his own resources prematurely due to the caretaker's failure of protection and at the price of developing a false self (Mahler 1968), I am stretching the term to include a role taken by the therapist when an adult or child is temporarily overwhelmed by stimuli. In early infancy the role of caretaker as auxiliary ego was expressed through voice, tone, touch, manner, and action. In this adult version I believe that tone, manner, and action still apply but we can add to this list the offering of suitable interventions. For instance, at an appropriate point during the initial consultation with parents, when one has gained a sense of what they're like, and of course if it seems appropriate to the situation, we can offer a statement along these lines: "Let's see what this is about, get to understand it, and then we'll know what to do about it."

The implication that if we understand a situation we'll know what to do about it is so simple and so obvious to us that it's all too easy to leave it unstated, but it's difficult to overemphasize the importance of this idea and the value of stating it in words. Perhaps this simple truth holds particular importance within the context of a consultation with parents who are basically adequate in dealing with the ordinary problems of childhood and have come across a problem that baffles them. It's the basic adequacy of these parents and the normalcy of their child that make their current difficulty so upsetting to them. These are people who have navigated well through early infancy and toddlerhood and have managed to deal with all the issues, all the dilemmas and conflicts and frustrations that arise during these early months and years.

Suddenly, no matter how they try, they can't manage a problem and the problem persists. They consult a child therapist and she tells them that when the problem is understood the solution will be found. This is startling news to them for they thought they understood the problem. The problem is that Sally has started wetting her bed after having been fully trained, or that Kevin has become unwilling to talk to his teachers, or that Peter is suddenly having a terribly hard time leaving home for school.

The fact that parents often consider the symptom to be the problem is not surprising since the symptom is indeed causing a problem for everyone. But we therapists tend to be more curious than that and wonder what caused the symptom, and as we draw the parents into this broader view, this inquiry into what is cause and what is effect, this collaborative exploration of their situation, there is often a shift in their attitude. First there is the immediate relief of not being alone with the problem. Then there is the reassurance of knowing that the problem appeared for a reason and that it is possible to uncover that reason and eliminate it. Finally, it is comforting to be in the presence of a professional who sounds as if the process of finding the cause and the solution is nothing unusual or mysterious, but rather all in a day's work.

One of the requirements of our profession is to have the ability to tolerate not having answers, not knowing where we are going; accepting ambiguity as normal and even interesting is intrinsic to our work. How could I as consultant possibly know why Sally is wetting her bed, Kevin refusing to talk to his teachers, or Peter experiencing distress during the morning transition from home to school? I only know that these symptoms are indicators of psychic distress and that in each case the distress is manifested by a regression. I do know that if I engage the parents in exploring their total situation, ask all the questions I feel to be relevant, observe their interaction and their effect on me, and if necessary meet their child, it is likely that I will find out what I need to know and what to do about it. During this process I will lend these parents my confidence in my knowledge and training and let them make use of it until they have regained confidence in their own insight and common sense. This is my view of the role of the consultant: the consultant as auxiliary ego. This is not my view of the role of a child or adult psychotherapist or psychoanalyst, although the role of auxiliary ego can at times be temporarily called upon in these more usual treatment situations. When that occurs it is more along the lines of employing a parameter (Eissler 1953) that is eliminated when no longer needed. In brief consultations to parents on commonplace childhood problems the consultant as auxiliary ego is the moving force, the catalytic agent that enables the normal rhythm of family life to be resumed.

It is important to mention that during the early stage of the consultation process it is sometimes difficult to tell whether what is being presented to us is really a commonplace developmental difficulty or whether the familiar nature of the presenting problem masks more pervasive disturbances in child and/or parents, requiring more intensive treatment. I consider some of the commonplace problems of early childhood to be difficulties around going to sleep and staying asleep, fussiness about food, protracted fear of strangers, difficulties around ordinary transitions such as going out or leaving a friend's house, difficulty with ordinary routines such as bathing and dressing, and, in the decade of the '90s, the increasingly common difficulties around toilet training.

Some of the difficulties common to childhood are present to varying degrees in each child's development. These taxing moments for children present parents with challenges and dilemmas and a job to be done. Many parents are up to this job and are able to serve as auxiliary ego for their children to help them master each of the developmental tasks as they arise. The great challenge for parents is to find the proper balance between protecting their children from experiencing excessive anxiety, which as we know can be crippling, without swinging too far over into protecting them too much. Overprotective parents do not allow their children to experience ordinary struggles and frustrations; consequently children who have been overprotected often experience particular distress in mastering these difficult moments. It is often the parents who cannot find the right balance between their expectations of themselves and their expectations of their child who come to us for help. And so we enter into their situation for a short while, provide the dimension they're lacking, and help them achieve the balance they need. We become an auxiliary ego until they recover their bearings and can once again find their own way.

9

❦

Brief Treatment of a Bowel Retention Problem

*I*n this chapter I describe one of my earliest experiences in helping a mother–daughter pair who were caught in a dreadful impasse and needed help in order to move on. I believe that this case serves as a particularly good example of the consultant's role as auxiliary ego; in fact it is this case that precipitated my conceptualizing this aspect of the role occasionally played by both the consultant and the therapist. I could find no other way of understanding why my presence had such an immediate effect on the stalemate between the mother–child pair I am about to describe.

When I first met her, Zoe was a strikingly clever and engaging twenty-three-month-old child. She quite took my breath away when I saw her in the waiting room where I had gone to greet her and to invite her into my office. There she was, sitting comfortably in one of my straight-backed chairs, swinging her legs back and forth; their great distance from the floor accentuated her tininess.

"Are you Diana?" she asked. "Diana the poop lady?"

There was something so forthright and earnest about her question, and so poised was her manner that it was difficult to believe that she was not yet two years old.

The previous week Zoe's mother had come to see me in a state of desperation. For many weeks Zoe had been withholding her bowel movements for eight-, ten-, and even twelve-day periods. Mrs. Z. was extremely worried about both the psychological and physical damage this problem was causing her daughter. Medical consultations with two pediatricians had ruled out any physiological reason for this situation. Suppositories and enemas were suggested but Mrs. Z. was reluctant to use them as she was aware of the detrimental effect that their invasive nature could have on her child's body integrity and sense of autonomy.

Mrs. Z. had consulted another child therapist before calling me, and while he had been concerned and sympathetic, he told her that he had no prior experience with such a young child or with this particular problem. He felt unequipped to deal with this combination of unfamiliar factors, but was so interested in the progress and outcome of this case that he told Mrs. Z. that he would very much appreciate hearing from her to learn how the situation finally got resolved. Mrs. Z. spoke to a few more child therapists on the phone and found that none of them worked with children this young. She then called me with a mixture of reluctance and relief.

Mrs. Z. and I had met each other some years earlier when she had worked in a related field and our professional paths had crossed while we participated in a research project. Our contacts had been brief, cordial, and marked by mutual respect. Because of this prior association, Mrs. Z. felt awkward about calling for my professional help for herself and for her daughter. She felt that she should be going to a stranger, someone with whom she had no past association. At the same time she was also enormously relieved to be consulting me because I was not a stranger, because she knew and trusted me. The shame she felt at having to reveal what she considered a failure in her ability to mother her child was tempered by her awareness of the respect I had for her and further offset by her expectation that I would be able to help her. It was in this highly ambivalent mood, this combination of shame and hope, that she approached me. And much as she wanted my help, it pained her terribly that she needed that help and that I might be able to do for Zoe what she could not.

Mrs. Z. was a talented mother. She had good judgment in childrearing matters, confidence in herself as a mother, and pride in her thriving child. She had been attuned to her daughter from the beginning and she enjoyed her thoroughly. Except for the current problem, motherhood had been consistently rewarding.

Because of the unusual nature of his work, Zoe's father had mostly been out of the picture since Zoe's infancy. He was out of the country 90 percent of the year. Consequently his visits home were both brief and spaced far apart. For all intents and purposes Mrs. Z. lived the life of a single parent and did so without the help and support of other family members. Her parents were both dead and she had no siblings, nor did she have other relatives to pitch in and help. She had a circle of very close friends whose company she cherished, but where her child was concerned she made all the decisions, bore all the responsibility, did all the caretaking, and did this well, gracefully, and decisively. Then this problem arose, with a symptom that was worrisome and difficult to get a handle on. For the first time since becoming a mother Mrs. Z. was baffled, distressed, and filled with a sense of helplessness.

At this point in my narrative I would like to describe my conscious attitude about taking on this case. As mentioned in previous chapters, the response of the therapist to the parent (or parents) to the child, to the entire situation, including the presenting problem itself and what it might stir up in the therapist, is as important a source of knowledge as the information presented by the parent or child or gained from the bulk of our theoretical knowledge.

Just as with the first therapist Mrs. Z. had consulted, I too had no prior experience in working with a bowel retention problem. He was unwilling to take on the case despite his obvious interest because he found the problem too intimidating to approach. I felt sympathetic to his decision not to try to do something that seemed beyond his expertise and field of confidence. That seemed like a wise decision, protective of self and patient. Our work is demanding enough without our stretching ourselves beyond a reasonable comfort level. I too felt reluctant to undertake working with such a serious and unfamiliar situation. I also felt unease at possibly failing to be able to help this former colleague. The existence of our prior contact intensified my desire to help and my concern that I might fail her and her daughter and fail in retaining her good opinion of me. The objectivity that is so essential to our work was definitely compromised by our prior association. I had to assess to what degree these factors would interfere with my ability to do my work. I decided that on balance this was a situation I would be able to work with.

Several factors influenced my decision to take this case on despite my misgivings. Unlike the other therapist, I did have experience with children this young, felt comfortable with them, and particularly enjoyed working with them. Of equal importance was my belief that I could work well with this mother despite her ambivalence about receiving my help. And now, here's something curious. I find myself wanting to say that most of all I took this case for a simple reason: I wanted to be helpful to this mother out of concern for her intense distress and out of the wish to help her little girl who was suffering. But how can I make such a naive comment in a book that places such emphasis on the complexity of motives, on unconscious factors, and on the transference and countertransference that unfailingly arise in our work? Therefore let me say that my wish to help had a countertransferential dimension that I would need to examine, learn from, and use productively. I knew it was there but at the beginning of our work it was unanalyzed.

There was also another consideration that influenced my taking the case. I couldn't think of anyone to refer Mrs. Z. to who would see her right away and work with her and help *her* do the work that needed to be done, rather than doing it for her. I knew that this mother could not financially or emotionally afford the

expense of child analysis or lengthy psychoanalytic psychotherapy for Zoe. I strongly suspected that a treatment approach
in which Zoe was viewed as the primary patient would cause
Mrs. Z. to feel painfully excluded. I felt, with strong conviction,
that this mother needed to be helped to do the major share of
therapeutic work, that she needed to remain the principal player
in the impasse she had reached with her daughter.

Some parents are able, or willing, or even eager to place their
child into the hands of a psychotherapist or psychoanalyst. There
are many reasons for this, ranging from despair at their own failed
efforts, recognition that their ability to help their child is no
longer equal to the situation, childhood pathology so severe that
parents cannot cope, extraordinary external events, and all manner of variables ranging from enormous faith in the therapeutic
process to parental depression, indifference, and abdication of
caring.

I was recently told by a mother who had brought her young
son to me that she wanted to be very much involved in his treatment. I took that statement to have great importance. In fact,
although she didn't say so, I took it as a condition for the child's
treatment. I can imagine the thoughtful reader asking: "But what
did that mother mean? Involved in what way?" I didn't know the
answer, but I knew that I would have to find out. I would make
sure of that. I might find out that it was not exactly a sincere
statement, but rather a reaction formation against her too mild
involvement. Or I might find out that it was a cool territorial
statement, or a real plea for inclusion. Whatever the underlying meaning, it would eventually emerge as a vital factor in the
dynamics of that family, dynamics in which the therapist is assigned a variety of roles by the various family members. And what
I did find out, eventually, was that this mother did not want her
child to be in treatment; she wanted to be told that it wasn't
necessary, that whatever had seemed a problem turned out to
be just a passing phase, one that she could handle best. When
I first met her she assigned me the role of wise, experienced
expert; within a few meetings my role was changed to kindly

superfluous stranger. The case didn't last long enough for me to be assigned any other roles. And I think she was right in deciding that she probably could handle the situation well enough without my help. I told her so, and that in itself was greatly helpful to her.

Once having made the decision to treat Zoe and her mother I began to organize my thinking. First, I took stock of what I knew about the total situation so far. I reminded myself that the bowel retention problem was the symptom, the outward manifestation of something gone askew in the mother–child relationship. Of course the choice of symptom is always significant and yields information about the nature of the problem, but it's important to remember that it's a manifestation of the problem rather than its core. One outstanding feature of this symptom was the pressure it created to alleviate it, to not let it linger too long because the longer it remained the greater the damage it would cause. The sense of urgency this symptom evoked in the mother, in me, and in anyone who heard about it was an important clue; it stirred up concern but also anxiety and helplessness. I noted that some of the affects that Zoe's problem roused in the adults around her were the ones most unhelpful to her, for nothing could help Zoe less than being surrounded by adults who felt helpless and unequal to easing her out of her predicament. What could it mean that so many adults were rendered powerless by this symptom?

To counter some of the anxiety I felt, I reminded myself that as I got to know Zoe and observed the interaction between her and her mother, I would discover clues, have a better sense of what avenues to pursue, and gradually gain the insight I needed to proceed. I reassured myself that despite the alarming nature of this symptom and its unfamiliarity, I had much to help me find my way. There was the training and knowledge of our profession, and our ability to observe and organize our observations. I reminded myself that the tools of our work are applicable to all situations and this would be no exception.

As is my practice, I saw Mrs. Z. alone prior to my first session with Zoe. I consider it important to begin the consultation or evaluation process by seeing the parents alone. In many consultations it is not necessary ever to see the child, as was true in the case of Bonnie, the little girl who wouldn't sleep described in Chapter 7. But even when treatment of the child is indicated from the beginning, seeing the parents before seeing the child makes sense on many counts. Although it gives me a chance to gather the information that I think I need, that is only part of the reason for seeing them alone. The preliminary sessions with the parents become a preparatory period during which we get to know each other and take stock of whether we think that we can work well together. The parents need to assess whether they feel comfortable with me and find me competent enough to entrust their child to me. I in turn have to evaluate whether I can work well enough with them. In these early sessions with the parents it is often possible to sense whether and with whom a working alliance may develop, and this too is valuable information in planning a treatment approach.

My session with Mrs. Z. had given me a developmental and family history and a description of the current symptom. The mother vividly described the progressively increasing physical discomfort Zoe experienced the longer she withheld her feces and her refusal to try to move her bowels because "it hurts." When she finally defecated, it required heroic efforts and caused her pain.

During the initial session with Mrs. Z. I also learned about the exclusive nature of this mother–child pair. There was a two-hour play group that Zoe attended once a week; there were occasional baby sitters; there was the circle of close friends, many of whom were also mothers of young children, but there was no constant intruder on the close-knit pair. The visits from the father were so far between as not to provide the normal disruption of the mother–child dyad. There was no important "other," no father, father substitute, or other woman to disturb the closeness between mother and child. Would I be assigned that role? Would I become that missing other?

I learned that Zoe had been developing well, was precocious in speech, motor development, awareness of her animate and inanimate environment, ability to reason and comprehend and grasp abstractions. I also learned that she was friendly, communicative, affectionate, and generally in a good mood. In other words, she sounded like a well-endowed child regarding object relations and ego functioning. Her precocity was a possible concern since it could have caused her to be aware of her separateness before being emotionally ready to deal with such awareness.

It was difficult to get a sense of Zoe's attitude about the symptom that was bringing her to see a therapist. The mother reported that she had been uncharacteristically uncommunicative about her discomfort in this area. As was my custom, I advised Mrs. Z. to tell Zoe the real reason for her appointment with me: that she was being brought to see a woman who knew a great deal about children and who would help her with the problem she had been having in moving her bowels.

I got my first clue about Zoe in the waiting room but it wasn't a clue that registered consciously. It was one of those subliminal clues that we respond to unknowingly, that perhaps slip into our observing ego but are not formulated or articulated right away. The clue had to do with her readiness to see me and her stated understanding of my role, that of a poop lady. There was already a divide between me, the poop lady, and her mother who was not a poop lady. I had from the first moment of contact been invested with the special power that poop lady represented to her, or perhaps this investment, this cathectic energy, had already been vested in me when her mother first told her that they were going to see a lady who knew how to help children who had poop troubles. The name poop lady, this invention of Zoe's, was a wonderfully economical condensation of name and function, not unlike the designations we associate with primitive tribes.

Within a few minutes of entering my office Zoe gave me a second clue; this one I consciously registered. She had looked over the toys on my shelves and picked out a tiny metal motor-cycle carrying a rider. She placed it on my table and it fell over. She looked disappointed so I asked her if she wanted the motor-cycle and rider standing up. She nodded. I asked if she was going to stand the motorcycle up or should I. She told me to do it and I did. She pushed it around a bit, pretending the rider was riding around, then she let go and it fell over again. She again looked unhappy. I told her that she looked unhappy when it fell. Did that mean that she wanted it to be standing? She nodded "yes." I asked whether this time she wanted to stand it up by herself, and she nodded, stood it up carelessly, and again it fell, at which point she squinted, shook her head and said rapidly: "Oh, I can't do it, I can't do it, I can't do it." I asked her whether she wanted to try again and she nodded and tried once more and again it fell. This game continued for a while longer, and each time Zoe tried to stand the motorcycle up, it would fall and she would squint, shake her head and say: "Oh, I can't do it, I can't do it, I can't do it."

I was struck by the contrast between the poise and compe-tence of her verbal communications, of the way she moved around my office, exploring, naming things, telling stories about them, giggling at some of the puppets, all the while including her mother and me in her observations, and the extraordinary lack of patience she displayed regarding the motorcycle falling down. What was such a low threshold for frustration doing in this otherwise super-competent child? That was my clue and I incorporated it in the most general and surface way in my first intervention. I said something like this:

> Some things are easy for you and some things are too hard. You have trouble when things are too hard. Your mommy told me that making poops is too hard for you, and that's why she brought you to see me. Pooping should be easy for you and we are going to figure out how to make it easy.

Zoe nodded and said that pooping was too hard. I then re-peated my little speech, this time directing it to Zoe's mother. I added something to the effect that Zoe shouldn't have to work so hard to get her poops out and that we were going to make pooping easier for her because that's how pooping is supposed to be, easy, not hard.

Zoe's mother agreed and added that the doctor had given them some medicine that would make pooping easier for Zoe by keeping her poop soft. She said that soft poop is easier to get out than stiff, hard poop. I heartily agreed and said that the medicine should help Zoe a lot, and that certain foods also help to keep poop soft: prunes and prune juice, raisins, all kinds of fruit, and drinking lots of water were some of the ways that I knew that kept poop soft and made pooping easier. Mrs. Z. said that the one problem was that Zoe won't take her medicine or eat any of those foods. I asked Zoe about the medicine and she said it was "yuck." I asked whether it was "yuck" even when it's mixed with something like applesauce. Zoe said that her mommy never gave it to her with applesauce. I could tell by the shocked look that crossed Mrs. Z.'s face that this must be untrue. I asked Zoe if she would try it with applesauce and she said yes because applesauce was her favorite, and prunes, prune juice and raisins, all these were her favorite foods.

I could feel Mrs. Z.'s indignation at her daughter's enthusiastic acceptance of these foods that I had casually mentioned. I assumed, correctly it turned out, that Mrs. Z.'s efforts to get Zoe to eat them had been rejected over and over again. Here was another clue of twofold importance. Zoe was turning some aspect of her mother's role over to me, and her mother, recognizing this turn of events, was furious. I had to accept the role that Zoe cast me in without further angering her mother. With that goal in mind I ended the session by offering the next appointment to Mrs. Z. and the one after to Zoe with her mother again present. I addressed my explanation to Zoe:

> Now that I've gotten to know you, and you've gotten to know me and what I look like and what I sound like and how my room looks, and what toys I have, now I'm going to help you make poop-

ing easier. I'm going to see your mommy in seven days and she will tell me how you are, and we will talk about how to help you, and then I'm going to see you again. That's the plan.

After they left, as I reflected on the session, I decided that it would be important that I place myself equidistant between mother and child, positioned so as to move closer to one or the other as the situation dictated.

A week later I met with Mrs. Z. who told me with some indignation that my name now came up in every other sentence uttered by Zoe. It was always in regard to her diet. When she was offered her stool softener mixed with applesauce, or her prunes or raisins, she always asked: "This is what Diana said, right?" or "Diana wants me to eat this 'cause she says it will make pooping easier, right?" or "Did Diana say this much raisins?"

She even on occasion asked whether her mother was remembering everything that Diana told her to do. While Mrs. Z. was exasperated by this constant overriding of her authority in favor of mine, she couldn't help but also be amused, almost despite herself, by the success her not-yet two-year-old had in causing her to feel jealous, betrayed and dismissed. Being the insightful person that she was, she understood that what was happening was a way out of the impasse between her and Zoe. My prominence in their lives had already shifted their dynamics. Zoe was now expressing anger overtly and in words, rather than just in her silent withholding mode. That was a big change, and it made Mrs. Z. feel more optimistic. She felt that any change was a good sign; even the slightest change brought them a little closer to ending their awful deadlock. Zoe had already had a bowel movement while attending her morning play group and had allowed her teacher to clean her up and change her diaper. This had occurred only six days after her last movement and consequently had not been quite as painful an ordeal as the ones of the last two months. Following this incident Zoe had complained for the first time about being messy inside her diaper, and Mrs. Z. wondered whether Zoe should be taken out of diapers and whether an effort should be made to get her to use the potty for bowel movements. Should she, for instance, be suggesting that Zoe try to use the toilet for bowel movements? Mrs. Z. was uncertain about what position to take on this matter since Zoe used the toilet with ease when needing to urinate. When she was home and on occasion not wearing a diaper, she went to the bathroom and urinated on the potty quite on her own, but of course this independent use of the potty was infrequent since she normally wore diapers and had to ask for help in having her diaper removed in order to use the potty. She had never moved her bowels on the potty.

We discussed what would make the most sense for Zoe at this point and decided that any suggestions to poop in the toilet could wait until we had made some progress in understanding the current situation.

I told Mrs. Z that with our plan of seeing her alone every other week and seeing her with Zoe on the alternate weeks, I planned to write to Zoe on the weeks that I did not see her. As soon as Mrs. Z. left my office I wrote the following message on a card for her:

Dear Zoe,
Today I saw your mommy and she told me that you were eating prunes and raisins and other fruit and taking your medicine mixed with applesauce and drinking lots of water and juice. I think that will help you. I'm going to see you again in seven days and we will play and talk some more and think of more ways to make pooping easier for you. I hope you like this card.

Fondly,
Diana [1]

---

1. It was not my custom to be on a first-name basis with a child patient but I made an exception in this case. Mrs. Z. and I had been on a first-name basis during our prior association and since she introduced me to her daughter as Diana, I went along with this informal mode, recognizing that it perhaps diluted the professional role that I had assumed in their lives and thus made my presence more acceptable.

At the time I happened to have had a supply of cards depicting a mother and child hippopotamus in a variety of situations: climbing a mountain, sitting on a lawn having a picnic, food shopping at an outdoor market, riding a bicycle built for two, and so on. These cards were attractive, clever, and gentle, and had nothing distorted, weird, or coy about them. Cards like that are hard to come by and when I happened to see them displayed in a store I stocked up on them. I decided that I would use these cards whenever I wrote to Zoe; in that way she would recognize them and know that they came from me. I decided that I would write to Zoe whenever I saw her mother without her and always refer to some of the things that her mom and I said about her in her absence.

The reader might wonder at how I arrived at such a plan and my answer will sound too simple to be the whole story, but it's as much of the story as I myself understand. This was a difficult case for me. The symptom was extreme and caused this little girl physical discomfort and pain. I had no prior experience with such a condition and the colleagues I consulted, while aware of this childhood symptom, had no direct experience with its treatment. I asked a pediatrician about the physical consequences of such infrequent bowel movements and he reassured me that there was no immediate health risk, but he did express concern should this continue. All in all I was in a precarious position. Not only was I unused to working with the particular symptom that Zoe manifested, but in addition, I was in an increasingly delicate position regarding her mother.

Zoe had conferred on me greater power and authority than what she was granting, at least overtly, to her mother. It appeared that she had assigned to me that role of "other," the intruder who is given sufficient stature to disrupt the closeness between mother and child. That role, customarily played by the father, is instrumental in allowing the separation-individuation process to unfold; it was a role that had not been filled in Zoe's life. Upon learning Zoe's history, particularly regarding the absent father and the intense closeness and exclusivity of the mother–child pair, I had wondered whether that role might come to me. Now it appeared that Zoe had not only given it to me but that she had done so with urgency, from the very beginning. That it had already been apparent during our first encounter in the waiting room suggested that she had probably assigned it to me prior to our even having met. Her mother must have described me as a helping expert and Zoe, eager to regain the omnipotent mother she had lost and whose help she needed, appointed me to that role.

This displacement, this cathectic shift from devalued mother to powerful "other" had been a fortuitous development; in the long run it would benefit her and her mother. But how well her mother would stand the constant reminders that a stranger now had this lofty place in Zoe's life was a concern. And I was told that Zoe's questioning of her mother didn't let up. She reported that throughout the days it went something like this: "Did Diana say this much raisins? Diana said prunes too? Give me prunes now. Diana said medicine and applesauce, no apples! Don't want apple, want what Diana said. Diana said juice, give me juice!"

I mentioned earlier that my decision to see Mrs. Z. alone was prompted by my awareness of the effect that Zoe's continuous challenging of her mother's authority, in contrast to the lofty place she had granted me, was having on this mother. Mrs. Z. reported with great anger and distress that Zoe wouldn't eat or drink anything unless assured that "Diana" would approve. I wanted to preserve my alliance with this mother; indeed it seemed to me that the outcome of the case would rest on my ability to accomplish this goal. Mother and child were both suffering and both needed help. Most likely the child was experiencing a rapprochement crisis that was severely intensified by the current problem. In response to this disequilibrium the mother too was experiencing a crisis, and if such a thing can be imagined, the mother's crisis was not so different from the child's. It appeared to be an adult version with some of the same features. One difference between them was that no matter how much Zoe devalued her mother, no matter how deep her disillusionment, she still had her as the loving and devoted caretaker that she had always been and still continued to be. But Zoe was imperious, disdainful, and rejecting of her mother much of the time and that, combined with Mrs. Z.'s sense of helplessness in dealing with Zoe's problem, made Mrs. Z's sense of loss at their former closeness extremely painful. For this reason I thought that Mrs. Z's need of me was more pressing. It seemed important to see her more often.

The thoughtful reader might wonder why I didn't see them both more often. As mentioned earlier, there was a financial problem. I had already substantially reduced my fee, but my offer to reduce it even more to allow for more frequent appointments had felt like charity to Mrs. Z. and she had refused. We agreed to try this approach for a month and if no significant progress was made she would reconsider my offer of reducing the fee.

The cards I sent to Zoe were a transitional device. Of course they served as a reminder that I had a place in her life even when we weren't together, but that was of secondary importance since Zoe had a mental representation of me. My primary purpose was reflected in the content of what I wrote, the references I always made to her mother, and my careful way of representing my role as that of joining *with* her mother on her behalf. It seemed very important that Zoe be reminded that her mother and I were a pair, allies joining forces to help her. I considered conveying this view of my role equally important to the mother and to the child.

I asked Mrs. Z. to telephone me on the eve of my second appointment with Zoe. This was another way of compensating for the less-than-ideal frequency of sessions for it provided me with up-to-date information about Zoe. However, the request for a telephone update prior to seeing a child is not an uncommon feature in the treatment of young and latency-age children, for it allows the therapist to have the kind of information that children rarely provide that might prove useful in the session with the child.

Mrs. Z. told me that Zoe had been showing signs of needing to defecate, was very uncomfortable, but wouldn't let herself, despite having continued on her improved diet and use of the stool softener. Mrs. Z. sounded quite discouraged and told me that she was eager to bring Zoe to see me the next morning.

This time, the minute Zoe heard my office door open she slid off her waiting room chair and ran into my office. She headed straight for the toy cabinet and took the motorcycle and rider. By the time her mother caught up with us she had already failed to stand the motorcycle up and was chanting: "I can't do it, I can't do it, I can't do it."

Before I had a chance to respond her face became contorted, the veins stood out on her neck, and she ran to a corner of the room and, slightly squatting, began to move her bowels. After a minute or two she straightened up, ran around the room and began again, squatting, straining, the veins on her tiny neck bulging. I have never seen a tiny child in such a state of distress. During the pauses, when she just ran around, I would murmur something inane like:

> Now I can really see how hard it is for you. I think you waited to do it here, to show me, so I could see how hard it is. That's not the way it's supposed to be. It's supposed to be easy and your mom and I are going to make it get easy for you; we're going to make sure that you don't have to struggle and work so hard and be uncomfortable when you poop.

It really didn't matter much what I said. My tone was soothing and my concern must have been apparent to her. Most important was the assurance that help was on the way. Sometimes when I spoke I addressed these repetitive comments to her mother, inviting her participation, and she would respond by agreeing that it should not be so hard to poop and that we would help to make it easy for Zoe.

In between these spasm-like episodes Zoe played quietly for a few minutes; then another spasm would overtake her and she would squat and strain. When it was over she would run around a little, then play for a couple of minutes, and then the cycle would start all over again. After about thirty-five minutes she seemed to have finished and Mrs. Z. took her to the bathroom to clean her up and put on a fresh diaper. The last five minutes of the session were spent with Zoe quietly drawing a picture while her mother and I spoke softly to each other in a way that included her.

I commented that Mrs. Z. had told me how hard it was for Zoe to poop and now I had seen with my own two eyes how very hard it was. We agreed that this was going to change soon.

I asked how pooping had been when Zoe was a baby, difficult or easy? Mrs. Z. said that when Zoe was a baby, pooping was really easy, very, very easy. Zoe looked up and smiled when she heard that. We agreed that with the new diet and medicine it would get easy again very soon. I said that Zoe's diet is going to keep the poop soft and that's important for making pooping easier. Mrs. Z. said that another important way to make it easy is to do it as soon as you feel you need to poop. If you hold it in, the poop gets hard and then it doesn't come out easily.

I said it might be difficult for Zoe to believe how easy pooping can be; she probably forgot how easy it was for her when she was a baby and it just came out with no trouble at all. Mrs. Z. said that when Zoe was a baby it was hard to tell when she was making a poop. Sometimes she wrinkled her little nose, and Mrs. Z. wrinkled her nose to show Zoe and me the way that had looked. Zoe smiled and imitated her mother's grimace. Mrs. Z. continued her narrative by saying that more often than not she didn't even know that Zoe was making a poop, that's how quiet and easy it was. When Zoe was a baby she often didn't know until she went to change Zoe's diaper and there it was, baby Zoe's secret poop. Zoe looked very pleased.

They left in a quiet, warm mood and just before they left I made the next appointment with Mrs. Z. alone for the following week, and another one for the two of them together two weeks hence. After they had gone I reflected on the session and on the dramatic change in their affective connection. It seemed to me two factors affected their change of mood. The first had to do with my verbally expressed resolve that Zoe would not have to continue to endure the struggle that I had now witnessed firsthand.

I believe that my deeply felt confidence in our ability to resolve this awesome problem had swept them both into a more hopeful mood. Then the reminiscence about Zoe's babyhood had been an affective bridge to a time when their connection had been intensely satisfying. No wonder they left in a better state.

At my next session with Mrs. Z. she reported that during the past week Zoe had asked several times if pooping was really easy for her when she was a baby, and she had been assured that yes, it had been easy. These questions were followed by Zoe's then wanting to hear the story of how easy pooping had been and Mrs. Z. repeated what she had told her in my office. During that week Zoe alternated between bossy questioning about whether her mother was doing what "Diana said," and requests for stories about pooping being easy when she was a baby. She moved her bowels only three days after our tripartite session and did so with not very much difficulty.

Mrs. Z. told me that it had generally been easy for Zoe to move her bowels until two months ago when she had become constipated. She had occasionally been slightly constipated when changed from breast milk to cow milk and then to a more varied diet, but these incidents were very easily remedied by adjustments in her diet. Then, several months ago she told her mom that her poop wouldn't come out, that it got stuck and hurt. Mrs. Z. tried her customary dietary adjustments, confident that they would take care of the problem, but nothing she tried worked and Zoe was very uncooperative about these dietary changes. That was how the current problem began. Mrs. Z. told me that Zoe had always had an easy time eating and digesting her food, and had never before had gas or any of the gastrointestinal problems so common in early childhood. Maybe it was because Zoe had been so free of problems that Mrs. Z. didn't react with sufficient seriousness to her first complaint about constipation. Mrs. Z. looked at me and said:

> No wonder she's so mad at me. I really let her down. I didn't help her when she really needed me. There she was with this hard poop hurting her and she didn't know what to do except keep it

from coming out. If I had paid better attention I would have given her some stool softener right away and the whole thing would have been over in a couple of days. No wonder she's put you in charge of her life.

I reminded her that while hindsight can make us all wise, she had no way of knowing when this first happened, having no prior experience, that it could turn into such a big problem. And there were other factors that contributed to the situation becoming so extreme. I enumerated the ones I had come to understand.

One factor was Zoe's precocity, her extraordinary facility in learning new things, solving problems, and being able to do so much at such a young age. Yet, as we observed from her reaction to the motorcycle falling down, when something was not very easy for her, she gave up quickly. That may have been her reaction to the first sign of constipation; she didn't try very hard.

Another factor was the nature of the problem. It was inside Zoe's body and for the first time in their relationship, in a situation of duress, Zoe had to do the actual work of helping herself while the most that her mother could do for her was to provide indirect help, such as reassurance, encouragement, and only later, stool softeners and alterations in diet. The constipation had thrown Zoe into being in sole charge of her body. This abrupt shift from her body being at least part mommy's body to that of its being entirely her own had happened before she was ready to take charge.

This problem also manifested itself shortly after toilet training had been discussed (not instituted but simply discussed with her) as something that was planned in the future. But with her characteristic ambition Zoe immediately took on toilet training and began to use the potty. She had an easy time urinating in the potty but found herself unable to use it to move her bowels. At that point she began to retain her bowel movements. It's possible that her newly developed standards regarding using the toilet placed a self-inflicted burden on her and caused the constipation. Or it's possible that the timing was such that she happened to be constipated at a particularly inopportune time. It's

difficult to reconstruct. Whatever the cause, the problem esca-
lated rapidly. I reminded Mrs. Z. of how very promptly she had
sought help.

I was concerned about the degree of self-blame this mother was
experiencing and wondered whether I could ease some of this by
giving her some information about the confluence of forces that
produced this symptom, forces that were beyond the reach of even
the most caring parent. Because this mother was in a related field
I considered whether I should discuss with her the fact that this
occurred during the rapprochement subphase. With a parent not
in the field or a related field it is still possible to provide some
educational information on those somewhat rare occasions when
we feel this could be helpful. Because of Mrs. Z.'s knowledge of
developmental theory and because of what I knew of her as a
person I decided I could present some of my ideas about how the
interplay of developmental forces, and circumstances due to hap-
penstance, combined to produce this condition.

This was my thinking and I shared some of it with her. The
normal rapprochement crisis involves the child's acute realization of her state of separateness from the mother, and this realization brings about the loss of belief in their shared omnipo-
tence. One central and inevitable feature of this crisis is the
child's disillusionment in the self and in the mother. In Zoe's
case, the mother's inability to eradicate the discomfort and pain
caused by her constipation, to stand by helplessly while this
condition persisted, must have dramatically intensified the normal disillusionment of this stage. But by devaluing her mother
at a time of such intense need for her, Zoe found herself in a
terrible predicament. Considering all the forces at play, it was
not surprising that she latched on to me, the potentially omnipotent stranger, and granted me all measure of power and authority.

Mention also needs to be made of Zoe's outstanding intelligence and verbal ability and of the part that these traits played
in her development and in this brief treatment. The use of language provides the child with a formidable tool for the communication of affects, experiences, needs, desires, observations,

areas of curiosity, and so forth. It involves such ego activity as observation, organization, synthesis, and integration, and it requires and aids in the delay of drive discharge. The intelligent child who has acquired language can think and reason much more affectively than the intelligent child whose language has not yet developed. With language, the object world becomes accessible in a new way; communication can now operate on a more specific and explicit level. Although Zoe's language development was exceptional, she was unable to use it to express her feelings during the rapprochement crisis. Her symptom was a kind of silent withholding and with it came a more general withdrawal. With the introduction of another person who was from the beginning identified as a helper, she moved out of her regressed silent mode of punishing her mother (and herself) to a more active mode of expressing her anger verbally. She very quickly shifted to using language for superbly articulated renunciations of this mother who had "failed" to meet expectations, and with expressions of allegiance to the newly cathected "other," in this case the therapist. Zoe's verbal ability, in turn, greatly aided my work with her, both in what she could tell me and in what I could expect her to understand in the way I responded to her.

There were, of course, many other forces at play here, not the least that all this was happening during the anal phase of psychosexual development when the power of withholding might gain a prominent position in a child's quest for autonomy. There was a tragic element in the way this worked out with Zoe. In rushing into toilet training she made a gallant effort to gain mastery of her body and body functions, but this flight into independence foiled her and she lost the very control she strove to gain. What should have been a good and satisfying developmental spurt caused her bewilderment and pain.

As I reviewed some of these developmental milestones and the way they had played out for Zoe, Mrs. Z. was comforted. She was relieved to be reminded that things happen for a reason, even when the reason is not readily apparent. She was both comforted and disturbed by being reminded that some things are beyond her control. But most of all she found it reassuring that some progress was taking place.

After this session with her mother, I wrote to Zoe and mentioned some of what her mom and I had discussed, which this time included their preparation for Zoe's two-year-old birthday party. I wrote that her mom had told me about how easy it was for her to use her potty to urinate and so I was thinking of buying a potty for my office so it would be there should she need it during our appointments. I asked her to tell her Mom what she thought of the idea and to ask her mom to call me with a yes or no answer. A few days later I got a telephone message from Mrs. Z. saying that Zoe wanted me to buy a white potty.

This time Zoe raced down the corridor to my office looking for the potty, which she found in a corner of the room. She asked to use it, and I said sure, but her mom would first have to take off her diaper. Zoe and her mother looked at each other and smiled, and then Zoe shouted "no more diapers" and pulled up her dress to show me her underpants. I asked what had happened. Zoe asked her mother to tell me and she pulled her pants down and urinated on my potty.

Mrs. Z. told me that all week they had been talking about pooping as soon as you feel a poop coming and not waiting and holding it in. Then, after Zoe got my letter, she asked how people can do that when they don't wear diapers. What if they feel it coming and there's no toilet near, like on a bus or on the street? Mrs. Z. said that one good way is to get used to pooping in the morning before you go out for the day. That's what a lot of children and grownups do. That way you're usually finished with pooping for the day. But if that doesn't always work out, there are toilets in restaurants and large stores, and at friends' houses, and many other places. Zoe said that she wanted to learn to poop on the potty and to stop wearing diapers.

This discussion between Zoe and her mother was another example of the use to which this very young child was able to put her extraordinary verbal ability. Through language she could express curiosity and find reassurance and understanding in the information her mother gave her. Then she was able to make an informed decision.

Mrs. Z. continued filling me in on their week. All week pooping had been easy for Zoe. All that fruit and medicine and water had helped. Zoe had pooped every day in her diaper and it had been easy. But this very morning, just before leaving the house to go see "Diana," Zoe said she felt a poop coming and wanted to poop on the toilet. She sat down on the toilet and pooped. And so, now she's wearing big girl pants.

I looked at Zoe and at her mother and they both had big smiles. I asked Zoe's mother what kind of a look Zoe had had when she pooped on the potty. Before Mrs. Z. could answer Zoe shouted: "A big girl look! And no more diapers 'cause I'm two!"

I saw Zoe with her mother two more times and her mother alone also two more times. Then I saw Mrs. Z. occasionally over the next many years. They were doing well. The crisis was over and development was moving along. The Hippo cards from me to Zoe were placed in a special box and I added to the collection for the next few birthdays until she was too old for such young cards and too involved in her life to be reminded of me. She looked at the cards now and then and liked to talk about when she was little and had come to see me and what that had been about.

After my work with Zoe ended, Mrs. Z. asked me whether I would be willing to call the first therapist she had consulted to describe what had happened in Zoe's treatment. Since it was someone I knew and liked I was comfortable about making the call and he in turn was very pleased to receive my call and interested in how I had approached this problem. But at the end of our conversation I sensed in his tone that he was perhaps a trifle disappointed at my attempt to convey the essence of what had transpired. Perhaps it seemed to him that the way I put it was too simple to explain the magnitude of what had happened. I could understand that he might feel that way, for this whole case was in some ways very simple and in others complicated beyond explanation.

I told my colleague that my understanding of the case was that at the height of the rapprochement period, in this unusually close mother–child pair, the child found herself in a difficult predicament and her mother, for the first time ever, was unable to help. The mother found her own failure so intolerable that she suffered a regression that compounded her sense of helplessness vis-à-vis her child. The child, now very frightened, angry, and further disillusioned by the mother's loss of power, latched on to me as a source of help and made good use of me. Although the child's investment in me and disinvestment in her mother angered Mrs. Z., it also gave her time to step back and recoup, because now someone else was there for her child. Despite her rivalry with me, this mother was able to join me, lean on me, and make use of my help. I told this fellow therapist that during a time of crisis in the life of this attuned and well-matched mother–child pair, I had served as auxiliary ego, a job that only works when it is self-eliminating, and in this case it was.

10

✌

A Tripartite
Treatment Approach[1]

*I*n this chapter a case will be described in great detail to illustrate a treatment approach in which the mother was a full-fledged participant in the treatment of her son's developmental difficulty. Later in the chapter I will explain how I arrived at this particular treatment plan, or rather how this treatment plan evolved quite naturally.

Max was referred to me by his nursery school because his parents were unable to toilet train him. He was three years and six months old at the time of the referral. The appointment for that first session was made by Max's mother and it was made very efficiently. She did, however, request that I have no further communication with her child's school. I agreed to her request, noting, but not exploring with her, this wish for privacy.

Both of Max's parents were present at the first session. They told me that Max, age three-and-one-half, refused to give up

---

1. An earlier version of this chapter, titled *"Max and His Diaper: An Example of the Interplay of Arrests in Psychosexual Development and the Separation-Individuation Process,"* appeared in *Psychoanalytic Inquiry*, volume 14, #1, pp. 58–81, 1994: The Analytic Press, Hillsdale, NJ. Copyright Diana Siskind.

wearing diapers and would only urinate and defecate when his diaper was on. He was also reluctant to talk much in school and would only speak when he needed something, and even that was rare. He liked going to school, talked normally at home, played well, ate well, and seemed to be a well-developing child in all other ways, according to the parents, who were intelligent, articulate, and appropriate in their concern. They told me that Max said that he could not give up his diaper because he would have an accident and "that would spoil everything." He was unbudgeable on this subject. The parents assured me that they were not un-usually neat or demanding of absolute cleanliness, and they did not know how their son got the notion that an accident was such a drastic matter. I noticed that they were deferential in their attitude toward their son and sounded as if his problem must be entirely their fault. They mentioned that perhaps they had done him harm by requiring that he say "please" and "thank you" and such mannerly things. Could this have had a constricting effect on him? I questioned them and learned that their require-ments for good manners were very reasonable and appropriate.

I asked whether they had ever made it clear to Max that they wanted him out of diapers and using the toilet.[2] They assured me that no, of course they would not make such a demand.[3] After all, that would place additional pressure on Max. How could they do such a thing to their little boy who was already so worried about having to give up his diaper? They were perfectly willing to wait as long a necessary for Max to pick the time most comfortable to

---

2. This is the *key* question referred to in Chapter 7, the one I al-ways ask during the course of a consultation. In Chapter 7, sleep was the issue; in this chapter it was relinquishing diapers. Whatever the issue the question is directed at whether the parents have actually voiced an expectation.

3. As is typical of these consultations, Max's parents assure me that they wouldn't voice an expectation for fear of putting pressure on their child. Consequently the child is not enlisted as a participant in deal-ing with the problem at hand.

him. After all, wasn't Max the only one who would know the right time for this big step? The father added that surely Max would do it on his own eventually. After all, children learn to use the toilet sooner or later. Why make a big deal out of it if it takes some kids a little longer than others?

As I listened to them talk this way about their son, I became increasingly aware of their diffident tone. I wondered how much power and control Max was given in the home. I decided to explore this and asked how normal routines were handled: meals, baths, getting dressed, bedtimes, outings, and so forth. To what degree were decisions left up to him and to what degree were they presented to him? The parents assured me that Max was very reasonable about general routines. Going to sleep, eating, dressing, and such were accomplished smoothly. The parents found it unnecessary to present him with rules and regulations. He was very sensible and when matters were left up to him he made very reasonable choices and decisions.

I wondered out loud about not having rules. Sometimes rules are helpful even with reasonable children like Max. Sometimes freedom can be burdensome. The father commented that there was something paradoxical in my suggesting that a little boy who hadn't been able to take control of his toilet functions might be handed too much control in other matters. He said that Max was, if anything, too cautious. He was not independent enough. How could presenting him with rules promote independence? I agreed that it seemed paradoxical, but one aspect of what we were dealing with was Max's sense of danger, for what else could explain his need for caution and his fear of making a mistake? These could be indicators of not feeling quite safe with his own decisions. Therefore, I assumed that feeling in charge might be increasing that sense of danger, whereas if the parents were more in charge he might feel safer.

I told these parents that toilet training is much more than a practical matter, much more than a convenience. It is a developmental leap that involves mastery and results in self-regulation. This achievement enhances a child's sense of autonomy in a profound way. Max had not yet taken this step; therefore the quality of his taking charge, making decisions and choices, was of a different order. Even when these actions were based on real preferences and good thinking they probably lacked the sense of conviction and confidence he would discover once we helped him take this necessary step. I added that while they described Max as not a bossy child, some children who act bossy appear to be taking charge, but they are only imitating what they think is "in charge" behavior. Ultimately, bossiness is a form of posturing, an unsatisfactory and unsatisfying substitute for feeling strong and sure and comfortable.

As I presented to these parents some aspects of the developmental growth that was a requisite substratum to gaining control of the body functions involved in toilet training, I was aware of their differing reactions to this unfamiliar view of early development. The mother was very interested; the father, restless in his chair and glancing at his watch, was eager to be done with the session.

Clearly this was not going to be a one-shot consultation. These parents conveyed caution and reserve. The information they provided was, on the whole, limited to the factual. This was consistent with their very articulate and reasonable style, a style that edited out affects. Whatever disappointment they might have been experiencing about their's son's inability to be toilet trained like other children his age was well guarded. Only a few clues gave me any sense of their response to me or to the consultation. The father had made the statement that Max's problem would take care of itself and became restless towards the end of the session; the mother seemed more consistently interested, but on the whole their reserve was striking. I would need to understand how it served them. I would need to find ways to get to know them and to gain a footing into understanding their situation. My first approach would be to meet Max directly.

I asked Mr. and Mrs. M. whether they would be willing to bring Max to see me. I explained that seeing him would allow me to gain insight into the situation. The parents looked at each other and nodded, almost in unison. They said they had quite expected that I would need to meet him. What should they tell him? I said that it was most helpful to tell a child, even one as young as Max, the real reason for the appointment. That way the child knew in advance that this was not a social visit, but something different, important, and about him. I suggested that they tell him that they had been to see a woman named Mrs. Siskind who knew a lot about children and who would help him feel less afraid about giving up his diaper. I suggested that Max be told that the parent who brought him would stay in the room, and that I had toys. I added that I would want to see Max for as many times as it took to figure out what was going on, what was making him so fearful in this regard. Once we'd figured out what was going on we'd know how to help him. My plan was accepted without question and the parents left.

SESSION 1 WITH MAX

I saw Max the next day. He arrived with his mother and easily but slowly came into my office. He was a cute three-and-one-half-year-old with blond hair, fair skin, big blue eyes, and of average size and weight. He moved quietly and cautiously and looked at me as he accepted my offer to show him my toys. He chose a box of wooden blocks, began to build on my rug, and of course everything fell down. I suggested that the rug was too soft, not a steady place to build, but that the desk was. Would he like to build on the desk? He accepted my suggestion and announced that he wanted to build a bridge. His handling of the blocks was haphazard. I noticed that he used right and left hands interchangeably with only a slight preference for the right hand. He was uninvested in his play and did not react much to his blocks falling down. I made a couple of comments about "things falling" and "not steady" and mentioned that I would help if he would like that. I noted that he was facially responsive when I spoke. After a few minutes of block building he spotted some scissors and tried to cut paper with his left hand. He did so with difficulty and seemed unaware of his awkwardness.

His mother was watching intently from her chair at the other end of the room and I commented that Max used both his hands for his work. She said that he always liked to use both hands interchangeably.

Max now picked up a magic marker with his right hand and managed somewhat better. He made a picture for his mom, slipped off the chair, gave it to her, and she gave a friendly response. He returned to his seat. I commented that it was very warm in the room, would he like to take off his sweater? He said yes, he was hot, and unbuttoned the buttons very smoothly and removed his sweater slowly but quite expertly. He made a picture for his dad and wanted to mail it to him. I handed him a box and called it a mailbox and he dropped his letter in the pretend mailbox. He then discovered my Scotch tape and tried to cut and paste with it, but again had difficulty in performing this task, as the tape just kept getting stuck to itself. This did not appear to bother him; he simply asked me to help, to hold it for him while he tried to cut, and I did. His mom said that tape was his favorite material. It was the first time she spoke on her own initiative. I took that as an indicator that she was growing somewhat less tense.

After a while Max slipped off his chair and walked over to an old-fashioned swivel piano stool (used as a side table) next to his mom's chair and twirled it around a bit. Our time was pretty close to over by then and I said so and told his mother that I would like to see Max again. We made an appointment for ten days hence as the family was going on vacation at the end of the week.

I told Mrs. M. that if she wanted to speak to me she could call me that evening, or next day since I would not see her for over a week, and that might be a long time to wait. She heartily agreed that it would be too long to wait and thanked me for making that option available. Since she had theater tickets for that evening we arranged a telephone appointment for the next day.[4]

---

4. Use of the telephone is common and helpful in child treatment for a variety of reasons. In this case it gave the mother the opportunity of touching base with the therapist and allaying some of the anxiety

As Max heard this conversation and realized that the session was about to end, he walked over to a chair in the far corner of the room where his mother had placed his knapsack. He carefully positioned it to make the zipper accessible, opened the zipper with quite a bit of skill, removed its contents, which he carried over to the piano stool, and there placed two neatly folded disposable diapers. He then stood back and waited. I leaned forward, looked at him and said, "So that's what you brought in your knapsack; that's what you wanted to show me, your diapers."

Mrs. M. called the next day as planned. She said she didn't have anything specific to discuss, but wanted to touch base after Max's session. She had been surprised at how outgoing he had been, much more than she had expected. She asked if I had any observations to share and I told her that he was a bright and engaging child but I was in the early stages of getting to know him and would prefer to wait until we had gotten better acquainted. Mrs. M. thought that made sense and went on to say that Max had been very upset the night before because she had been unable to find his brand of diapers and had brought home an unfamiliar brand. She mentioned that it was hard to find diapers big enough to fit Max, since he was beyond the usual age when diapers were worn.

She sounded a bit more animated than during the two office visits and spoke of feeling discouraged that Max clung to his diapers so. She asked whether she had been wrong not to have exerted pressure on Max regarding giving up his diaper. Should she take a firmer stand while they were on vacation? I suggested she and her husband hold off trying to deal with the diaper issue until they got back and I saw Max a few times and got to know him better. I said that something about giving up those diapers was frightening to him and it was important to understand how to

---

that this consultation evoked. The offer of the telephone contact to this reserved and stoical mother, who would not have initiated the call without invitation, set a more relaxed tone to the consultation and contributed to the developing working alliance.

help him be less afraid. Mrs. M. then reminded me that they weren't leaving until the next afternoon. Couldn't I see him later that day or the next morning or both? I said, no, it wasn't possible. We would wait until they got back and then I would see him a few times. We made two appointments for after their return. Then we talked a bit about Max placing the diapers on the piano stool at the end of the session and wondered together whether it was his statement of recognition about the purpose of his visit.

After we hung up the phone, I wondered a bit about something puzzling in this exchange and realized that I had sounded markedly definite in my responses. Why did I sound that way? After all, I had very limited knowledge of Max and his mother, and it was not like me to take such a categorical tone. Then I realized that I was reacting to something in Mrs. M. Something about her formal manner, her struggle for composure, and the anxiety that nonetheless communicated itself had evoked my "in charge" manner. It seemed to me that she needed me to be definite. This recognition of the interplay between her tentativeness and my sureness became my first clue.

SESSION 2 WITH MAX

The next time I saw Max he too was a bit more animated. He went right over to the chair he had sat in last time and climbed into it. Although he stuck to the same toys he had used the time before, he did everything with a little more spirit and was a bit more playful. He was also more verbally engaging. His mother, sitting at the back of the room as during the first visit, said that their vacation had been nice and Max had had a good time. Max did not volunteer anything about this but was interested in listening. Max did remember the "mailbox" into which he had placed his father's letter the week before and asked to mail another letter. He appeared to enjoy knowing where things were and having my office now be a familiar place and I said all that to him. I said:

"This time when you came to see me you knew just what to expect. You remembered what I looked like, how this office looked, my toys, and everything about this place. I think you like that a lot, right? It's nice to know how things are going to be."

And Max answered: "Come on, let's cut some tape."

Toward the end of the session I told Mrs. M. that I wanted to see her alone at our next appointment and had an open time Friday morning at 8:30. She said that was a perfect time for her.

Max and his mother left very slowly with a lot of negotiating about the jacket, the wool scarf, the flavor of ice cream to be eaten on the way home, taxi versus bus, and so on. It was late in the day. They were my last appointment and I had to close up my office before going home. A couple of minutes later I put on my coat and stepped into the lobby. There, to my great surprise, was Max, right in front of my office door. He stood there with fist on hip, and with a facial expression of great authority was saying to his mom, "Oh no, you aren't going to see Mrs. Siskind alone Friday at 8:30. I'm coming with you to see her Friday morning at 8:30."

His mother was trying to stifle a smile. When Max saw me, he went right on with, "Oh yes, I am coming with you to see Mrs. Siskind tomorrow morning at 8:30, oh yes I am!"

And as he spoke this way, he stared right at me. His mom said that he would see me again another time and I agreed and walked right past them. As I rounded a corner of the lobby on my way out, I could still hear Max insisting, with mounting vehemence, that he was coming with his mom the next morning at 8:30. And then he asked, "But where is she going now?"

By now I had seen Max twice and I was pretty sure that this was not a simple battle of wills over toilet training. Do such simple things ever exist? Max and his parents were caught up in something subtle and complicated that I did not yet understand. I would need to see them a while and wait for the clues to emerge.

Little as I felt I knew about Max's dynamics and the root of his fears, I had developed a definite opinion about the role that Mrs. M. would have to play in Max's treatment. I felt that it was important for this very capable and caring mother to be the primary player in helping her little boy over his fears. I wanted to see whether I could take a back seat and use my observations of Max in helping Mrs. M. deal with this delicate situation.

It is hard to know with certainty how I reached this formulation, and in reconstructing my thinking something will probably be left out. The specific factors that I am aware of might seem slight but their cumulative effect shaped my thinking. For instance, there was Mrs. M.'s quiet intensity as she watched every move that Max made and every move of mine. There was the feeling I had about Max's lack of playfulness in the first session, giving way to a lighter, more playful mode by our second meeting, and his eagerness to not miss any sessions, as expressed so passionately in the dialogue with his mother in my lobby. And there was another thing. I know that playfulness comes very naturally to me, particularly in the presence of young children. This characteristic is so much a part of me that I tend to experience it without particularly observing it in myself. In the presence of Max and his mother I was very much aware of it in two ways. Max, in his own quiet way, seemed drawn to it. I sensed that he wanted more, as if it were a form of ego nourishment for him. And there was my awareness of the contrast between my playfulness and Mrs. M.'s sober demeanor. This created a dilemma for me. Max obviously needed to be playful. It was a quality that he didn't spontaneously express but was drawn to. He was so serious and cautious that I wondered what he had been like as a toddler. Had he had "a love affair with the world" (Mahler et al. 1975) during his practicing subphase? Had he ever experienced that level of exuberance? My immediate problem was to offer him the opportunity of being playful without leaving his mother behind. There was the danger that Max and I might play and that she might feel excluded. If play was a factor in his "stuckness," and the mother rather than I had to be the principal helper, how could I help her open the gates and let in play?

Based on my conviction that I must enable Mrs. M. to do the major share of the work with Max, I decided to alternate tripartite[5] sessions with one-on-one sessions with Mrs. M. That way my most intense contact would be with her and I would use my observations of Max and of their interactions to help her along. She would also have the opportunity of observing him interact with me. By this time she trusted me enough to be able to sit back and just observe during Max's sessions. It is a uniquely enlightening experience for some parents to spend an hour just watching their child without having any pressures and interruptions.

At 8:30 the next morning I presented Mrs. M. with my plan. For the next four weeks I would see her alone once a week and with Max a second time per week. Since my plan was based on an idea that might or might not work well, I did not explain the thinking behind it, nor did she act at all curious about it. I suspect that she assumed that this is the way child treatment is always conducted. I told Mrs. M. that it was important that I also see Max's father alone and asked that he call me to make an appointment. We talked about Max's temperament, his caution, his fear of making mistakes, such as, for instance, a toilet mistake. The mother wanted to know what she should be doing to try to get him to even consider giving up his diaper. She said that at school all of the children go to the bathroom before going outside to play. They are all trained except for Max. If he minds that, he doesn't let on. Should she now be putting pressure on him? I suggested that she simply tell him that we are going to figure out how to help him be less afraid to give up his diaper, and when we

---

5. The tripartite approach (mother-child-therapist), was developed by Margaret Mahler in her work with psychotic children. In this therapeutic design, "the therapist serves as the catalyst, the transfer agent, and the buffer between child and mother" (1968, p. 115). I use this approach for entirely different reasons. I find it invaluable in the brief treatment of very young children who are experiencing a mild developmental impasse. In these cases I generally obtain the most significant clues regarding the root of the problem, by observing mother–child, and/or father–child interaction.

know how to help him, he will feel comfortable about wearing big boy pants. She said that he doesn't tell her when he is wet or soiled and in fact he even gets rashes from being wet so long.

I said that this might be a good place to begin to have some expectations of Max. She could transfer some responsibility to him by telling him that it was now going to be his job to tell her when he needed to be changed. I suggested that she demand this of him and if he refuses she not be afraid to be annoyed and to show her annoyance. Mrs. M. agreed to the plan in every regard, and we made appointments for her and for Max for the next four weeks.

The next afternoon Mrs. M. telephoned and asked, "Could you please explain what you meant when you said that I should not be afraid to show my annoyance?"

I told her that her question addressed the heart of the matter. I said that in order for Max to take this step she is going to have to be able to tolerate his frustration, his anger at her, her anger at him, and the temporary distance between them. I told her that in practical terms what I meant was simply that if she finds him wet or soiled and he did not ask to be changed, she can tell him that he has a job to do, that it is *his* job to let her know when he has urinated or made a bowel movement, and that she is very annoyed with him for not doing his job. After such a speech it would be best to just walk away, go about her business, and not be too ready to make up with him right away. Of course that meant that she would not allow herself to be too concerned with his mood and whether he was happy or not.

I added that it was important to convey to him that letting her know when he needs to be changed was now the "rule." I stressed that it was very important not to act tentative in the way she informs him of the new order of things. A firm manner would let him know that this was a non-negotiable matter.

It was clear from Mrs. M.'s tone and manner that she understood me perfectly and realized that this little exchange was indeed directed at the heart of the problem.

Throughout this book I have made reference to the fact that we do not make interpretations to the parents of our child patients or to the parents who consult us about their children. Yet my little speech about showing annoyance was very close to being an interpretation. In it I addressed the reaction formation that was blocking the normal irritation and frustration that Max's behavior should evoke, but I addressed it in a prescriptive rather than an interpretive way. My approach worked in this situation and curiously had the same effect on Mrs. M. as that of a well-timed and well-executed interpretation. I had taken a therapeutic chance and it had worked.

I would like to stop the narrative of this case for a moment to discuss the importance of this communication. I think that we can all agree that Max's development was hampered by failure to take a developmental step at the age-appropriate time, that step, on the surface, being the achievement of toilet training. What did this symptom reveal about Max's development?

1. He was still tied to his mother in regard to toilet functions and had not taken over this task as a separate and autonomous person. Transfer of function (Blanck and Blanck 1986) is an intrinsic aspect of separating from and identifying with the parental object. It indicates that the self representation has expanded to incorporate some of the attributes that have been part of the object representation. This psychic shift in the self representation is indicated by a child's willingness to do for himself some of what was hitherto done for him by the parents.

2. In order to relinquish the pleasure of messing and the wish to be a passive baby, the child must be eager to please the object. In fact, the wish to please the object must be stronger than the wish to be a "messing" baby. This can only happen smoothly if the parents make their expectations known with firm authority and not in a diffident or apologetic manner. At this developmental juncture it becomes essential that the

child experience his parents as strong and powerful figures. One important reason for this is that the new parental demand is likely to evoke anger and defiance on the part of the child, and his sense of danger at the force of these negative affects will be intensified if he perceives his parents as unequipped to deal with his anger.

3. In order for the child to take this giant step, he must have developed the defense we call *identification with the aggressor* (A. Freud 1946). This defense allows the child to identify with the powerful and (in fantasy) threatening parental imago, and thereby protects the child from the fear that his anger will destroy the love of his objects. Identification with the ("no"-saying) aggressor allows the child's aggressive drive to operate without being overwhelmed by conscious destructive wishes. It allows him to use the aggressive drive to serve psychic separation without severing the libidinal connection. This synchronicity of drive expression in turn facilitates *and* keeps in pace the dual processes of separation and individuation.

4. The circularity and interplay of these processes needs to be stressed. As a child takes charge of his toileting, he is taking ownership of his body, and this marks the end of a form of intimacy he shared with his parents. Both parent and child need to let go of babyhood and be able to bear the frustration caused by the temporary dislocation of affection that this step often entails. In fact, such frustration in tolerable doses is essential to promoting growth insofar as it propels the child into higher levels of integrating external and internal reality. This process of integration involves selective identification (Jacobson 1964), the taking in of characteristics of the object representations, and making those attributes his own. Here is where we can talk of the evolution of higher and higher levels of autonomy. When a child takes ownership of his body, this represents the culmination of intricate processes involving internalization and identification, resulting in individuation. When the young child

begins to take over his toilet functions, and does so with a measure of pride rather than fear or compliance, this becomes an indicator that development is moving in that propitious direction.

These were some of the issues addressed in the telephone conversation about the mother showing her annoyance. Thus, the very specific directives offered to this mother were largely based on how developmental theory aided the therapist in understanding what was happening to this child, to his mother, to their relationship, and to the insufficient influence of the father, that is, his inability to modify the forces at the root of the mother–child problem.

At the beginning of this book one of the questions raised was about the wisdom of giving advice to parents. It was not answered then but is discussed in Chapter 12. In this case example I gave the mother certain directives that might appear to be no different from advice, but I see them as operating on a level quite different from simple advice. I see them arising out of the role I took, that of auxiliary ego, a role designated to help the mother take hold of something that she could not yet, *for unconscious reasons*, grasp on her own. This therapeutic role can take many forms, and in my directive that Mrs. M. allow her annoyance at Max to be visible, it addressed her defense of reaction formation and worked similarly to an interpretation. It allowed her to become conscious of her anger at Max, and this freed her and spurred the development of both of them.

SESSION 3 WITH MAX

The next time I prepared for my session with Max I had two important matters on my mind. The first was the memory of the scene in my lobby and of his passionate insistence that he must see me "Friday morning at 8:30." That had established quite clearly that I had become valued by him. The second was my awareness that his mother had, at my suggestion, made a new demand of him. He was now required to let her know when he had wet or soiled his diaper and needed to be changed. But even more important was my awareness that his mother had understood that allowing herself to feel annoyed was in some inextricable way essential to the resolution of the problem.

The session began smoothly with Max, as usual, playing at my desk with blocks and tape. He then found some cars and trucks and began to ride them around my desk. Now the tempo of his excitement quickened and he asked me to take one of the cars and help him make them crash into each other. He then took two puppets and said that they were policemen and would stop the crashing. But the policemen began to crash into each other. He talked to me as he played and I noted his mounting intensity and how much he included me in his play. Taking another puppet he said, "This is the fixer person. This person can stop the fighting and fix everything."

I took a therapeutic chance[6] and said, "Oh, like me, I'm a fixer person."

Max put down the puppet, slipped off his chair, and walked over to his mother and asked, "Can we go now?"

She looked at me for help and I said quietly but very firmly, "No, you can't go until our time is up and we still have some time to be together." I was aware of my unequivocal "no!"

While Max did not overtly balk at my firm stance, he began to act distracted. He walked over to the analytic couch and asked what it was. I told him that it was a couch and that some people who come to see me lie down on it and talk to me while lying down. He walked over to the toy cabinet and got some plastic snowflakes, spilled them on the floor, and sat down to examine them and asked me what they were, and I told him. He then

---

6. The therapeutic chance this time was an attempt to bring the content of the play closer to the present; it was the equivalent of a transference interpretation in the treatment of an adult.

returned to the couch and started talking in nonsense words and gibberish and acted babyish, but very much as a performance. His mother said that he was very tired because he had had an active day at school and no nap and our appointment was late in the day.

My view of what we were witnessing was different. I felt that Max's regression was probably triggered by my referring to myself as a "fixer." After all, he had been enacting a fantasy that contained some hostile aggression (Parens 1979), and my use of the word "fixer" might have brought to consciousness some of the hostile content of the fantasy. While I had intended to introduce that word as representing my helping role, my timing was unfortunate and resulted in "fixer" being perceived as threatening rather than helpful. I believe that my firm yet matter-of-fact way of dealing with his wish to leave allayed some of his discomfort and was a helpful communication to his mother.

For the last few minutes of the session, Max lay under the analytic couch and pretended to be asleep. He tried to suppress a smile that kept emerging despite his efforts. He left quietly when our session came to an end.

The next day when I saw his mom alone, I mentioned the dramatic reaction to my referring to myself as a fixer. She had noticed it and was puzzled but not too interested. She had her own agenda, which consisted of complaints about Max, particularly his lack of cooperation in letting her know when he needed to be changed. She said that at first she forced herself to feel annoyed and to show her annoyance, and since I had granted her "permission" to be annoyed, she soon found that it was quite easy. She discovered that she really was very annoyed. She smiled, adding that she hadn't realized that expressing annoyance could be so freeing.

She reported that Max's teacher told her that for the first time ever, Max had gone along to the bathroom at school when the other children went as a group, and showed some curiosity about the toileting activity. In the past he had always stayed in the room at such times. We were both encouraged by this bit of progress.

SESSION 4 WITH MAX

On this day Max dragged his feet on the way in to my office, and although he played with the blocks and cars and tape and magic markers and puppets, he did so in a slow, laborious manner, going through the motions rather than really feeling invested in what he was doing.

I commented that Max didn't really seem too interested in what he was doing today. He did not respond. After about thirty minutes of half-hearted play, Max slipped off his chair and brought the basket of colored plastic snowflakes over to the coffee table where his mother sat. I sat down in my big chair across from his mom and he sat down on a little stool between us. After holding the basket of snowflakes on his lap he placed it on the table. There was total silence, which I broke by saying, "Could I please have two green snowflakes?" He picked them out of the basket and touched my hand with them; he then yanked them back and dropped them in the basket. I asked his mom, "Would you like any snowflakes?" She said she would and asked for one red and one green. Max picked them out and again just touched her hand with them and yanked them back. We continued in this manner, our requests becoming more elaborate (one green, two white, and one blue etc.) as we went along. Gradually, Max stopped just brushing the snowflakes by our hands on their way back to the basket. He began to release them, allowing us to keep our "order" of snowflakes until the next request was made, at which time he grabbed them back. He was quite excited and pleased with this game and soon was echoing our orders as he made the delivery. The atmosphere in the room was a combination of calm and intensity. I was acutely aware of what was happening and I could tell that Mrs. M., while quite engaged, was puzzled by this game. When our time was up Max went out of my office through a side door with the plan of meeting his mother in the waiting room; in that instant that I was alone with her, I said, "What a fascinating session."

The next morning at 8:30 sharp Mrs. M. came into my office and, as if a minute rather than fourteen hours had elapsed since my parting words the night before, asked, "What was fascinating about the session?" I said that the whole twenty minutes of snow-flake play had turned into a practice toilet-training session. At first he acted as if he was going to let go, to give us the snowflakes, but would not let go. Gradually he was able to let go and soon he began to enjoy letting go and giving, the mastery of remembering our "order," the reciprocity of the experience, and the pleasure of feeling big and in charge.

I told Mrs. M. that the child experiences all of these emotional states during the toilet-training process. These states are part of the emotional growth that occurs during this stage. Sometimes children feel the need to give presents during this period as well as to hoard and to hold on. I said that Max had been through a practice run. That's what I had found so fascinating about the snowflake session.

I added that sometimes during this stage children also need to receive "gifts," and that it is helpful then to gratify some of that need. Mrs. M. told me that this must already be happening, for Max had seen a rifle advertised in the paper on Sunday and told her that he wanted it. He was quite impassioned about this wish of his. She told me that since she was a pacifist and hated guns, she had told him that guns were awful, violent things and that she hated them and they were not allowed in the house. I recognized that Mrs. M. and I were in dangerous territory here. I wondered whether the working alliance was sufficiently established to weather what was going to be a serious difference of opinion between Mrs. M. and me. I decided that she really believed in what we were doing together for Max, and that I should go ahead and say what needed to be said at this point in the treatment. I took a deep breath and told her that to a little boy a gun is not just a gun, it is also a symbol of power and phallic prowess, so we need to look at this request very carefully and understand it well.

I said that by asking her to give him a gun, he may be asking her to permit, and even admire, his boyishness and strength. I asked her whether she would be willing to reconsider this gun issue. She wasn't sure. I told her that I treated adults in psychoanalysis, and that in the memories of some of my male patients there existed the feeling that their maleness had not been valued enough, and the wish to repair this appeared in dreams as a desire for a better pen, pipe, tower, sword, and so on (Siskind 1987).

I said that Max was a peaceful, fair boy and he could be trusted with a gun. I reminded her that it was a toy gun. I said that he needed an incentive to get out of diapers. I asked her whether she would be willing to do the following. Could she tell him that the reason she had talked about not liking guns was because when she was his age, being a little girl, she had liked other toys and not guns? Some little girls like guns, but she had never liked them. Max, on the other hand, was a boy and boys usually like guns and for that reason she would be willing to give him a gun. But there was one problem. Guns are for big boys who don't wear diapers. He would have to stop wearing diapers before he could have a gun.

As I finished this sample speech, Mrs. M. looked at me with amazement and exclaimed that I was suggesting bribery. I said that I knew that it sounded like bribery and of course that was unappealing, but there was a subtle but important difference between a bribe and an incentive. I was viewing the gun as an incentive, a way out of a very difficult situation. Max wanted to take the next step, was on the verge of taking it, but just could not get himself to do it. He was feeling small and helpless and probably quite ashamed. The twenty-minute experience with the snowflakes indicated that he might be ready to move on. I told her that this might or might not help him but that I thought it was worth a try. He wanted to be big and he should be given this chance. She hesitated for a few seconds and then said that she was willing to follow this suggestion. I asked her to think about it and only do it if she believed it was all right.

At this point in the session I realized that I had not asked about masturbation when I had taken a developmental history of Max. This omission had been an oversight on my part since questions about masturbation are a standard part of history taking. I asked about it now and Mrs. M. told me that sometimes, when she changed Max's diaper, he asked her to wait a minute before putting on a fresh diaper and held his penis. She said that because he was so big the diapers were quite tight and he could not really reach inside them. I told her that I was concerned about his not being able to masturbate. It was such a natural thing to do at his age and he was missing out on the pleasure of his genital by having it trapped inside his diaper. We ended the session with the understanding that she would offer Max a gun as an incentive for relinquishing his diapers.

I worried a great deal the next day. I questioned whether I knew enough of Max's problem and dynamics to have suggested such an intervention. I also questioned whether Mrs. M. was ready to take this step: perhaps it was precipitous. Did Mrs. M. really understand the difference between a bribe and an incentive? My formulation was based on my knowledge of development and allowed me to distinguish between the two. A bribe was a form of seduction that bypasses the ego, while the offering of an incentive could strengthen intentionality and the executive functioning of the ego. In addition, the nature of this incentive could also serve as a crucially important communication regarding the mother's acceptance of Max's masculinity (Parens 1989b). Thus my suggestion about the gun was a dramatic intervention designed to end a derailment in Max's development. Here was a little boy who, chronologically, should be entering the phallic phase of development and who was stuck, in a complicated way, with protracted anality as a symptom. This was clearly not a typical toilet training battle of wills. This was a situation that involved coinciding and interconnected developmental difficulties: one along the separation-individuation continuum, the other along the psychosexual phase progression. His tentative moves into the phallic phase caused such castration anxiety (Galenson and Roiphe

1980) that he retreated to the anal phase, just as his struggle to move beyond the rapprochement subphase caused him too severe separation anxiety, and his solution again was to retreat. This type of developmental impasse could have far-reaching consequences, such as jeopardizing his identity formation, which of course always includes gender identity. Maybe such a serious move required a few more sessions.

Prompted by my worry I telephoned Mrs. M. in the late afternoon of the day after our session,[7] planning to suggest that she wait until we talk some more before offering Max a gun. Before I had a chance to speak she announced that Max was out of diapers and that she had just put him down for a nap and was about to call me.

She told me that the night before she had made her speech about not having liked guns when she was his age since girls usually like other toys, but that guns are fine for big boys and she would like him to have one since he wants one very much, but the problem was that guns are for big boys and big boys don't wear diapers. She asked him whether he could give up his diaper and wear regular big boy pants.

Mrs. M. said that as she finished her statement, Max slipped off his chair, and with his hand pulling off the diaper tab, asked when they could go get the gun.

They went to buy the gun the next morning and he picked a water gun. He spent a couple of hours in the bathroom the next afternoon shooting water into the bath tub. Except for nighttime and his nap, he had been out of diapers since the evening before and had urinated in the toilet with great frequency. Even with all of that urinating he had a couple of accidents, but did not get upset

---

7. The use of the telephone comes up again, and while I had earlier mentioned that it was useful in allowing parents access to their child's therapist in between sessions, it was very unusual for me as the therapist to initiate the call and to do so out of concern that I had made a recommendation prematurely.

about them. Since her tone was, as usual, neutral, I could not tell how she felt about these developments. I asked her. She paused for a long time and said, "I'm in ecstasy!!"

I suggested that she throw out all of the diapers so that she would not be tempted to put them on for naps or nighttime. I also suggested that she tell him that his body sends a signal to his brain telling him when he needs to go and that the signal is even strong enough to wake him when he is asleep. We agreed that since he had not yet made a bowel movement we still had a way to go, but so far it sounded very good.

I asked her to call me on the eve of my next appointment with Max so as to bring me up to date on the course of events. She did and reported that he was completely out of diapers and had made several bowel movements in the toilet. He had used the bathroom at school and at several people's houses during visits over the weekend.

She said that she would sometimes ask him when he appeared to be wiggling and squirming whether he needed to go, and once when she asked him he looked annoyed. She asked him what was wrong and he said, "You don't know when I have to tinkle or make a poop. Only I know 'cause my body tells *my* brain, not *your* brain."

This declaration of independence seemed such a dramatic indicator of Max's developing sense of autonomy, as well as pride in his separateness, that I felt that our work was nearing its end.

I told Mrs. M. that we needed to talk about how much longer I would be seeing Max. I said that it sounded as if the series of appointments we had made for him would work out just right. I did not want to stop too abruptly, but since it did appear that we had accomplished our objective I would prepare Max for ending our appointments. The next time I saw him I would tell him that we would only need one more appointment. She agreed with my plan for Max but told me that she would want to continue to see me a few more times after Max stopped. "And after I stop," she added, "I will have your telephone number, and that will make me feel very secure should anything go wrong."

SESSION 5 WITH MAX

The next day Max walked in looking slender and more coordi-nated now that he was unencumbered by the bulky diaper. He barely greeted me, so busy was he humming. He sat down at the desk and spent a good twenty minutes trying to connect two tow trucks with a paper clip. It was a difficult task and he per-sisted until he succeeded, all the while humming in a show-off way: Ta tatata, bumbum and bum, and abarum rum, and so on. He referred to himself as the "fixer" who brought broken cars to the garage and fixed them to be "good and fast."

At one point during the session he went to the bathroom as if it was nothing special. When he returned, I told him that his mom told me that he didn't wear diapers anymore. I reminded him that he had come to see me because he had been afraid to give up his diapers and now he was no longer afraid. We had done the job we had set out to do together. Now he wouldn't need my help anymore so we would only meet one more time and say goodbye. What did he think of that? He didn't answer and seemed quite content to hum and twirl the piano stool up and down.

When our time was up he walked over to the chair in the far corner of the room where his mother always placed his knapsack, unzipped it, and took out a pair of training pants and put them on the piano stool. He then picked them up and said to his mother, "This is for you." She thanked him but said that those were boy pants and she wore girl pants. He then offered the pants to me and I too thanked him and said the same thing as his mother had said and added:

> Those are big boy pants and they belong to you because you don't wear diapers any more. You're comfortable about leaving those diapers behind and wearing big boy pants and using the toilet like all your friends. It must be a very good feeling to feel safe and big at the same time.

The next day I met with Mrs. M. and she told me that Max was alternating between being very loving and very aggressive. She laughed and said that very morning he had tried to lock her in her closet so she would not be able to leave the house. For the first time she talked a bit about her husband's relationship with Max. She said that he tended to be laissez-faire about Max's routines, but was generally happy to play with him. Despite my frequent reminders, I had not yet seen the father alone. We had an appointment scheduled for the following week.

When I met with Max's father I learned that he had good insight into Max's personality and expressed some sound ideas about what might help Max be less tentative and more venturesome. Yet, he was reluctant to implement his ideas because he believed that they would cause friction between him and his wife. He expressed an optimistic attitude about childhood problems working themselves out. While I had little or no impact on him, and he had not participated in Max's treatment, he had not interfered with its progress and for that reason I considered him a tacit ally. He clearly wanted things to work out well for his son but felt unable to take an active role in fathering him, at least at this point in Max's development. Some therapists would have been more insistent on his participation, but that's a matter of individual style and of differing attitudes about the therapeutic process. I am not comfortable about insisting that both parents participate equally unless equal participation is essential to the progress of the case. The solid working alliance with Mrs. M. was enough to move this case along. Mr. M.'s participation was not essential. Had I insisted on it I might have increased this father's skepticism and turned him from tacit ally into resentful rival.

SESSION 6 WITH MAX

My last session with Max was uneventful until the final minutes. He was not very interested in me or my toys. He had a play date following our session and that was the object of his interest as well as a bag of pretzels that his mother had left in the waiting room for after our session. When our time was up and he was allowed to pick a pretzel, he became very upset upon discovering that the one he chose had a broken section. He left in tears.

I wondered about the tears and speculated that the broken pretzel might have triggered castration anxiety and accompanying feelings of humiliation at this unexpected loss of power at a time when he had been feeling so cocky. I also understood his tears over the broken pretzel as overriding his disavowal of the importance of our goodbye.

I continued my weekly sessions with the mother and it was clear from her reports that this difficult chapter of their lives was over. Diapers were a thing of the past and Max had become quite matter-of-fact about using the toilet on his own.

DISCUSSION

Let me discuss what happened in this case from several different points of view. To begin with, how do we begin treating a three-and-a-half-year-old child? Obviously that would depend on what needs to be treated. In Max's case it appeared to be a developmental impasse that the parents were unable to handle. Who, then, was to be the patient? I decided that the parents' difficulty with this developmental snag was the primary problem and therefore something in the parent–child relationship would need to be the focus of the treatment.

My primary goal was to enable these parents to help their child take an ordinary developmental step so that he could be back on track in his psychosexual development and the separation-individuation process, thus allowing for the structural change implicit in such growth. I saw my job as disturbing the status quo of helplessness that was afflicting all three family members. I had to do this carefully, using all the information I had gathered about the family. And, to meet my goal of helping the parents bring about the necessary change, I had to do this without becoming too prominent a player in the family constellation. That meant that as each therapeutic opportunity arose I would do less rather than more so as not to intrude in the parent–child relationship more than was absolutely necessary.

The bare essentials of what I learned during the initial consultation with the parents was that Max's sense of safety was in some way connected to clinging to his diaper. The mother, for reasons that were buried in her own history, was not able at this point in her son's life to act as a good auxiliary ego that would provide the safety net that he needed, to take what appeared to him too dangerous a step. The father, for reasons buried in his own history, was also not able to be the kind of father who promotes his child's phallic strivings. The freedom to be phallic eases separation from the mother, thus accelerating the separation-individuation process.

Because of these vulnerable spots in the parents, I had to become a temporary bridge. I had to serve as an auxiliary ego until everyone was, more or less, back on track.

The therapist has to assess each family member not only from a diagnostic point of view, but also in regard to forming a therapeutic alliance. In this case I sensed from the first session with the parents that the alliance could best be formed with the mother because she wanted my help. The father, in contrast, had the need to minimize Max's difficulty and downplayed the need for our consultation. I have found that many fathers take this position about seeking psychological help for their children when their children are very young. For many fathers, problems in young children are not taken very seriously and are viewed as falling under the jurisdiction of the mother. These same fathers often become more active as their children grow older. I felt that something like this might be at play here and that I had to respect Mr. M.'s wish to *not* participate, whatever his reasons.

My impression of the mother was that she was a woman of high intelligence, excellent ego functioning, sensitivity, and abounding love for her son. The father was also highly intelligent, accomplished, and a caring and concerned parent, but since I had such limited contact with him I did not get to know him well.

Max presented a confusing picture at first. On the one hand he appeared uninvested in his projects, he had poor small muscle coordination, he had not yet developed right-left hand dominance, he spoke very little, he had indifferent standards for his play, he seemed somewhat passive, somber and un-childlike. On the other hand his coordination in dressing was quite good, he understood my abstract communication about mailing a letter, he made that stunning move at the end of the first session when he placed his diapers on the piano stool. By the second session I felt more confident that he was a well-endowed child with good ego functions: memory, anticipation, intentionality, reality testing, object comprehension, and so on. I still wondered about the degree of his constriction but was encouraged by his being drawn to my playfulness.

I speculated that this was a transient developmental problem and that I needed to observe Max and his mother together to understand the underlying dynamics. Having established for myself a tentative working diagnosis of mother and child and feeling that I had a working alliance with both, I presented the mother with a plan that alternated between tripartite and bipartite sessions. What unfolded as the case moved on was that I could share my observations of Max with his mother. His mother, being receptive and insightful, was able to put my observations to use and be an active participant in Max's treatment. I believe that because of the mother's prominent role in our work, rivalry between mother and therapist, a feature that so often sabotages child treatment, did not develop in this situation. And I could be relatively confident in guiding Mrs. M.'s work with Max since we were dealing with a transient developmental derailment in a well-endowed child with a stable object environment.

I believed that Max's derailment was caused in part by the mother's difficulty in saying "no." This difficulty in the mother was certainly not insignificant, since the "no" has such far reaching consequences in promoting growth and psychic organization

(Spitz 1959).[8] When Spitz formulated his theory about the organizers of the psyche, he placed the "no" at eighteen months as being the child's first abstraction. The attainment of abstract thinking facilitates displacement of aggressive cathexis, which is necessary for identification with the aggressor: the "no"-saying parent (Spitz 1965).

Mrs. M. felt enormously relieved at being helped to say "no," and, as described earlier, this had immediate beneficial results. Her readiness to use help in this area established that her difficulty with "no" was not caused by serious maternal inadequacy, such as a boundary problem in an adult whose own separation-individuation process was incomplete. More likely, this mother's lack of firmness in this matter stemmed from her anger at and disappointment in Max, and her reaction formation against this unacceptable affect in herself. In other words, I had to help Mrs. M. accept her aggressive cathexis, which had been too effectively repressed by the reaction formation.

It is significant that the father waited until it was all over before coming to see me. The rivalry he might have felt toward me that appeared, though fleetingly, in the first session, returned in this final session as we reached the end of the hour. He stood up and said that all that happened was nothing much, just as he had known from the beginning. But it had made his wife feel better and that, he supposed, was worth something. But he had known all along that things would straighten out; after all, who ever goes to college wearing diapers? These things take care of themselves. He reached out to shake my hand as he said goodbye, and then turned at the door and asked, "A pistol for a diaper? Is that something very simple or is it something very Freudian?"

---

8. I am extending Spitz's concept of "no" to include the mother's and/or father's "no"-saying capabilities, since the parents need to be perceived this way by the child in order to become objects for identification.

We cannot reconstruct with certainty the reasons that Max became so fearfully dependent on wearing a diaper. We can, however, speculate that the convergence of certain forces in his ego endowment and his object environment created this particular situation. What is striking is how easily the manifest problem was resolved and how serious the consequences could have been had his mother not sought professional help.

Let us consider the fact that this little boy felt out of control without a tight diaper covering his genital area. We could examine this from many different points of view, but let us just look at the implications of Max's predicament vis-à-vis the oedipal situation. Here is a little boy who does not get to masturbate or admire and enjoy his phallus in the ordinary way that little boys do. How, then, is the necessary libidinal investment in the phallus going to occur prior to the oedipal phase? Freud (1924) stated that in the positive oedipal stage, the boy has to choose between his highly cathected genital and the longed-for love object, the oedipal mother. The implication is that if the genital is not highly cathected the boy will not be able to make the oedipal choice and establish a firm masculine identity.

Let us consider an even earlier area of developmental vulnerability. If concern over pleasing the parents does not occur during the anal phase, a precursor of reciprocity is not established. What emerges is the possibility of a narcissistic personality structure in the making. Viewed this way, the brief intervention described in this chapter is a good example of how the repair of an early developmental derailment serves as both primary and secondary prevention (Parens 1990) of more serious pathology.

Max's development seemed satisfactory as this brief intervention came to an end. He felt like a big boy and was quite pleased with himself. He had finally taken ownership of his own body and was able to accept, without undue fear, the sexual differences (Roiphe and Galenson 1981) that his diaper had (ineffectively) obscured. His self-satisfaction, exhibitionism, and cockiness suggested that he had moved into the phallic phase. It appeared that with both psychosexual development and the separation-individuation process back on track, Max had been provided with a stronger position for tackling the next developmental challenge, the passage through the oedipal phase.

SUMMARY

In the brief treatment of this mother–child pair, the tripartite sessions revealed the nature of Max's problems along the lines of psychosexual development and separation-individuation and his mother's difficulty in allowing adequate expression of aggression, a core obstacle in facilitating Max's development. The bipartite sessions allowed the therapist to address the mother's difficulty with aggression. When this was interpreted, a crucial shift (belatedly) occurred in the emotional climate of the home, a shift that allowed for this mother's more "normal" expression of aggression. Consequently, Max was finally able to identify with the aggressor. The use of this defense finally freed him to use the aggressive drive in a non-destructive way and released energy that spurred his growth in the areas that had suffered an impasse.

The ego's ability to employ and regulate the aggressive drive allowed him to move out of the ambitendent position of the rapprochement subphase to: "on the way to object constancy" (Mahler et al. 1975). Concurrently, the ego's ability to harness his aggressive strivings liberated the expression of phallic exhibitionism without being burdened by the intense castration anxiety that had previously caused regression to the anal phase. Phallic exhibitionism allowed for a range of affective experience of pleasure, power, and age-appropriate grandiosity that in turn firmed up Max's sense of identity as a boy and as a separate and autonomous person.

Although psychosexual development and separation-individuation are being discussed as two separate processes, they are inextricably intertwined. In Max's case we saw that the appearance of a symptom indicating a developmental problem in what appeared to be the area of psychosexual development soon revealed corresponding problems in separation-individuation and in the ego's ability to deal with the drives. Conversely, when development proceeds well, these processes often stay in pace and quicken each other with synergistic force.

EPILOGUE

I made reference at the beginning of this chapter to a characteristic of playfulness[9] in myself that is generally evoked by the presence of young children, and of Mrs. M.'s apparent awareness of this quality in me. I believe that she too wanted to be able to play and couldn't, and wanted Max to be more playful than he was able to be. Playfulness became an important part of the climate of our sessions, and with each session Max became a bit more playful and so did his mother.

Playfulness is a perfect vehicle for the expression of libido *and* aggression. Powered by the drives and converted into creative and pleasurable activity by the work of the ego, playfulness was just what this mother–child pair needed. It was indicative of Mrs. M.'s sensitivity and insight to recognize this lack in herself and in her son and to recognize its value. And I believe that it was essential to the outcome of this case to help her release this latent quality in herself. It allowed for a whole new dimension of communication between her and her son. A lighter, freer climate became available to them. I believe that my helping the mother become a major participant in the treatment process was essential to bringing about this fortuitous development.

When our work was done, Max could feel safe and big at the same time, an achievement of high order for a person of any age.

---

9. Sanville (1991) refers to this aspect of the therapist's role as *play ego*.

11

Examples of Brief Interventions with Mixed Outcomes

$\mathcal{T}$he parents of Justine, a twelve-year-old girl, a young scholar, and a budding intellectual, consulted me because she was so attached to home and parents that her social development lagged far behind what they considered to be appropriate for her age. The precipitating factor for requesting my help was their daughter's upcoming class trip involving a weekend away from home, which she refused to even consider because she would be too "homesick." She had always been unwilling to go on these or any other trips that did not include at least one of her parents. The consultation took place only two weeks before the scheduled trip and they stressed how very eager they were to see her able to go off with her class.

Mr. and Mrs. J. did a good and thorough job of telling me their story; they were articulate, well-organized, and not lacking in humor. I picked up on their humorous tone and commented that they must think me a miracle worker, for who else could resolve such a long-standing problem in so little time? To be humorous was not a conscious decision on my part but one of those intuitive responses that occur silently in work and life. Only with hindsight do I realize that in joining their light tone I was respecting their need for distance.

Their story was of a very close tie between mother and child and of a father who was often away from home because his work required much travel and long work hours when he was not away. They were both lawyers, he in a large, prestigious, high-pressure firm, she in a branch of law that had more regular hours. There were two older children, both sons, both at college. Mr. and Mrs. J. tried to hide their disappointment that both sons had gone in the direction of the performing arts, but the disappointment was there. All the more reason these parents were pleased with their brilliant daughter who so perfectly met all their academic aspirations. Their only regret was that unlike her socially adept brothers, she was awkward and had few friends.

We set an appointment for Justine for the next day and I asked, as I always do, that she be told the real reason for the appointment: discomfort at leaving her parents, expressed by her refusal to go on the forthcoming class trip. Mrs. J. telephoned in the evening to report that Justine had been furious at being "forced" to see me and had stated that she wouldn't talk during her appointment.

Justine arrived the next day with her mother and when I saw her in the waiting room I was startled by her outfit; she was wearing one green and one yellow sock, one orange and one blue shoelace, dark purple nail polish, and a ring on every finger. Based on her parents' description of her social isolation and scorn of the "trendy and frivolous" pursuits of her contemporaries, I had expected a nondescript outfit. The one she wore indicated that she had joined her peers in the eccentricities of dress typical of their age. Her appearance provided me with invaluable information. It announced that she wanted to belong. Furthermore, she was letting me know this through her dress. I also realized how blind her parents were to this obvious communication on her part.

Justine was true to her pledge; she remained silent throughout her session. For forty-five minutes we sat in our facing chairs with the silence broken only by my increasingly tired and hollow comments. I said all the customary things: why her parents had come, their concern about her feeling uncomfortable about the forthcoming trip and her refusal to go, that sometimes a therapist can help with these situations, and would she tell me a little about herself and her feelings about coming to see me?

There we sat, this sullen, multicolored, tall, pale, pubescent girl and I, caught in the deadlock of my offerings and her refusals. As our time drew to an end I finally said the following:

> Our time is almost up and before you leave I want to say one more thing. You told your parents that you didn't want to come and that you wouldn't talk to me. Well, it's true that you didn't talk to me in words, but you talked to me in socks and shoelaces and rings and nail polish. These adornments tell me a lot about you and how much you want to fit in but won't admit it out loud. Would you like to come back to see me again in a few days and figure out what's getting in your way?

To my amazement she smiled briefly, nodded, then resumed her blank look and joined her mother, who had waited for her. They left quietly, wordlessly, her mother's questioning look unanswered and eager smile unmet. That evening Justine's mother called to say that I had indeed brought about a miracle. With some embarrassment Mrs. J. reported the following. Justine told her that the time spent with me was one of the worst and most boring hours of her life. She never wanted to see me again. She said that I had suggested another appointment to which she had agreed just to placate me and end the session more quickly. She told her mother that the time with me was so awful that she would even be willing to go on the class trip if her mother swore that she need never come back to see me. Justine was assured that now that she had agreed to go on the class trip there would be no such need.

I saw Mrs. J. alone right after Justine's class trip and learned that Justine had managed the trip well. I also gained a clearer picture of how much this woman held on to her daughter. For instance, Mrs. J.'s unabashed delight in Justine's dislike of me made me wonder what she might have fantasied prior to my encounter with her daughter. Did she fear that had Justine liked me her own position with her would have been undermined? She certainly expressed much relief at Justine's passionate rejection of me. Also, her belief that Justine's dislike of me was intense enough to "shock" her out of her lifelong fear of being apart from either parent seemed naive for so intelligent a woman. Mrs. J. ended her session with me by chuckling and saying that from now on whenever she wanted Justine to do something odious to her, she could bring up my name and Justine would do it for fear of having to come to another appointment. What comfort she found in my lower-than-low standing with her daughter and the increase of power this apparently gave her! As she stood up to leave, Mrs. J. said that we had accomplished our objective with Justine and she felt much relieved by that, but she also had concerns about herself, and she would like to see me a few more times to talk about them.

After Mrs. J. left I took stock of the situation and decided that this case was taking a clear direction. Although Justine had been presented as the reason for a consultation, there seemed to be general agreement that it was Mrs. J. who was to be the primary patient. Justine, Mrs. J., and I appeared to be in agreement on this score. Mr. J., in his characteristic way, was busy with other matters and his opinion on this was not available. I did learn later that he was very pleased that his wife wanted to continue our sessions.

Although I didn't agree with Mrs. J. that Justine's problems were over just because she had gone on the class trip, I did agree that her going was an important developmental step and that both mother and daughter would be served best if the mother became my patient. Since Mrs. J. had already suggested this direction by requesting "a few" appointments, perhaps the time limit she imposed could be lifted during our sessions, allowing her to have as much time as she needed. I had by then observed, beneath her humorous facade and subtle denigration of me, a tone of resignation and a disparaging attitude about herself. It seemed that a mild depression, perhaps of long standing, was present and probably played a part in her leaning on her daughter. If she counted on

Justine for emotional supplies, what would happen to her now that her daughter had taken license to go off with her peers?

With this understanding of who needed to be and seemed willing to be the primary patient in this family, at least at this time, I was ready to explore the prospect of treatment with Mrs. J. But I also marveled at the cleverness of her twelve-year-old daughter, who had seized on an excuse that allowed her to go off with her peers without upsetting her mother too much.

The reader might say that's fine as far as the mother is concerned, but what about Justine? True, she finally found a way to join her peer group, but what about all the years that she stuck so close to her mother? We know that her problems aren't over. Shouldn't she also get some help? The reader might also wonder why it took me so long in the session with Justine to make the interpretation I made at the very end. After all, I had my clue about Justine's interest in conforming to her peer group the minute I saw the flamboyant touches to her outfit. Perhaps if I had made the interpretation sooner she and I would have formed a connection and she might have been more receptive to treatment. It's possible that all this might have happened, but we will never know where a path not taken leads to. In our work we don't have complete answers but rather use whatever information we've gathered to guide our clinical decisions and the direction we take. I will touch on this, including any errors of which I am aware. But first, a digression into the general topic of communications made by our patients through their appearance and our response to these sometimes conscious and sometimes unconscious communications.

I am generally reluctant to comment on a patient's dress or appearance. That type of observation conveyed to a patient seems tactless, intrusive, and likely to make the patient feel self-conscious. Also, what the patient is communicating by dress or other appearance-related phenomena is usually not actively offered by the patient in the same way as is, for instance, a dream or even a parapraxis. Also, by commenting on appearance the therapist would be selecting material for the patient rather than allowing the patient to do his own selecting of material. Most likely, such an intervention would be resented, misunderstood, or ignored.

I have had patients appear in outfits that very obviously had unconscious meaning. For instance, a middle-aged man I treated in psychoanalytic psychotherapy, a radiologist living a conventional life, periodically arrived for his sessions in bizarrely split outfits. Once he came dressed with the top half in a sport shirt and crew-neck sweater, bottom half in tuxedo pants, black silk socks, and patent leather formal evening shoes. He sat down, crossed his legs, and looking at his formal trousers, volunteered the explanation that that very evening he was going to a black tie dinner, and while in the process of dressing for it realized the time of his appointment with me, and "dashed out midway between being Joe College and Cary Grant."

The split outfits appeared at least monthly, (shirt, tie, and jacket on top, tennis clothes from the waist down, and so forth), sometimes with explanation and sometimes without, and while I noted them, understood them to express, in part, his general identity confusion and lack of groundedness, I never explored what elaborate fantasies might exist in his wish to exhibit himself to me in these costumes. My decision to refrain from such exploration was based on my diagnostic impression of him; I saw him as a fragile person with a shaky defensive structure who was coping surprisingly well in his daily life. It seemed to me, during the particular phase of treatment when he appeared in these curious outfits, that his need for distance was paramount. He wanted as little as possible from me and would even get upset when I stood up at the end of his sessions. When it first happened he looked pained and I wasn't sure what he was reacting to, but some time later he blurted out that I need not disturb myself that way, that I should remain seated. After I explained that I stood up because it was good for me to stretch a bit, he felt relieved; my action had nothing to do with him. He was the kind of patient who for years seems to have one foot out the door, despite arriving weekly on time and never canceling. For many of these reasons I felt that what he showed me and what I acknowledged seeing were two different matters. This, of course, was my approach with this particular patient. Others might see a situation as dramatic as that of the split outfits I described as one crying for interpretation. I preferred waiting until the therapeutic climate became safer for him, and eventually it did.

In those instances when a patient directly asks for comments about a haircut, a new coat, the loss of ten pounds, or some such appearance-related matter, the situation is quite different because the patient has, verbally and consciously, raised the issue. Then I am naturally interested in exploring what he is asking me to comment on. Often patients present these questions and comments as if they were extra-analytic communications. It is my job to dispel this notion; these communications are grist for the mill, along with anything else the patient brings in. Even when children arrive wearing a new pair of sneakers or a first pair of glasses, or bringing a new toy, I do not react like other people by saying something social and enthusiastic. I stick to my role of looking at things differently from others in their life; I ask them about the item in question.

I do remember one incident that made me lose my professional composure. One day a young woman, a long-time patient in analysis, arrived with her waist-length, straight, light brown hair transformed into an exact duplicate of my short curly dark hair. Although I said nothing, she burst out laughing at my look of utter surprise. "I got you this time," she said and I had to agree, but we then went on to analyze why she had cut her hair and gone to such lengths to "get me" and what that was all about.

This detour was to explain that the interpretation that I made to Justine about her appearance was completely out of character for me. I believe that my straying so far from my customary style was in reaction to her unresponsiveness and out of anger that she had rendered me useless and invisible. Thus, out of frustration, I grabbed hold of, and threw back at her, the only information she had made available to me. I used it to let her know that I was not the useless fool she had created. I realized right away that this was acting out, a countertransferential outburst. Fortunately, this lapse on my part turned out all right.

Had I not made my interpretation would she still have thought of turning a second appointment with me into a greater evil than going on the trip, of using not wanting to see me again as her excuse for leaving her mother and going off with her peers? Perhaps, but maybe not. We did have a moment of connecting and I believe that in that moment she admitted to herself how much she wanted to emancipate herself and then found a way to do it. In her fierce rejection of me, she offered a gift to her mother—the more "bad" I was, the more "good" was her mother. As to the question of whether Justine would have become more receptive to treatment had I made my interpretation earlier in the session, I can only repeat that there is no way of knowing something that didn't happen. Perhaps even more important than worrying about the possibility of a lost opportunity is placing faith in the clinician's feel for a situation. I'm not even referring to anything as conscious as the timing of an interpretation, for that involves choice. In the case of Justine I couldn't have made my interpretation sooner because I didn't have it available to me. I made it when I had it to make. I suspect that she might have rejected the interpretation had it come earlier in the session, that she was more able to hear me because we were almost finished and she was on her way out. So all in all it seemed that by default the consultation took this unexpected turn, Justine was able to make her getaway, and Justine's mother found herself in the position to consider treatment for herself.

The case of Gus will illustrate a very different outcome. With Justine, my most useful piece of information was that her appearance did not match the image presented by her parents, and although my sole intervention was fueled by frustration rather than wisdom, the outcome was a good one. In the case of Gus the information provided was extensive and gave me all the knowledge I needed in order to do my work, but I neglected the most vital component, and, as the reader will see, the result was not very good.

Gus's mother first called me at the recommendation of her own therapist, when Gus was eighteen months old. She told me that **Gus could not tolerate change of any sort and would react by screaming, hitting, and biting. He even screamed when either parent came home from work.**[1]

The parents worked long hours in the city where I practice but lived in a distant suburb. Scheduling an appointment was difficult for them, and despite the considerable accommodations I was willing to make at my end, Mrs. G. let me know that the time we settled on was far from ideal and a disruption of their normal routine. That was my first clue about these parents. **Why were they so difficult, so inflexible about making an appointment?** This was particularly striking since this was only to be a one- or two-session consultation to determine whether they should find a therapist for Gus near their home. It was revealing that such a minor change in their routine would elicit such dissatisfaction, particularly since they had rejected several other appointment times I had offered. I was not surprised when Mrs. G. called shortly before we were to meet and canceled. She had found a psychiatrist near to her home and seeing him was more convenient.

Mrs. G. called again when Gus was two and said that she and her husband had to see me. The psychiatrist had helped some but the problem was far from resolved. Again it took a few phone calls before an appointment time was arrived at, but this time an incident occurred during one of these calls that provided some additional information about this mother. As she and I talked, Gus began to play with the phone and I heard her laugh as she asked

---

1. Bold print will be used to alert the reader to information about Gus or his parents that was diagnostically significant.

him to stop. Then the phone dropped and we were disconnected. She called back and while still laughing, apologized, and **a minute later Gus again began to play with the phone and Mrs. G. laughed uproariously.** The phone dropped and we were disconnected a second time. This time when she called back we were able to make the appointment. It was late at night and I felt a bit annoyed that making this appointment took so much of my time. In Chapter 7 I described another mother who also took a long time in making an appointment, but something in the way she did it had a very different tone and actually allowed a beginning connection to develop between us. This was not so with Mrs. G. There was something disjointed in her manner with me and I was very mindful of that same quality toward her little boy and of her inability to take charge when he needed help in controlling himself. It seemed that rather than being able to take charge she joined him and also regressed to a state of disorganization manifested by silliness and wild laughter.

When I finally met with Mr. and Mrs. G. they told me that the psychiatrist they had consulted had met with them and Gus on the first visit, had observed Gus, and had concluded that Gus had learned to hit from his baby sitters and that he should be stopped from hitting by a firm "no," and a slap on the hand. This had worked a bit, but now he was biting, and biting hard, and they felt that they needed more substantial help.

The parents provided the following information. Pregnancy and birth were uneventful. He was bottle-fed, had some digestive problems which caused spitting up and gas, but these cleared up once the formula was adjusted, and after that he was an easy baby. He slept through the night at two months, staying asleep for twelve hours and **has continued to sleep 12 hours per night without a single exception.**

The mother **was eager to return to work and did so when Gus was eight weeks old,** leaving him with a baby sitter who was competent and nice but who left after six months. After that there was a series of sitters, each one lasting several months. **The parents described the sitter who was fired shortly**

before their consultation with the psychiatrist as "dreadful, negligent, and dishonest." She allowed Gus to get such a severe diaper rash that the diaper area became raw and bled. She had a brusque manner and a nasty tone. It was assumed that she must have hit Gus and was the one who had "taught" Gus to hit. Later they discovered that she had stolen clothes, money, jewelry, and other items.

I asked the parents why **they had kept this sitter for four or five months,** and the mother replied that she had wanted to fire her much sooner, but her husband had dissuaded her on the grounds that it was a terrible hassle to find and train a new person. The father nodded, saying that he hadn't wanted to believe that she was as bad as she was because each change of help is so difficult. He now recognized that this had been a serious mistake on his part. This was said so objectively that I was puzzled. He didn't sound very disturbed that his young son had been mistreated for many months.

I asked some of the customary questions about the early history, about Gus's development, and about the current picture, and learned the following. Gus was erratic in his eating habits, eating a lot some days but not others. He loved to drink and consumed large quantities of liquids. He drank from a cup and bottle but wanted only milk in his bottle. He began walking at twelve months and shortly after that developed a small vocabulary of words. Now, at age two, he spoke in phrases. He was very observant of how things work, had learned to unlock the screen door, and had taught himself to fast forward and rewind his cassette player and could skip and replay sections of tapes. He loved listening to music and dancing and was quite exuberant when engaged in these activities.

Gus interacted well with adults and older kids but not with children his own age or babies, whom he hit and bit and pushed around. When with his age group, Gus had to be watched every minute as, for instance, in the sandbox, where he was a menace to others, grabbing their toys, throwing sand, hitting, and biting.

Gus's difficulty with change extended to new sensations as well as to people and situations. When first placed in the sandbox he had gotten hysterical at the feel of sand. Then he became accustomed to it, but cried and screamed if any got on his clothes. Also, he became terribly upset if he spilled any food or drink on his clothes. Thunder terrified him, as did sirens or any other unexpected noises. He hated to have his diaper and clothes changed and **every night it took him a while to become accustomed to his bath, and then he screamed when it was over.** He loved Lego, trucks, and cars. **He did not have a favorite blanket, did not suck his thumb, and rejected a pacifier when it was offered to him.**

Gus had a bedtime routine that he liked, so long as no changes and interruptions occurred. His father played with him for a while and then his mother took him to his room, read to him, and then put him into his crib and told him go to sleep, reminding him that when he woke up the baby sitter would be there and mommy and daddy would be at work. **He always went to sleep willingly and always woke up twelve hours later.**

The parents went on to tell me that when they got home from work they had about two hours with Gus before his 8:30 bedtime. They live in a sparsely populated area, houses are far apart, and, unfortunately, there are no young children in the immediate neighborhood. Consequently Gus is alone with his baby sitter for about ten hours each day. Thus they feel that they have to make up for Gus's isolation during the day by offering him stimulation and exposure to learning situations during their evening hours with him and on weekends. Two evenings a week they take him to a gymnastics class that meets from 7 to 8 PM in a nearby community center. They take him to local events such as fairs, dances, ball games, and so forth, that work into the schedule of their homecoming and his bedtime. When there is no place to take him, they rent educational videos for him and the father builds sophisticated Lego structures with him. They take him to museums and various events over the weekend, trying to expose him to as much culture and information as possible.

The mother described a recent scene with Gus that had upset her. For lack of anything better to do one evening they had taken him to a shopping mall that offered rides in miniature cars. These cars were set to a timer and for fifty cents Gus got the standard three-minute ride. **He screamed for the first minute, whimpered for the next, was sort of beginning to enjoy himself for the third, and then the ride was over and when his mother lifted him out of the car he screamed and hit and bit her hard on the arm.**

She described another very recent scene. She had taken him to a video store that she goes to often. He began to play with the light switch, flicking it on and off repeatedly. When she told him to stop, he ignored her. Then he spotted a stack of video tapes that he was on the verge of overturning so **she ran over, grabbed him, and as she lifted him, he smacked her in the face, hard. She said that she was mortified to be slapped by a two-year-old and in front of all the people in the store who knew her. She blushed with indignation as she told me this story and I could see how still vivid was the pain of it, and how narrow was her perception of the incident.**

At that point in the consultation I felt that I had been given a fairly comprehensive picture of Gus but needed to check out more about the relationship between him and his mother. I told the mother that it would be helpful for me to have a more detailed description of the incident in the video store and that I would ask her some questions that might seem trivial, but that the best way for me to do my job was to have the clearest and most vivid picture of some of the incidents she had described. She nodded in acquiescence.

I asked how she asked Gus to stop flicking the lights. Was she right next to him, touching him, looking into his face, or was she at a distance? She said **she was at a distance, at the counter. Gus was at the entrance, a good twenty-five feet away from her, and she shouted over, but he paid no attention.** He seemed excited and happy, and then when he was about to overturn the stack of video tapes, she ran over and grabbed him and yelled at him, and that was when he smacked her.

I said that from all that they had told me, Gus was a little boy who had trouble regulating his states of excitement. That was probably the reason that he liked sameness. Change, surprise, and the unexpected were upsetting even when these were exciting experiences, such as the events they offered him for his pleasure. Probably because he was so bright and alert, it was hard to recognize that his mood swings were enormous and beyond his control. He could fast forward his own cassette recorder to the exact section he desired, and yet became hysterical at being put on a kiddie ride. Then, as soon as he got used to it and liked it, he was again hysterical at being taken off it.

I went on to say that what was striking to me was that I was pretty much repeating back to them all their observations of Gus, yet I was beginning to suspect that the way I registered this information was different from the way they registered the same information. I added that this difference of perspective was partly my role as consultant. They came to see me hoping that I would provide a way of understanding Gus that differed from theirs and would help them deal with him more effectively. I told them that their very thorough description of Gus, and of the kiddie ride and video store incidents seemed a good place to begin.

I said that the kiddie ride served as a dramatic example of our differing views of the same event. Their most outstanding concern about Gus is his inability to tolerate change, and that the distress this causes him is manifested by screaming, hitting, and biting. These were, in fact, the symptoms that brought them to this consultation. Now here's a puzzling factor. In some curious way they behave as if they don't really believe that Gus has an extremely adverse reaction to change, even though they described his difficulty in such painstaking detail and of course see it in action all the time.

The parents looked amazed and said that of course they believe that Gus can't tolerate change. That's what they came about.

What could I possibly mean? Well, I said, in the three minutes with the kiddie ride they have a perfect example of the type of situation that Gus finds most disturbing. At first he is terrified of the new experience, and just as he is becoming a bit confident and interested he has to get off. So for three minutes he experiences three changes and this throws him into a state of disequilibrium. What seems puzzling is that they are inclined to expose him to these situations. A kiddie ride is not something essential like a necessary though unpleasant medical procedure, or even an injection. On the contrary, it's meant to be a treat, but for Gus it's not a treat, but a rather disquieting experience. It appears that they are so eager to give him treats that it's hard for them to distinguish between real treats and experiences that are too stimulating for him.

I told them that some children are not able to tolerate much stimuli. This trait is usually part of a person's temperament, and Gus appears to fit the characteristic of children who react strongly to stimuli of any sort. Change of any kind is overstimulating for him; at least this is so at this point in his life. He is still very young and this is likely to change as he grows older. If they accepted this personality trait as fact, they would avoid kiddie cars and other experiences of that sort.

I said that the incident in the video store served as another excellent example of how Gus reacts to certain situations, what that tells of his temperament, and how that in turn informs us about what he can and cannot handle. I said my understanding of what happened to Gus in the store is that he probably got so carried away flicking the lights on and off that his mother's voice was actually blocked out. In fact, flicking the lights might have been his way of dealing with the overstimulating atmosphere of the store, its bigness, its brightness, the isles full of merchandise, the people walking around and talking, and so forth. While flicking the lights he probably found a way of maintaining his equilibrium. This might have involved a regression to a younger mode, in which reliance on this very simple action of on and off became a way of maintaining focus and control.

As they have undoubtedly noticed, Gus, and other children his age, are often capable of moving rapidly through a range of behaviors, and while they regress quite easily under stress, they tend to recover easily when given some help. I said that going into a store is probably so stimulating to Gus that it's hard for him to feel safe there on his own. He probably needs the adult to actually hold him at first, and then stay very close and connected to him in order to help him not lose his bearings. Once he loses his bearings he really is out of control and that is such a frightening experience for him that he will hit and bite and scream because at that moment he has no other resources available to him to deal with the state of distress that he is experiencing.

I explained that to arrive at this view of what had happened in the video store I was working backward and using Gus's reaction, his out-of-control behavior, to reconstruct the emotional state that could have precipitated such behavior in him. This of course was speculative on my part and based on what they described and on my general knowledge of young children.

I stressed the need for protecting Gus from becoming overstimulated. What I had to say was very simple. If they would avoid the situations that are difficult for Gus and stick to sameness and predictable routines, and avoid surprises and the unexpected, they would be giving him something much more valuable than all the workshops, museums, educational events, and so forth.

Mrs. G. said she could understand that, for she too was easily overstimulated and preferred a quiet and predictable routine, but she said that her husband wanted Gus to get used to change and to have maximum exposure and learning opportunities. Mr. G. said that his wife was correct; it was true that he wanted Gus to have a lot of exposure to different experiences. He said that he disagreed with me and with my recommendations. He could not accept that Gus would do better with sameness. He didn't want Gus to be a narrow person.

I tried to engage the father, looking at this matter from a different perspective and making a distinction between the kind of learning that Gus experiences while doing simple things, where he is in command, and the arbitrary nature of a ride that has been timed for several minutes and then stops. I talked about little children learning from simple, safe, ordinary experiences, in a safe environment with familiar people, like the Lego and books and trucks and puzzles that he has at home.

The parents talked some more about only having two hours with their child at night, how guilty they felt spending so little time with him, and their wish to make those two hours as productive as possible. I responded by agreeing that of course they wanted to make the most of their time together, but Gus is only two years old and they have so many years together ahead of them. They need to be mindful of the fact that two-year-old children are not uniform in their development. Some aspects of intellect, physical maturation, and emotional development mature more rapidly than others. Gus is probably precocious in understanding cause and effect in the mechanical sphere and is probably most comfortable in that area. In contrast, a sandbox filled with other children his own age is full of the unpredictable, and he falls apart in that situation. It's for good reason that he feels safer with adults and older children, for they are more predictable than kids his own age and younger.

I told these parents that they are excellent observers and can usually predict those situations that Gus will thrive in and those that are difficult for him. The problem is that they don't make use of their observations. Their concern for compensating for their long hours away from home seems paramount and overshadows their awareness that their homecoming is in itself so exciting that it needs no embellishment. My recommendation was to set aside their notion of compensating for their time at work, make sure that he has competent care while they are away, and provide him with a quiet and predictable environment. I said that if Gus feels safe and competent, the rest will follow. The safe feeling that he needs to develop will be nourished by their acceptance of his unique temperament. In accepting him as he is they will be able to stay in step with him, and he will feel supported to grow and develop at his own pace.

I added that sometimes they almost sound afraid of him—are they aware of that? The mother said that this was true of her but not of her husband. For instance, her husband would have picked Gus up in the video store sooner than she did. She sometimes avoids physical contact with him because she is so afraid that he will hit her or bite her.

We went on talking this way a while longer but our time ran out and they said that they wanted to come back and talk some more. We made another appointment, which they canceled, and I never heard from them again.

I will review what went wrong in this consultation and how it came about. It was obvious from the beginning that Mr. and Mrs. G., while good observers of their son, were unable to accept his unique temperament and consequently unable to accommodate to who he was and what he needed. Their repeated failures with him, painful as they were to them as well as to Gus, did not provide these parents with insight. They seemed to have a fantasy of an ideal son, tried to turn Gus into that ideal child, and could not let go of this futile quest.

Gus sounded like a child at risk for the following reasons: his extreme need for sameness; his lack of reliance on the object environment, composed as it was of his parents and a changing cast of caretakers and his preference for the inanimate environment; the absence of a transitional object (Winnicott 1953) or any self-soothing habits such as thumb or pacifier; and his oddly unwavering sleep pattern. All these suggested an ego deviational picture. Ego deviation refers to a constitutional deficit in the ego equipment itself. Weil (1970) refers to the infant's inborn "basic core of fundamental trends" (p. 442), which the environment either aggravates or attenuates. Of course it is difficult to reconstruct what Gus's ego equipment was like at birth, and certainly we know from his history that his parents were unattuned and that the care he received from sitters ranged from poor to inconsistent. According to the description of his parents, by age two he had symptoms and characteristics that very much fit the general pattern of ego deviational children.

We know that many children raised in similar and even far more inadequate environmental circumstances do not present a symptom picture similar to the one presented by Gus. There are children whose constitution makes them more resilient, tougher, less vulnerable than Gus appeared to be. It seemed likely that Gus was the kind of infant who needed a better than "good enough" environment but this, sadly, was not his fate. The combination of Gus's vulnerabilities and of his unattuned parents did not bode well for the future and had probably already exacerbated his innate deficits.

This was not a suitable case for the type of brief consultation described in the other chapters of this section of the book, consultations on transient problems in cases where the child and parents are basically healthy. In this case the child was fragile and the parents not up to the extra care he needed. Such a combination of factors generally requires long-term treatment with child and parents in combination with a therapeutic nursery, when one is available.

My job with Gus's parents had been to evaluate the need for ongoing treatment. This needed to be done while taking into account the parents' guilt, their blind spots, projections, and their need to be beyond reproach. Instead of discussing treatment with these parents I tried to educate them. I embarked on this endeavor despite knowing quite well that a big part of their problem was that they didn't listen and they didn't hear. That's where my countertransference became manifested. I became as unattuned to them as they were to their child. I expected them to be able to use what I offered, all good stuff to be sure, but just as misplaced as their offering to Gus all those stimulating activities they believed to be good stuff.

The countertransference was demonstrated in the loss of a professional attitude, which encompasses all aspects of a case. I took into account what Gus needed and bypassed his parents. This case was an example of the therapist forgetting who the patient was and what needed to be treated.

If I had recommended treatment for Gus and for his parents, explained a bit about why I thought it a good idea to begin at this time, and been able to do all this without alarming them, would they have listened to me? Probably not. We have all met parents who put off beginning treatment for their child for years. When it's recommended in consultation with a therapist they find fault with the therapist; when it's recommended by the nursery school or kindergarten where their child is floundering, they change schools; when a friend takes them aside and suggests it, they find fault with the friend. Then, finally, at some point they run out of options; every nanny quits after a short time or the last available school delivers an ultimatum, and only then does treatment begin. With it sometimes comes unimaginable relief or the opposite in the form of dissatisfaction with the therapist.

While it is true that in some of these cases the failures and disappointments have to run their course before treatment is initiated, I cannot be sure that this would have been so with Gus's parents. Had I not overly identified with Gus, felt disapproving of his parents, and tried to work a sixty-minute miracle by trying to alter their perception of him and replace it with my own, who knows what might have happened?

This case serves as an example of a therapist not taking an equidistant stance among the participants in the family drama, and therefore losing sight of who the patient was and what needed to be addressed. In this consultation, my patients were the parents. Had I maintained clarity in this regard I could have done a better job to the benefit of all three family members.

While the consultation with and about Justine serves as an example of the therapist's countertransference not having a harmful effect on outcome, the one with Gus illustrates the opposite. What is so particularly striking in the case of Gus is that I had such important information about this mother from the first phone call, from the extraordinary rigidity she manifested in making an appointment, in her unawareness of my attempt to accommodate her, in her striking difficulty in understanding mutual accommodation. These were preverbal and rapprochement-tinged communications that revealed important diagnostic information about Mrs. G., but which I registered with irritation rather than with professional interest. The affect of irritation is sometimes unavoidable, since we are, after all, human, and patients can be very irritating at times, but when we feel such affects we need to pursue them and search out the countertransferential component. Mrs. G. was letting me know, through her attitude in making an appointment, that I would have to do the major job of adapting, and when a patient lets you know that, there really is no choice. It's a preverbal communication, one that the patient is not aware of but that is fundamental to the work ahead. It tells us what our role will have to be, at least at the beginning. In these cases we have to fit with the patient because we can and they cannot. When we don't, the case doesn't get off the ground and that is precisely what happened in the case of Gus.

Ongoing Work with the Parents of Children in Treatment

12

~

Guidelines for Establishing Patterns of Contact with Parents

*I*n Chapter 1, I listed seven questions that typically arise when child therapists meet and discuss their work with the parents of their patients. Throughout this book only one of these questions has been addressed directly, Question #2:

> *When the parent of a child in treatment is seen by his or her child's therapist, is the parent to be viewed as a patient or as something other than a patient?*

I've concentrated on this question because I see it as most basic to understanding this aspect of our work. Being clear about the patient status of a parent, or being unclear about that status and knowing that one is unclear, helps us make clinical decisions based on the real situation before us: this child and these parents. It not only gives focus to our work with parents but also helps us think diagnostically about them and aids us in uncovering distortions created by countertransference.

This question is especially useful at the beginning phase of treatment but we need to keep this concern alive throughout; it keeps us alert to shifting currents and to the changes that occur

as treatment progresses. Because being clear about the patient
status of parents is fundamental to the work of every child therapist, it can be used as an organizing principle in our child cases.
It can help us with all the questions that follow. Question #1:

> *Should the child's therapist also work with the parents or should the
> parents be seen by a different therapist? Should the parents be seen
> as a couple, individually, or should they each be seen in individual
> treatment by separate therapists? If other therapists are involved in
> treating the parents, how much communication, if any, should take
> place among the various therapists?*

Here, within a general heading, we have a series of very specific interrelated questions, all valid, all important, and all needing to be addressed. But it is not possible to address such questions outside the context of the clinical material that raises them
because the answers must be shaped by the total conditions of
each case. We must look at each particular case with its unique
circumstances before we can arrive at a treatment plan; we must
first of all understand *what needs to be treated*. That is not to say
that we cannot set down some of the factors that need to be considered in planning our contact with the parents of our child
patients, factors that would help us reach a beginning understanding of the case before us.

We need to consider the following: the age of the child, the
nature of the problem, the relationship between child and each
parent, and the relationship of the parents to each other. We need
to explore the attitude of each of the parents to the child's treatment and gain an impression of how psychologically minded they
are. We need to have a working diagnosis[1] of the child and of the
parents; we must be realistic about the availability of therapeutic
resources, and aware of the parents' time constraints and their
financial picture. We need to know whether treatment is volun-

---

1. A working diagnosis would involve charting a patient's primary
psychosexual stage and anxiety level, object relations and identity formation, and adaptive and defensive functioning.

tary or mandated by an outside agency. Finally, we need to arrive at what might be an ideal plan, and then, if necessary, trim
it to what is realistically possible.

These are some of the important background questions we
need to consider in our work with the parents of our child patients. But let us remember that the core issue to be clear about
is this: What is the nature and purpose of the work with these
parents?

Sometimes our work with parents is in response to their wish
to be a part of their child's treatment, and by meeting with them
regularly we respond to this wish, gain their cooperation, and make
it easier for them to tolerate their child's need for treatment. Sometimes our purpose is to try to help them deal with a difficult family
situation more effectively and our role might be to give them a
time and place to air their concerns and perhaps provide information that could help them feel less helpless and more competent.

Some therapists feel strongly about having regular ongoing
contact with parents in order to be informed of all and any events
at home that affect their young patient. They would not agree with
Anthony (1980), who writes: "One does not really need an information service from the mother because the patient is generally
an excellent 'newsboy' and carries the family 'headlines' with him"
(p. 25). Of course the child's age would play an important part
here and many agree that with a young child there is more need
for ongoing contact with the parents, especially since a young child
would not be likely to provide information about home and school.

Sometimes work with parents rises out of our concern that the
climate at home will not accept and support any of the changes
in the child that we strive for and are at the heart of our work. In
such cases we would make every effort to enlist the participation
of parents in the hope that we might help them develop some
insight into their child's changing needs and behavior. In most
child cases there are many reasons for seeing the parents, particularly if the child is young. Sometimes, however, there are good
reasons for not seeing the parents, and this would be determined
by such factors as the degree of their unwillingness to participate,

their hostility towards the therapist, and their very fixed negative view of psychotherapy.

As with everything else we do, we need to be clear about why we have or don't have ongoing contact with the parents or with one parent. Anna Freud makes a distinction between "helping the mother and seeing her in order to get information about events at home" (Sandler et al. 1980, p. 214).

This might sound like too rigid a demarcation, since, in most cases, gaining information and helping the mother and father are complementary processes. The point is that raising questions of this sort helps us to be clear about our focus and the primary thrust of our contact with the parents.

With some mothers and fathers the working alliance is best protected if their primary function is to provide information about the child's life outside our office. I refer here to parents who are not sympathetic to treatment, not psychologically minded, and not eager to become so. For this group of parents, bringing their child, meeting with the therapist, and paying the bill is doing a great deal. As long as that's all we expect of them they will cooperate. It is essential to be respectful of parents who limit their contacts with us to the concrete level of providing information and transportation. Only by accepting their terms do we protect the working alliance. When a parent joins forces with us on behalf of his child, whatever level it's on, however faint we might find the effort, we must accept it. Some parents have a high stake in *not* having a place anywhere on that patient-to-non-patient continuum, and with such parents any effort to be helpful might be experienced by them as a transgression. Certain parents need to believe that their child needs help but that his problems have nothing to do with them; *they* don't need help. To offer it could destroy an already fragile alliance.

The important matter in planning parent contact is for the therapist to be clear about what has been decided about the role of the parents in the child's treatment. With this basic issue as a guide, it is easier to determine who should see them, how often, and with what objective.

Outside of agency practice, with its tradition of dividing child cases into a therapist for the child and other therapists for the parents together or separately, it is customary for the child's therapist to work with the parents. When contact with the child's therapist has been of a positive nature it is not uncommon for a parent to seek her own treatment. Often the exposure to the child's therapist introduces a parent to a whole new way of thinking, reflecting, and observing that the parent experiences as growth promoting. The parent may then recognize that some of what is problematic for his child has some connection to his own past and present difficulties. In such cases treatment may be viewed as an opportunity rather than a punishment or stigma denoting failure. When this most favorable turn of events occurs, there is no reason for the contact between the parent and the child's therapist to end. The parent's own treatment should be viewed as operating independently from the treatment of the child. There is no reason for the parent's therapist and the child's therapist to be in contact and good reason for them to not be in touch, since there is nothing for them to learn from each other that would not have been more appropriately conveyed to them by their patient.

This leads us into the second part of this question regarding communication between the various therapists of family members. Respect for patient confidentiality applies here and is always a prime concern. There would have to be a strong reason to justify discussion among therapists of family members, strong enough to override the issue of confidentiality. This does happen at times but before I illustrate some of these situations I would like to discuss the concept of confidentiality from a broader perspective than that of client privilege.

The assurance of confidentiality provides our patients with the guarantee that what they tell us is for our ears alone. We recognize that our pledge to keep private all information provided by the patient allows the patient to be self-revealing. Self-exploration cannot freely take place without a climate of trust. When a therapist betrays that trust by discussing the patient's communications, something vital in the relationship between patient and therapist erodes; something sacred is trivialized.

The dyadic nature of the patient–therapist relationship and its exclusivity cannot be overstressed; its presence is an underlying theme in psychotherapy and in psychoanalysis alike, and exerts a constant force through the vicissitudes of the transference, the therapeutic alliance and the various phases of treatment. While we generally think of this dimension of dyadic exclusivity from the perspective of the needs of the patient, I propose that it is also integral to the work of the therapist. It contains an element of "fitting together," Hartmann's (1958) elegant concept regarding the mother's adaptation to her infant, which requires of her a regression to a primitive and preverbal level of perceptual awareness, to the place inhabited by her infant. To do our work, to stay in pace with our patients through their forward moves and regressive phases, their rational discourses and intellectualizations, and their journeys into the often obscure landscape of dreams, we have to simultaneously maintain a place in the present while abandoning the dramatic unities of time, place, and action. To fit with our patients we too have to allow ourselves these regressive shifts.

Because this aspect of the connection between therapist and patient is subtle, delicate, and reaches beyond technique and into an affective realm, discussions regarding the patient with other therapists dilutes something deeply personal in the patient–therapist connection. I propose that confidentiality is vital not only to the patient, but to the therapist as well. It would then follow that the corroding effect of discussions with other therapists is unaltered whether these discussions take place with the patient's permission or without.

Of course exceptions exist and some circumstances warrant discussions among therapists. The following will serve as an illustration of such a situation. Johnny, a ten-year-old boy in treatment, lives alone with his mother. The father was never in the picture and his whereabouts are unknown. The mother is seriously depressed and she and her therapist are planning her hospitalization. The mother's sister, who lives far away and is a stranger to the child, has agreed to come and take him to her home and keep him as long as it takes for the mother to return home and feel strong enough to resume caring for her son. This depressed mother feels unequal to preparing her child for the separation. She's afraid that if she tries to explain the situation to him she'll get confused, cry, and alarm him further. She wants her therapist to call Johnny's therapist, apprise her of the situation, ask her to tell Johnny about the hospitalization, and prepare him for their separation. The two therapists talk and the child's therapist agrees to do as the mother asks.

This is an extreme situation in which the communication between therapists of family members seems warranted. What needs to be mentioned though, is that in this situation the therapists are stepping out of their customary roles and into those usually carried out by family members. Since no family members are available to do this job, these therapists are stretching their role on behalf of mother and child, and in this sense are being very helpful. They are filling an important vacuum, but this is not exactly the kind of help that they were trained to provide. Sometimes expedience is everything, but it is not psychoanalysis or psychotherapy, and it is useful to be aware of the difference.

In the next example, two therapists of family members choose to talk to each other in a situation that seems very different. In this case, each therapist is treating one of the children of divorcing parents. The parents are engaged in a custody battle and the two therapists are subjected to constant demands for information. They receive calls from the parents' attorneys and from court-appointed attorneys, and are threatened with having their records subpoenaed. The therapists are concerned that these extra-analytic activities pose a threat to their work with the children. They try to explain this to the parents but their concern is not taken seriously and the barrage of demands continues. The therapists request permission from the parents to consult with each other. They wished to establish a unified approach in dealing with all the legal questions to try to prevent the complete collapse of the children's treatment. They recognize the fierce nature of the custody battle. Parents and lawyers seem to be joined in wanting to win at any cost. They recognize that much damage can be done in this warlike atmosphere and they want to maintain a level and consistent approach to the custody dispute so they won't inadvertently say or do anything that might be used destructively and undermine the children's treatment.

In this example, it again makes some sense that the therapists talk to each other, and while this sort of situation is by no means unusual in the practice of child treatment, it does require therapists to stretch their role beyond what falls within the domain of our training, realm of expertise, and responsibility. So, while the circumstances around these two case examples are very different, the common denominator is that the therapists are faced with situations that take them beyond their basic role.

In another example, the mother's therapist calls the child's therapist and says, "I haven't told my patient that I'm calling you, so don't say anything to her about this call, but I need to know how disturbed her son is. The way she talks about him makes him sound psychotic one minute and like an ordinary kid the next. I need to know where he really fits."

Why does the mother's therapist need this information? Of what possible use will it be to him? That the mother has such divergent impressions of her child is the more profound information. Why does he fail to recognize that? And why is he calling without his patient's permission? That certainly is not all right. Had he asked for his patient's permission to make this call, that too would not have been all right, for the call itself is inappropriate. Most likely the therapist's action was motivated by his anxiety rather than his concern for the patient. The therapist and patient would have been better served had the therapist analyzed his countertransference, rather than expressing it through action.

In Chapter 5, I described some of the problems that may occur as early in our work as the initial referral of a patient when the one who refers and the one receiving the referral blur the lines between relevant information about a potential patient, the therapist's wish to satisfy his curiosity, and other forms of acting on countertransferential impulses.

Members of our profession are as curious as anyone else or perhaps more curious than other people. After all, an inquiring mind and the courage to explore are intrinsic aspects of our work. We are also very interested in our patients and everything about them. Our interest grows out of concern and empathy, vital ingredients in our effectiveness as therapists. It is not surprising that we might be curious about a patient's child, a child we've gotten to know in the particular way that we get to know the families of our patients. We might have first met that child as the mother's fantasy before his conception. Then during her pregnancy the fantasy changed, grew more detailed, and combined with earthbound hopes and concerns. Then, after delivery, we grew to know that child as a now real and idealized infant, toddler, nursery school child, and then first grader. Might we not be curious to hear what impressions our colleague formed of him when his mother had that consultation about his daily distress over going to school following the birth of his baby sister? And might we not be tempted to ask our colleague about him and be distressed when we are told that the boy is terrific but if only his mom wasn't so controlling? What do we do with that information? Our patient controlling? Why that was not at all our view of her! No, our curiosity wasn't satisfied; it rarely is. More likely, as in this case, we are left with information we can't use and that sometimes gets in our way.

Our curiosity is a very good thing when we use it to further the patient's treatment. For this end the curiosity must have been sublimated and fits with the therapist's representation of an ideal professional self. That is a far cry from simply satisfying our curiosity by indiscriminately seeking information from patients and colleagues.

A good approach to assessing the potential value of speaking to therapists of family members is to examine why we are considering such an action. Is it arising out of some unconscious need on our part? The informed reader might ask how we would know if our motives were unconscious. We might get some indication of this being the case by asking ourselves some probing questions: Do we have the need to distance the patient, to polarize and dilute the patient–therapist relationship? Do we feel overwhelmed by the patient and therefore seek the support of a colleague because we find the patient difficult and draining? Do we want to complain to our colleague as we once complained to a parent? One can ask oneself various questions of this sort and then ask oneself once again what will best advance the course of the patient's treatment.

There are circumstances where consultation with colleagues is enormously helpful, particularly when the therapist has reached a difficult juncture and needs help, but that is different from casual discussion of a case. Generally, little is gained and much lost in these discussions, unless, as in the first two examples, unusual circumstances require that we depart somewhat from our basic role of dealing with psychic reality and psychic stress.

Question #3 has directly and indirectly been touched on in some of the chapters.

> Should parents be given direct advice regarding their children or would this represent the therapist as an authority figure who might undermine parental prerogative?

The second part of the question partly answers the first, but there's more to be said about it. Most often we don't have the knowledge to give advice. Our training has given us a great deal of information about human development, and hopefully our own treatment has given us a good deal of insight into our own. We have our particular skills, but when it comes to childrearing we are no experts. Speak to any teacher or school administrator and you will learn that psychoanalysts and psychotherapists do not have a particularly wonderful reputation as good parents. And haven't we all had patients describe the most obnoxious child in their son's class or the worst bully in their daughter's pre-kindergarten, and then tell us, with glee, that the mother (or father) is a psychiatrist!

There are other interesting issues regarding the giving of advice to parents. In Chapter 3, discussing Mrs. Kay's expectation that her two-year-old son clean up his room by himself, I proposed that given our diagnostic understanding of this mother, to have told her that a two-year-old is far too young to clean up his room on his own would have been an inappropriate intervention. This "educational" intervention would have failed to educate. Most likely it would have been experienced as criticism. Of course someone could have made a case for educational information, justified it on the basis of its accuracy, and amplified it with the kindly and sensible advice that the parent join her toddler in the cleaning of his room. I believe that at the time of the incident Mrs. Kay would only have heard in that advice that more and more was expected of her and less of others. A year later in her treatment she might have heard the same advice for what it was, good common sense, but by then it would have been superfluous, for she might have known it on her own.

There are some forms of advice that can be helpful. A long time ago the two embattled divorcing parents of an eighteen-month-old came to consult me. The father tended to fall in love with ideologies. At the time of the consultation he was devoted to the ideal of social consciousness. For this reason he wanted his daughter in a day care center with other children. The mother (who worked full time) was more attuned to the actual needs of her child and wanted Libby to stay home with her familiar and very competent nanny.

After meeting with the parents I had an appointment with their little girl and found her to be a well-developing, happy child. I then agreed to share with these parents the direction that my knowledge of child development pointed to. I voiced my preference for Libby staying home with her nanny. I explained my thinking along the lines of the separation-individuation process and the establishment of object constancy (more or less) around the age of three and suggested that day care be delayed until then, if finances allowed. Finances were a major concern. The mother was pleased, the father angry, but he agreed to this and elected to continue using me as a consultant whenever they got into disagreements about Libby. Three or four times a year they would appear over an issue and with the passing of time I noted how the father's originally doctrinaire approach mellowed, giving way to a more genuine and attuned relationship with Libby, while the mother's common sense and good judgment came with a certain coolness of spirit.

I very much admired these parents, whose love for their child always carried higher importance than their anger at each other and disappointment over their failed marriage. They consulted me about matters that many would have dismissed as minor: who should give Libby her allowance, disputes over amount of time spent watching television, bedtime, and, as she grew older and had more of a social life of her own, necessary adjustments around their joint custody arrangements so as to minimize the difficulties she encountered by living in two homes. When she was nine, they came to see me to help them agree on the proper age for sleep-away camp and continued to come to discuss all the other normal rites of passage that ideally are discussed by two parents without outside help. But these parents were not so lucky; they didn't have compatible mates to discuss things with, so they came to see me.

Except for that first dispute when I declared myself on the side of a nanny versus day care, I never voiced a direct opinion. I asked questions, explored, and made certain connections that their frustrations often obscured. Our meetings were a forum for discussion, and I believe that they perceived my presence as assurance that they would each maintain adequate self control, and, having that in place, arrive at acceptable solutions about whatever was on their agenda that day. They gave me a role to play and wanted me to play it well; that made it possible for me to be effective. It was a very satisfying situation for all three of us. The only advice I gave them, way back at the beginning of our long association, was the only advice I had a strong conviction about and the only issue they really couldn't resolve on their own.

Is this an example of a therapist stepping into a realm different from our function of psychoanalyst or psychotherapist, of taking on the role of part-educator, part-mediator? I think not. A psychotherapist acting as consultant needs to be informed about the subject matter of the consultation, and in the case of Libby, one level around which the consultation revolved was knowledge of human development, of the phases and stages through which we pass from infancy to adulthood, and of the psychic changes implicit in this growth. But that was only the more obvious, more surface subject of the consultation. The more substantial subject was the toll that a failed marriage took on their lives and their intense disappointment at not being able to love and raise their child together. Theirs was an unending state of mourning. It was very important to both of Libby's parents not to allow their anger to take over, but both recognized that their (ego) strength was not reliably able to deal with their lingering wish for union, or with the force of their anger and frustration, at least not when they were together. They had invested me with a function in their lives, and to have done that involved a powerful positive transference on both their parts, one that needed no interpretation. I simply had to accept the idealization it carried. My role as consultant was that of auxiliary ego, a role that requires all our training and all our wisdom.

It needs to be stated that therapists have no special monopoly on tact and sensitivity. Plenty of people outside of our field learn to listen well, to observe, and to combine intuition with observation. Of course the good parent combines these qualities (Pine 1976) as a matter of course, and in the experience of harnessing and using these cognitive and affective experiences with our children lies the origin of what we as psychotherapists develop into a professional attitude (Winnicott 1960). One difference between us and other people whose attunement is used in such helpful ways is that of attitude about being idealized. Because we understand the force of the unconscious and the effect of transference on perception, we have a more moderate and more objective response to being idealized (Freud 1912a, 1915). We try not to take too literally the patient's exalted view of our worth and power.

There are certain circumstances in which our information about child development can be shared with parents in a very helpful way. For instance, we know that there are pivotal stages in early life. Each of these stages represents the culmination of maturational growth and psychological development,[2] providing the base for a significant psychic leap. I refer here to the child's passage through the progression of psychosexual stages and those of the separation-individuation process. We know that each of these stages carries the potential for growth, but an increased level of anxiety is also present. If the anxiety level exceeds the ego's capacity to temper this affect, a regression rather than a progressive move might result. Because we understand these processes and their vicissitudes, we are sometimes in a good position to help parents plan the timing of an event. For instance, if a separation from the parents must be scheduled, we know that it is best not to plan it when their infant reaches the third quarter of the first year, the phase that Spitz (1959) referred to as *stranger anxiety*. During this period the child's attachment to his caretakers has become intense and is no longer primarily based, as it had been earlier, on his caretaker's ability to satisfy his momentary needs. The specificity of the attachment and its intensity are a welcome developmental landmark, but with it comes a significant increase of anxiety when the now highly valued caretaker is absent. Since object constancy is not yet established, the anxiety of a child at this age would be intense and cause a great deal of psychic pain. Knowing this, we would advise, all other considerations being equal, that a separation from the parents be planned at an ear-

---

2. Spitz (1959) makes the distinction between maturation, which is biological and has its own preset timetable, and development, which is psychological and is significantly affected by environmental circumstances.

lier age or later, when the child is more likely to have developed the inner resources to deal with such a separation.

Another example of using our knowledge to help parents plan the timing of events would be to consider how surgery might be experienced by a child at various developmental stages. For instance, a child at the oedipal phase would experience surgery differently than he would a couple of years later upon reaching latency, so if there was no pressing medical reason to perform the surgery right away, putting the surgery off might be a better plan.

Our knowledge about how children might experience various events and life situations has wide application, but often in consultation the use of our knowledge takes a different turn. The parents of an adopted pre-adolescent consulted me about the advisability of treatment for their daughter. They were worried about her constant state of anger, which was expressed in her unrelenting questioning about her biological mother, idealization of the biological mother, and devaluation of her concerned and loving adoptive parents.

Of course it was useful to be informed about the special problems of adopted children, to know that the absent parent is often idealized (Neubauer 1960), and that much of what the daughter was doing was typical pre-adolescent torment of parents, in her case with adoption as the theme because she knew that to be their most vulnerable area. This was useful background information. The more substantial job was to help the parents with their distress, a matter not even on their agenda. And here lies the difference between how a trained therapist deals with a request for information and what might be found in books, friends, and the profusion of workshops by minimally trained people who represent themselves as parenting experts. We are trained to listen to the question behind the question—the unstated and not yet known. What could lie behind this highly articulate request for treatment of an adopted daughter who seems pretty consistently angry and discontented is a story not yet told. It begins with two grieving parents whose devotion and best efforts are being trampled while they watch in joined helplessness. Before we can help them with their daughter, they will need to get to know their stories, and as this evolves the self-imprisonment they created will be given voice. Perhaps then and only then will their daughter's anger dissipate. It is always good to ask: Who are the patients and what needs to be treated?

This has been a long response to question #3, which turned out to be more complicated and more interesting than it appeared at first glance. No, advice is not our metier, but sometimes the special knowledge we have can be helpful to parents in dealing with certain situations and decisions. Hopefully our training helps us convey information in a way that can be accepted and used. With this in place it would be our job to not present ourselves as bigger and more important than the parents, but rather competent and useful in meeting their request. But then some parents would want us to be bigger and make us so and then accuse us of fitting the picture they created, and some would make us small and useless, and so it goes. A big part of our job is to stay the same size whatever comes along. Question #4:

At what age should we consider the child too old for us to continue to maintain regular contact with his parents?

This is another of those questions that, while unanswerable out of context, come up as real issues in our daily work. A simple approach would be to ask: (1) What is the purpose of seeing the parents? (2) Is the child's chronological age a significant factor? These diagnostic questions get us away from the standard and generally appropriate view that at adolescence we stop parent contact. In cases of severe pathology, chronological age might have little bearing on the total situation. Diagnostic considerations might need to be placed ahead of age-related factors. Psychotic states and severe depression would be two examples where contact with parents might continue well into the patient's adolescence and young adulthood. In such situations our patient's emotional development would be impeded by his pathology and he would not be able to reach the developmental landmarks that eliminate the need for contact with parents.

Now we can proceed and consider some of the situations that arise in our practices. Let's say that our new patient, Sam, is fifteen years old, appears to be chronologically on track, not seriously disturbed, and articulate and communicative. We don't need to see his parents from our end and he doesn't want us to see them, but they insist on having regular appointments and set this as a condition for their son's treatment. Most likely their demand has drawn us right into the heart of family dynamics and can't be ignored or avoided. In fact, the case can't even begin until we know what this is all about, so one approach would be to work with the parents for a while to explore with them what they want or fear from their son's treatment. This approach with the parents could clear the path for Sam's treatment or lead to a referral for the parents, together or separately, or the parents might insist on continuing with the original therapist and Sam would need to be referred to a different therapist. The point is that what the parents want matters and must be taken seriously. Many therapists have an easier time taking seriously the demands of the adolescent than those of his parents. When the requests of parents are taken more as nuisance factors than as communications that need to be respected and understood, the case is often doomed to fail.

In some rare situations, the child or adolescent wants us to see her parents because she has trouble communicating with them directly and wants our help. In some instances the therapist might want to see the parents of an adolescent in the hope of bringing about some environmental changes. None of these variations in contact with the parents of an adolescent should be undertaken lightly. They need careful consideration lest they serve the patient's fantasies of being rescued, the therapist's fantasies of being a rescuer, or other pursuits not grounded in therapeutic work. To make a good decision we need to take into account all relevant information about this particular case and with that in place it is usually possible to arrive at a plan that protects the effectiveness and continuity of treatment.

The next question is probably the only simple question on the list, Question #5:

*What is the child's right to confidentiality and what is the parents'
right to know what is going on in their child's treatment?*

I think we would all agree that the patient's right to confidentiality is absolute. Is this also true if the child is three years
old? Yes, I think it is, and for many children the promise of "our
work is private" becomes an important and unique aspect of the
treatment situation. The more complex part of the question
pertains to the parents' demand or request that they be told what
is going on in the child's treatment. One angry father told me
that he had taken his four-year-old son out of treatment after
six months of being told by his child's therapist that she couldn't
tell them anything about his son's sessions. This father asked
whether I too had such a policy, for if I did, I wasn't the person
for his son. He would not be shut out of his son's treatment and
thought that it was idiotic to expect any parents to bring their
child, pay the bill and be told nothing. His manner was loud,
bossy, and slightly menacing.

I agreed with this father and told him so. Then I tried to learn
what kind of information he would have liked to have about his
son's prior treatment. He was vague and said that he just wanted
to know what went on.

I considered his anger and the conditions he made key to working with him. Obviously his contact with my predecessor had made
him feel shut out, and judging by the force of his reaction this
had touched something deep and painful in him. I told him that
parents had a right to be part of their child's treatment and that
children also had rights, and privacy was an important aspect of
their treatment. I saw no conflict between these sets of rights. As
I got to know their son I would share some of my observations
with his parents and perhaps help make sense out of some of the
behavior that baffled them and brought them to a therapist. I could
easily share this knowledge without divulging its specific source.
What did it matter whether puppet play or time spent drawing
and making up stories was the source of some of my insights? What
was important was that I welcomed their participation in their
son's treatment.

I added that it was also important that his son be told that what we do is private from my end, in other words that I would not discuss with anyone what we did during our appointments. He, on the other hand, would not be bound by this rule and could either talk about his sessions or not, as he wished. He would be the boss in this regard.

I told this father that I always say this to my young patients because I find it to set a collaborative tone, one most conducive to effective treatment. I viewed this approach to the child as compatible and complementary with the right of parents to meet with me and be a vital part of the treatment process.

My purpose in spelling out this standard therapeutic position was twofold. It accurately informed the parents of what could be expected, but it also diluted the father's very aggressive tone. The reader might not be too surprised to learn that in the two years I saw his son in treatment this father kept only one of the many appointments we made, and although arriving thirty minutes late that day was barely able to focus on his child for the little time that remained of his session. What is the message here? Well, there are two messages contained in my vignette.

The first message is that children have a right to confidentiality and parents of young children have the right to have contact with their child's therapist and to get both feedback and help. The second message is that we need to explore what a parent means when he says that he wants to be part of his child's treatment. Sometimes it is a very strong statement of a parent's lack of readiness to separate from his child both physically and emotionally, and it could mean that a tripartite treatment plan is indicated, at least for the beginning phase. Sometimes it simply means that the parents want reasonable contact with their child's therapist, and sometimes, as in the example of the father who made demands but didn't show up to collect on his demands, we never get to know the person and are left with an incomplete diagnostic picture of the parent and of that aspect of the child's object environment. But whatever the case, we don't lock horns with the demands of parents; we discuss and explore. Question #6:

Should the parents' participation in their child's treatment be mandatory or voluntary?

This question raises some fundamental questions about the role of a child therapist vis-à-vis the parents of his patient. We would all agree that in cases where it has been established that the child is the primary patient, the therapeutic task is to treat the child. But what if the treatment of the child cannot proceed effectively unless the parents, or in some cases one parent, participates in the treatment? What if certain environmental changes are crucial to supporting any gains the child might make in treatment? How far do we reach into the family in our effort to provide our young patient with the best conditions for growth and change? What parameters do we set for ourselves as intruders on the status quo, as outsiders jolting the dynamics of family relationships?

Of course we would hope that parents would join us in wishing to do whatever is in the best interest of their child. When circumstances are favorable, parents participate in the child's treatment to the degree recommended by the therapist. What do we do when circumstances are less than favorable?

Let's back up and briefly examine the purpose of parental participation. I believe that most therapists would agree that the participation of parents in the treatment of very young children is usually an integral part of the treatment process. After all the child is still completely dependent on his parents and very much in their care; parents and therapist must work together cooperatively for the treatment to stand a good chance of making a substantial contribution to the child's development. Not only is an alliance between therapist and parents essential, but so is ongoing communication between these principal caretakers and the therapist. It is important for the people who play a primary part in the life of the child to share with each other their view of the child and their understanding of his temperament, personality, character, role in family dynamics, and so forth.

The need for parental participation in the treatment of children under six is pretty clear cut and would cause little disagreement among therapists, but what if only one parent is willing to participate? Do we insist that the abstaining parent be enlisted? To what degree do we insist?

Ferholt and Gurwitt (1982), in an article called "Involving Fathers in Treatment," suggest that the psychotherapeutic community has a tendency to neglect fathers and not make a substantial effort to enlist their participation in the treatment of their children. They would probably find support for their point of view in the cases presented in this book, for there is no question that more often than not, it was the mothers who were either the more active or the sole participants in their child's treatment. This pattern of greater involvement on the part of mothers than fathers has been true in my practice and that of my colleagues, and while we consider this a regrettable fact it is not one that we have been able to change. Yet Ferholt and Gurwitt conclude their article with

> To summarize, the commitment to involve fathers in treatment is not just a nicety but a necessity. The lack of such a commitment or capacity to implement it reflects incorrect beliefs and attitudes about the role of the father in the child's development as well as the powerful intrapsychic forces at work in clinicians and patients alike. . . . [p. 568]

The thesis of the authors appears to be that if the father's participation is not obtained it is due to the therapist's failure to bring this about. They suggest that perhaps the therapist's efforts to engage the father were blocked by countertransference, or perhaps there was a failure of effort or commitment stemming from other sources. Since their position is that it is the job of the therapist to enlist the father, the implication must be that his participation always carries positive value.

Where I disagree with this position is in the assumption that being a father implies certain positive things about a man's character, commitment, caring, sense of responsibility, and so forth. What if these qualities are not evident? Is it the job of the therapist to help these fathers develop fatherly traits? This would be possible in cases where these traits were latent and needed to be sparked, but we know full well that biological fatherhood does not automatically bring with it characteristics of fatherliness. The same of course is true of mothers. Some fathers and mothers are so disturbed and so dysfunctional that having a child is barely present in their field of consciousness. It seems a tall order for a therapist to tackle such extreme situations and draw these very disturbed parents into their child's treatment. And is it wise to expose children to fathers who are known to be abusive? Aren't their children better off freed of their influence? The same would of course apply to abusive mothers.

These extremes are not rare in our society and therapists working in what is now called the front lines, in agencies that deal with child abuse of every form, are achingly familiar with these *bondless* (Fraiberg 1977) men and women whose early lives failed to produce the vital attachments that make us human, and whose unbound aggression constitutes a danger to all who cross its random and capricious path. In addressing the needs of the children of this population, often the best we can do for them is to protect them from their parents and from having to repeat, generation after generation, the tragic cycle of abuse and neglect.

But what about the less extreme situations? What about those fathers and mothers who are closer to what we consider normal, people who love their children, function in society and yet don't want to participate in their children's treatment? Is it our job to change their minds, to induce them to meet with us, to persuade them that theirs would be a contribution of value to their child and ultimately beneficial to them?

Would it ever happen that an average, ordinary parent of a child would not want to get to know his child's therapist, not want to meet with him to make sure that his child was in competent hands? Not want to talk about the child and exchange impressions of the child's progress? Yes, it is possible. A parent could be of a different culture or simply totally unfamiliar with psychotherapy or prejudiced against it because of religious or other bias. A parent could be suspicious and uneasy with psychotherapy for a variety of reasons.

Our population of "average ordinary parents" is mixed and includes a very large number of parents whose pathology is not minor but who nonetheless function in the world, have children, and raise them. There are enormous variations in the care that the children receive. I made the point at the beginning of this book that we need to put in its proper place an image of the ideal parent who is loving, wise, kind, patient, and reasonable. That's our ego ideal, our wished-for parent, the one we wanted for ourselves, and the one we aspire to becoming when we have children of our own. The parents we meet in our offices cover the entire range of the diagnostic spectrum, and in order to know when and how to enlist their participation we need to know where each parent fits. Our diagnostic assessment and training as therapists help us determine how to approach a resistant parent, when to persevere, when to wait, and when to step back.

Let's take the example of the angry father who insisted on being involved in his four-year-old son's treatment but only showed up for one appointment in two years. How hard did I, as his son's therapist, work to engage him? Appointments were consistently offered and made, I was always cordial and welcoming, cancellations were accepted without interpretation, and although he was reminded of the importance of his participation, he was not lectured on this subject. It was recognized in this father's actions that a significant conflict was being expressed by this pattern of making appointments and canceling. Ultimately, this father avoided dealing with his conflict by staying at a great distance from me.

Although the term *resistance* is generally reserved for psychoanalysis and psychoanalytic psychotherapy, it can be borrowed to describe the behavior of certain parents in their child's treatment. Resistance refers to the ego's defensive efforts in regard to bringing into awareness "unacceptable childhood wishes, fantasies and impulses that would produce painful affects" (Moore and Fine 1990, p. 168). The father who canceled appointments is an example of resistance in a parent towards his child's therapist and the treatment situation. What do we do in such a situation?

The child's treatment was proceeding well and the father in no way undermined it. There was no reason to demand the father's active participation and good reason not to make such a demand. Resistance is a powerful phenomenon requiring long, careful work. It is not something that the child's therapist can tackle in occasional sessions. By respecting the father's need for distance, I, as the therapist, communicated something positive to him, and, however faint or tenuous, a working alliance at least flickered; he consistently *made* appointments, he paid his bills, and he made no disparaging remarks about his child's treatment.

In a very different example of parental participation we have Mr. Adams who, as described in Chapter 2, came regularly but initially stayed at such a distance that his participation was more a matter of form than substance. Then, at the end of the first two years, significant changes in the child began to be manifested. As his son became a more attractive and confident boy, Mr. Adams became less guarded. Several years later he entered his own treatment. In this case too, the father's need for distance had also been accepted by his son's therapist; Mr. Adams had not been asked to do more or move more quickly than was comfortable for him. Eventually he found psychic destinations for himself and pursued them at his own pace.

Mandatory participation only makes sense when it is the only way that treatment can proceed.[3] For example, it would be impossible to treat an infant at risk without the participation of at least one of that infant's caretakers. In such an instance the major thrust of the treatment would be work with the parents or with one parent. The outstanding work done by Fraiberg and colleagues in the now classic paper "Ghosts in the Nursery: A Psychoanalytic Approach to the Problems of Impaired Mother–Infant Relationships" (in Fraiberg 1980) attest to this treatment approach.

---

3. In the child guidance clinic mentioned in the Prologue, participation by both parents was mandatory in order to fulfill a research project.

To do our work we need to have our standards and also be flexible. We do the best we can with each situation at hand and are best off not giving ultimatums to the parents of our child patients. Policing is at extreme odds with the spirit and purpose of our work. What we need are working conditions conducive to treatment, and that generally means the participation of at least one parent when the child is young.

Question #7 has already been touched on from several perspectives, but it warrants a general statement.

> *What happens with divorced parents in regard to confidentiality, contact with both parents or with stepparents, the therapist's role in custody disputes, and so on?*

The more complex and unwieldy the situation the more useful is a simple reminder of our training and function. We need to stick to our realm of expertise and not be swept into roles that don't fit our knowledge and experience. Nothing in our theory and technique changes when the parents divorce. Confidentiality doesn't change, the purpose of contact with parents doesn't change, and our work with our young patient doesn't change. Yes, there are new strains, and the consulting room could become more crowded with calls from attorneys and demands from stepparents, but we don't have to take on demands that don't further our work. If contact with stepparents is deemed helpful, we do it; if not we don't. In these situations we have to be very clear about what we consider within our domain and what lies beyond. Our job is to protect the treatment.

13

ℳ

An Ideal Outcome

*A*lthough much mention has been made of difficulties encountered in work with parents, in many of our child cases this
area of our work is productive, straightforward, and rewarding
to the parents and to the therapist. We know that a solid working alliance arises from and promotes favorable conditions, and
absorbs some of the inevitable frustrations that occur even under
the best of circumstances. The strength of the working alliance
is affected by various tangible factors such as the skill of the
therapist, the parents' attitude towards treatment, the conditions
imposed by the child's problem, and so forth, but in some of
our cases the determinants in establishing rapport or producing discord are subtle, elusive, and hard to reconstruct.

We are all familiar with the wide range of reactions parents
experience when seeking help for their child. Probably the most
common initial responses are anxiety about what lies ahead, what
might be uncovered, what they have done wrong, and how they
will be judged. Often there is also a sense of defeat that their child
has problems serious enough to warrant professional help. But
these negative reactions are only part of the story; they usually
coexist with a sense of relief that help is on the way, that this new
intruder who might judge them might also understand them and
what they have been struggling with and will know what to do
about changing their situation. Parental ambivalence, so familiar

to child therapists, is a serious matter for all the players in the drama that is to unfold.

When negative feelings about the therapist and the prospect of treatment predominate, the case might be in jeopardy. Sometimes parents have such immediate intense negative feelings that we can assume that they were triggered by forces beyond the therapist's reach: an extreme instantaneous negative transference in a parent who is a stranger to us and who is inaccessible to any kind of dialogue would be such an example. But that would not be a case of parental ambivalence, for when there is ambivalence there is the possibility of establishing rapport and finding commonality of purpose. This is the place where the therapist's attitude towards the parents can tip the delicate balance between the parents' view of the therapist as competent helper or as harsh critic.

The therapist's ability to find within himself an attitude of receptivity, the result of a long and rigorous process of training and self-knowledge, is the subject of this book. The therapeutic climate it sets and the clinical decisions that flow from it allow us to combine the freedom and ease of not feeling pressured to know what we have yet to learn. It is by staying *in pace* with all that is happening that we gain insight and direction. The way we work, by entering a situation and also staying outside and observing it, is at the heart of what we do; it is the underpinning of our professional attitude. But there is more.

There is another turn that the story of our work with parents can take; it has to do with what may happen to a parent because of his child's treatment. This version of the story has a happy ending, but not one we hear much about. The child gets better and can now sleep with only occasional bad dreams, play with his friends with only occasional disagreements, and think his parents are unfair, old fashioned, and pretty dumb (when they really are that way or even when they are simply doing their job) without being terrified that his bad thoughts have killed them off. In this happy outcome the child goes about living his life without worrying every minute about how big or smart or popular he is.

That is not to say that he doesn't engage in self-evaluation and self-reflection. He does. He just doesn't ruminate or obsess the way he once did. The thing that happened that changed everything for him is that he found a way to move *into* his story. He used to be a withdrawn little boy who stood outside and watched himself, and it seemed to him that the boy he watched was clumsy and not cool and he wanted to be the coolest and the best. So he made up stories, fantasies in which he was a hero, but they were hard to maintain and grew thin and unsatisfying. And then something began to change for him; he began to know himself in a new way, a good way, and this freed him from living in stories of his making and helped him live and shape his real story. He became a regular ordinary boy, who lived in the present and woke each morning in the same red house he shared with his parents and siblings.

But that's only part of the happy ending. That's the one we hoped and worked for. There's more. There's what happened to the boy's parents because of their son's treatment. A lot happened to them, none of which they expected. They thought that their shy little eight-year-old boy would see his therapist twice a week and that they would occasionally meet with Mr. M. and get some useful hints on how to help him. They were glad of that, for Mr. M. seemed competent and knowledgeable and had come highly recommended. They felt lucky to have him. They had heard stories from friends whose children's therapists had been critical, authoritarian, unavailable, and not particularly helpful. Mr. M. was not like that at all. He was very interested in their ideas and their observations and even when they specifically asked for advice he tended to chuckle and remind them that they were the parents, he was the therapist, and they'd all better stick to their own area of expertise. Only twice in the three years that their son was in treatment did he make a suggestion. The year their boy was nine they wanted to send him to sleep-away camp and he suggested waiting another year. This was discussed at length and that's when they realized that an important theme in their son's upbringing was their tendency to follow the patterns of child rear-

ing of their own childhoods. They both came from very traditional families where certain things were automatically repeated
from one generation to the next. Sleep-over camp was instituted
at age nine, and here they were, blindly following this tradition
even though the boy's father, when asked by Mr. M., clearly remembered that first summer at camp to be the most miserable
eight weeks of his life.

The other time that Mr. M. made a suggestion had to do with
the boy's school. They had to choose between keeping him in the
neighborhood school he was currently attending or sending him
to a very prestigious school that would have involved an hour's
trip each way and separated him from friends and familiar sur-
roundings. Mr. M. suggested that they delay the change of schools
until he was older, stronger, and more confident. In discussing
this the parents were once again shocked by their lapse of awareness, by their tendency to repeat their own past rather than be
attuned to the needs of their son. What was particularly striking
to these parents was that they did this despite conscious disapproval of their very traditional upbringing and of the cold and
formal climate of their early years. They were united in their disapproval, had initially been drawn to each other because they were
both rebels with the same cause: to live warmer, freer, more spon-
taneous lives than did their parents, and to raise their children in
an atmosphere where individuality held higher rank than the
tidiness of tradition.

The boy's mother was the first to raise the question:

How can it be that having set out to live by a set of values so different from that of my parents that at times it seems as if my parents are still there inside me making the decisions and I don't even
notice this to be happening? Then when we meet and talk, or at
some quiet moment alone, I begin to recognize that there it is again
. . . that what I'm doing has nothing to do with what I really believe or the needs of my son! And each time I realize this, I'm
shocked that I even considered a course of action so out of keeping with my beliefs and so inappropriate as far as my son's needs
are concerned. How can I change this pattern in myself? How do
I free myself from this disquieting hold the past has on me?

The reader will not be too surprised to learn that the discussions that followed prompted the boy's mother to seek her own treatment.

The father took a while longer to follow suit and his path into treatment was somewhat different. From his first session with Mr. M., the father sensed something about the way this man thought that was different from what he was used to, different in an intriguing way. For instance, he was aware from early on that there were no correct answers to any of Mr. M.'s questions; these questions were different in tone, manner, attitude, in every way, from the questions he was accustomed to, the questions of his past and present. But it wasn't just that the questions had this interesting exploratory dimension. There was also something in the way they talked to each other. For instance, they would begin to talk about something simple, his son's squabble with a friend, or whether they should get him a pet, and end up in the most unexpected places. The boy's rivalry with his friend might take them into a rich and thought-provoking discussion and it would suddenly dawn on him that rivalry, as part of the human condition, had a constructive side and was nothing to hide. Or they would talk about anger and he would for the first time be left with respect for anger, see it as an emotional state with as much potential to do good as to do harm. So many of the fixed ideas he had always held began to shift. Increasingly he could see the other side of things, the other side of stubbornness (tenacity), the other side of crying (the release of feeling), the other side of stoicism (fear of expressing feelings), the other side of unwavering order (spontaneity), the other side of being objective (fear of taking a stand).

The boy's father looked forward to his monthly sessions with Mr. M. He wanted to be able to think this exciting way, he wanted to develop the ability to explore and grow, and it was in this spirit of inquiry and quest for "self-improvement" that he decided that psychotherapy would be "intellectually broadening," a worthwhile investment of time and money. Once he entered his own treatment it took quite a long time before he could admit to himself and to his therapist that having been so

tightly wrapped all his life was not only intellectually restric-
tive, it was painful. Discovering the painful part was hard, but
it was also very freeing; he had been so out of touch with it all
his life. Now that an affective door had opened for him and he
could feel more deeply on every level he could hardly believe
that he had ever envisioned psychoanalysis and psychotherapy
as being primarily intellectually broadening, like graduate school!
There were moments during his treatment that reminded him
of when he had gotten his first pair of glasses at age seven and
suddenly he could see so well. He hadn't known how hard he
had worked before to make things look less dim and blurry, and
then came the glasses, and now his analysis, and the world
looked different.

This is the extra bonus that can come out of the treatment of
a child. All the while the child is getting better, the parents begin
to rediscover themselves as they glimpse their own past through
their child's struggles and sorrows. And with sharpened vision they
discern the effect of their past on the present and observe and
learn to regulate the climate they are providing for their child and
for themselves. And they discover that they still have the chance
to grow and develop in ways they hadn't imagined before.

Of course a story with an ideal outcome is rare; rare and ideal
often accompany each other. But stories like that do happen, they
are not beyond reach, and there is something very lovely in remembering that, particularly since so much of our work does not result in such a picture-perfect outcome. It has been presented to
make the point that for some parents contact with their child's
therapist exposes them to an experience that can significantly
enhance their lives.

We do have a way of exploring, observing, and integrating, a
total way of thinking that is different from those who have not
had our training or been analyzed. When we put these professional skills to use with the parents of our child patients, our
impact on their lives can have great significance. When their
exposure to our orientation, and the high value we place on the
pursuit of insight prompts them to seek their own treatment, we

can feel a sense of satisfaction that they have seized an enriching opportunity for themselves.

And because throughout this book I have focused on difficulties in our work with parents, I wanted to end with this happy story of a family whose lives were transformed by their child's treatment. This can happen only when the forces of chance and the talent of the therapist attain a high level of synchronicity of spirit and purpose. Then termination may indeed be, as we would hope, a new beginning.

References

Abelin, E. (1971). The role of the father in the separation-individuation process. In *Separation-Individuation: Essays in Honor of Margaret S. Mahler*, ed. J. McDevitt and C. Settlage, pp. 229–252. New York: International Universities Press.

Anthony, E. J. (1980). The family and the psychoanalytic process. *Psychoanalytic Study of the Child* 35:3–34. New Haven: Yale University Press.

Benedek, T. (1938). Adaptation to reality in early infancy. *Psychoanalytic Quarterly* 7:200–214.

——— (1959). Parenthood as a developmental phase. *Journal of the American Psychoanalytic Association* 7:389–417.

Bernstein, I., and Glenn, J. (1988). The child and adolescent analyst's emotional reaction to his patients and their parents. *International Review of Psycho-Analysis* 15:225–241.

Blanck, G., and Blanck, R. (1986). *Beyond Ego Psychology*. New York: Columbia University Press.

——— (1994). *Ego Psychology, Theory and Practice*. New York: Columbia University Press.

Casement, P. (1991). *Learning from the Patient*. New York: Guilford.

Chiland, C. (1982). A new look at fathers. *Psychoanalytic Study of the Child* 37:367–380. New Haven: Yale University Press.

Edward, J., Ruskin, N., and Turrini, P. (1991). *Separation Individuation Theory and Application*. New York: Gardner.

Edward, J., and Sanville, J. (1996). *Fostering Healing and Growth: A Psychoanalytic Social Work Approach*. Northvale, NJ: Jason Aronson.

Eissler, K. R. (1953). The effect of the structure of the ego on psychoanalytic technique. *Journal of the American Psychoanalytic Association* 1:104–143.

Elkisch, P. (1971). Initiating separation-individuation in the simultaneous treatment of a child and his mother. In *Separation-Individuation: Essays in Honor of Margaret S. Mahler*, ed. J. McDevitt and C. Settlage, pp. 356–376. New York: International Universities Press.

Erikson, E. (1950). *Childhood and Society*. New York: Norton.

Ferholt, J. and Gurwitt, A. (1982). Involving fathers in treatment. In *Father and Child*, ed. S. Cath, A. Gurwitt, and J. Ross, pp. 557–568. Boston: Little, Brown.

Fliess, R. (1942). The metapsychology of the analyst. *Psychoanalytic Quarterly* 11:211–227.

Fraiberg, S. (1977). On the origin of human bonds. In *Every Child's Birthright: In Defense of Mothering*. New York: Bantam.

———, ed. (1980). *Clinical Studies in Infant Mental Health*. New York: Basic Books.

Freud, A. (1946). *The Ego and Mechanisms of Defense*. New York: International Universities Press.

——— (1965). *Normality and Pathology in Childhood*. New York: International Universities Press.

Freud, S. (1905). Three essays on the theory of sexuality. *Standard Edition* 7:130–243.

——— (1912a). The dynamics of transference. *Standard Edition* 12:97–108.

——— (1912b). Recommendations to physicians practising psychoanalysis. *Standard Edition* 12:109–120.

——— (1915). Further recommendations on the technique of psychoanalysis—observations on transference love. *Standard Edition* 12:157–171.

——— (1924). The dissolution of the Oedipus complex. *Standard Edition* 19:171–179.

——— (1926). Inhibition, symptoms, and anxiety. *Standard Edition* 20:75–174.

——— (1933). New introductory lectures on psychoanalysis. *Standard Edition* 22:1–182.

Galenson, E., and Roiphe, R. (1980). The preoedipal development of the boy. *Journal of the American Psychoanalytic Association* 28:805–827.

Geleerd, E. (1967). Introduction. In *The Child Analyst at Work*, pp. 1–12. New York: International Universities Press.

Glenn, J., Sabot, L. M., and Bernstein, I. (1992). The role of parents in child analysis. In *Child Analysis and Therapy*, ed. J. Glenn, 2nd ed., pp. 393–423. Northvale, NJ: Jason Aronson.

Greenson, R. (1967). *The Technique and Practice of Psychoanalysis*. New York: Hallmark.

Hartmann, H. (1958). *Ego Psychology and the Problem of Adaptation*. New York: International Universities Press.

Jacobson, E. (1964). *The Self and the Object World*. New York: International Universities Press.

Kris, E. (1952). *Psychoanalytic Explorations in Art*. New York: International Universities Press.

Mahler, M. (1968). *On Human Symbiosis and the Vicissitudes of Individuation*. New York: International Universities Press.

Mahler, M., Pine, F., and Bergman, A. (1975). *The Psychological Birth of the Human Infant*. New York: Basic Books.

Moore, B. E., and Fine, B. (1990). *Psychoanalytic Terms & Concepts*. New Haven: Yale University Press.

Neubauer, P. (1960). The one parent child and his oedipal development. *Psychoanalytic Study of the Child* 15:286–309. New York: International Universities Press.

Parens, H. (1979). *The Development of Aggression in Early Childhood*. New York: Jason Aronson.

——— (1989a). Towards a reformulation of the psychoanalytic theory of aggression. In *The Course of Life, vol. 2: Early Childhood*, ed. S. I. Greenspan and G. H. Pollock, pp. 83–127. New York: International Universities Press.

——— (1989b). Towards an epigenesis of aggression in early

childhood. In *The Course of Life, vol. 2: Early Childhood*, ed. S. I. Greenspan and G. H. Pollock, pp. 129–161. New York: International Universities Press.

——— (1990). Neurosis and prevention. In *The Neurotic Child and Adolescent*, ed. M. H. Etezady. Northvale, NJ: Jason Aronson.

Pine, F. (1976). On therapeutic change: perspective from a parent–child model. *Psychoanalysis and Contemporary Science*, vol. 5, pp. 175–208. New York: International Universities Press.

Roiphe, H., and Galenson, E. (1981). *Infantile Origins of Sexuality*. New York: International Universities Press.

Sandler, J. (1976). Countertransference and role-responsiveness. *International Review of Psycho-Analysis*. 3:43–47.

Sandler, J., Kennedy, H., and Tyson, R. (1980). *The Technique of Child Psychoanalysis: Discussions with Anna Freud*. Cambridge: Harvard University Press.

Sanville, J. (1991). *The Playground of Psychoanalytic Psychotherapy*. Hillsdale, NJ: Analytic Press.

Seinfeld, J. (1991). *The Empty Core: An Object Relations Approach to Psychotherapy of the Schizoid Personality*. Northvale, NJ: Jason Aronson.

Siskind, D. (1987). Preverbal determinants in a classical analysis. *Clinical Social Work Journal* 15(3):361–367.

——— (1992). *The Child Patient and the Therapeutic Process: A Psychoanalytic, Developmental, Object Relations Approach*. Northvale, NJ: Jason Aronson.

Spitz, R. (1959). *A Genetic Field Theory of Ego Formation*. New York: International Universities Press.

——— (1965). *The First Year of Life*. New York: International Universities Press.

Webster's New World Dictionary, Third College Edition. (1988). New York: Simon and Schuster.

Weil, A. (1970). The basic core. *Psychoanalytic Study of the Child* 25:442–460. New York: International Universities Press.

Winnicott, D. W. (1953). Transitional objects and transitional phenomena: a study of the first not-me possession. *International Journal of Psycho-Analysis* 34(2):89–97.

———— (1960). Counter-transference. In *The Maturational Processes and the Facilitating Environment*, pp. 158–165. New York: International Universities Press.

Index